BTEC Level 2 Technical Diploma

Sport and Activity Leaders

Learner Handbook

Tim Eldridge
Katherine Howard
Becky Laffan

Published by Pearson Education Limited, 80 Strand, London, WC2R 0RL.

www.pearsonschoolsandfecolleges.co.uk

Copies of official specifications for all Pearson qualifications may be found on the website: qualifications.pearson.com

Text © Pearson Education Limited 2017
Typeset by Phoenix Photosetting, Kent
Original illustrations © Pearson Education Ltd 2017
Picture research by Aptara
Cover photo/illustration © maxstockphoto / Shutterstock.com

The rights of Tim Eldridge, Katherine Howard and Becky Laffan to be identified as authors of this work have been asserted by them in accordance with the Copyright, Designs and Patents Act 1988.

First published 2017

19 18 17
10 9 8 7 6 5 4 3 2 1

British Library Cataloguing in Publication Data
A catalogue record for this book is available from the British Library

ISBN 978 1 292 19648 0

Acknowledgements

The publisher would like to thank the following for their kind permission to reproduce their photographs:

(Key: b-bottom; c-centre; l-left; r-right; t-top)

Alamy: Florian Kopp/Westend61 GmbH 2, National Geographic Creative 10, Alan Edwards 15, RosaIreneBetancourt7 16, Photo Yom Lam/Stockimo 17, Alan Edwards 20, Sport Picture Library 25, Ivan Vdovin 27, Blend Images 42, Enigma 46, Cultura Creative (RF) 49, LH Images 51l, Ulrich Doering 51r, ImageBroker 65, Peter Muller/Cultura Creative 85, Action Plus Sports Images 89, Nippon News/Aflo Co. Ltd. 96, Francis Joseph Dean/Deanpictures 99, James Maggs 102, Jim West 107, Daniel Swee 120, Colin Underhill 122, ImageBroker 126, Allstar Picture Library 128, Reuters 137, Jim West 138t, ImageBroker 144, ImageBroker 147, Kevin Nicholson 154, Vadzim Kandratsenkau 161, Edward Herdwick 171b, Julia Claxton 172m, Barry Lewis 172b, Agencja Fotograficzna Caro 182, Laurence Hardy 183, John Fryer 188, Peter Lane 190, Hero Images Inc. 195, Hero Images Inc. 202, Allstar Picture Library 205, PCN Photography 206l, Reuters 206r, Reuters 209, Action Plus Sports Images 210, Action Plus Sports Images 212, Allstar Picture Library 213, Reuters 214, Gary Mitchell 220, Cultura Creative (RF) 225, Aloisio Mauricio/Foto Arena LTDA 226, Nick Hanna 232, Rob Walls 236, Keith J Smith 237, Alexandre Sousa 238, Adria Malcolm/Albuquerque Journal/ZUMAPRESS Inc 241, Migstock 242, Henry Iddon 243r, Colin Underhill 243l, Tony Watson 253; **123RF:** Alexandre Zveiger 51m, Mirosław Kijewski, 58, Microgen 81, Cathy Yeulet 83, Cathy Yeulet 103, Dmitry Kalinovsky 146, Wavebreak Media Ltd 152, Cathy Yeulet 163, zabelin 181, Radist 196, Bela Hoche 215, Mauro Rodrigues 251; **Shutterstock:** Maddrat 29t, Sarawut Chamsaeng 29b, Robert Kneschke 53, Wavebreakmedia 58, Sireonio 66, Sirtravelalot 78, William Perugini 101, James Maggs 105, SpeedKingz 110, Monkey Business Images 113, Dreams Come True 115, Wavebreakmedia 116, Air Images 132, Fotokostic 148, Ammit Jack 157, Ammit Jack 168, Lpatov 171t, Dmitry Kalinovsky 172t, Ammit Jack 192; **Getty Images:** KidStock/Blend Images 84, KidStock/Blend Images/Corbis 138b; **Reuters:** Jason O'Brien 93, Erich Schlegel 98

Cover photo/illustration © maxstockphoto / Shutterstock.com

All other images © Pearson Education

Contents

How to use this book

This handbook is designed to support you in developing the skills and knowledge to succeed in your BTEC Level 2 Technical course. It will help you to feel confident in taking the next step and be ready for your dream job.

The skills you will develop during the course include practical skills that you'll need in your chosen occupation, as well as a range of 'transferable' skills and behaviours that will be useful for your own personal development, whatever you do in life.

Your learning can be seen as a journey which moves through four phases.

Phase 1	Phase 2	Phase 3	Phase 4
You are introduced to a topic or concept; you start to develop an awareness of what learning and skills are required.	You explore the topic or concept through different methods (e.g. watching or listening to a tutor or a professional at work, research, questioning, analysis, critical evaluation) and form your own understanding.	You apply your knowledge and skills to a practical task designed to demonstrate your understanding and skills.	You reflect on your learning, evaluate your efforts, identify gaps in your knowledge and look for ways to improve.

During each phase, you will use different learning strategies. As you go through your course, these strategies will combine to help you secure the essential knowledge and skills.

This handbook has been written using similar learning principles, strategies and tools. It has been designed to support your learning journey, to give you control over your own learning and to equip you with the knowledge, understanding and tools to be successful in your future career or studies.

Getting to know the features

In this handbook, you'll find lots of different features. They are there to help you learn about the topics in your course in different ways and to help you monitor and check your progress. Together these features help you to:

- build your knowledge and technical skills
- understand how to succeed in your assessment
- link your learning to the workplace.

In addition, each individual feature has a specific purpose, designed to support important learning strategies. For example, some features will:

- get you to question assumptions around what you are learning
- make you think beyond what you are reading about
- help you make connections across your learning and across units
- draw comparisons between the theory you are learning about and realistic workplace environments
- help you develop some of the important skills you will need for the workplace, including planning and completing tasks, working with others, effective communication, adaptability and problem solving.

Features to build your knowledge and technical skills

Key terms

Terms highlighted LIKE THIS are 'key terms'. It is important that you know what they mean because they relate directly to your chosen subject. The first time they appear in the book they will be explained. If you see a highlighted key term again after that and can't quite remember its definition, look in the Glossary towards the end of the book – they are all listed there! Note that these key terms are used and explained in the context of your specialist subject or the topic in which they appear, and are not necessarily the same definitions you would find in a dictionary.

Practise

These work-related tasks or activities will allow you to practise some of the technical or professional skills relating to the main content covered in each unit.

Practise
1   Identify the hazards relating to the facility, participants and activity that you would look for before beginning a hockey training session.
2   How would you deal with each of these hazards?

Skills and knowledge check

Regular 'Skills and knowledge check' boxes will help you to keep on track with the knowledge and skills requirements for a unit. They will remind you to go back and refresh your knowledge if you haven't quite understood what you need to know or demonstrate. Tick off each one when you are confident you've nailed it.

Skills and knowledge check
☐ What is summative feedback?
☐ Give an example of formative feedback in a sports coaching session.
☐ A sport and activity leader can split their review into four areas – what are these?
☐ What does SWOT stand for?
◯ I can provide a definition of self-evaluation.
◯ I am aware of how important it is to gain feedback from the participants in a session.
◯ I can produce a SWOT analysis of my own performance.
If you have been unable to give positive responses to any of the questions or statements above, please go back and review the section.

What if...?

Employers need to know that you are responsible and that you understand the importance of what you are learning. These 'What if...?' scenarios will help you to understand the real links between theory and what happens in the workplace.

What if...?

Christopher is a sport and activity leader working at a leisure centre. He has been asked to lead a new exercise session for adults. In total, 12 men and eight women have signed up for the session. Two of the women are pregnant and four of the men are aged over 50.

The exercise session will last for 45 minutes and will take place in the centre's aerobics studio.

1 What characteristics are specific to the participants in the group?

2 What does Christopher need to consider about the needs of the participants?

Link it up

Go to Unit 1 for more information about equality, diversity and inclusivity, as well as more on health and safety.

Link it up

Although your BTEC Level 2 Technical is made up of several units, common themes are explored from different perspectives across the whole of your course. Everything you learn and do during your course will help you in your final assessment. This kind of assessment is called 'synoptic'. It means that you have the opportunity to apply all the knowledge and skills from the course to a practical, realistic work situation or task.

The 'Link it up' features show where information overlaps between units or within the same unit, helping you to see where key points might support your final assessment or help you gain a deeper understanding of a topic.

Step-by-step

This practical feature gives step-by-step descriptions of processes or tasks, and might include a photo or artwork to illustrate each step. This will help you to understand the key stages in the process and help you to practise the process or technique yourself.

Checklist

These lists present information in a way that is helpful, practical and interactive. You can check off the items listed to ensure you think about each one individually, as well as how they relate to the topic as a collective list.

Features connected to your assessment

Your course is made up of several units. There are two different types of unit:

- externally assessed
- internally assessed.

The features that support you in preparing for assessment are below. But first, what is the difference between these two different types of unit?

Externally assessed units

These units give you the opportunity to present what you have learned in the unit in a different way. They can be challenging, but will really give you the opportunity to demonstrate your knowledge and understanding, or your skills, in a direct way. For these units you will complete a task, set by Pearson, in controlled conditions. This could take the form of an exam or onscreen test, or it could be another type of task. You may have the opportunity to research and prepare notes around a topic in advance, which can be used when completing the assessment.

Internally assessed units

Internally assessed units involve you completing a series of assignments or tasks, set and marked by your tutor. The assignments you complete could allow you to demonstrate your learning in a number of different ways, such as a report, a presentation, a video recording or observation statements of you completing a practical task. Whatever the method, you will need to make sure you have clear evidence of what you have achieved and how you did it.

Ready for assessment

You will find these features in units that are internally assessed. They include suggestions about what you could practise or focus on to complete the assignment for the unit. They also explain how to gather evidence for assessment from the workplace or from other tasks you have completed.

Ready for assessment

For this unit you will need to design and produce an activity plan that can be used for an activity session for five or more participants. You will need to show that you can plan, lead and review a sports or activity session. Your session plan will include all the details relevant to your session and participants. You will show you have considered the resources you will need, the activities you are going to provide and the leadership behaviours you are going to demonstrate.

During the session you will show all the leadership skills, qualities and responsibilities that you have developed throughout the unit.

After the session you will need to review your own performance and produce an action plan that helps you improve for the future.

The more experience of leading activities you can gain before your assessment, the better you will be. Consider work experience and voluntary opportunities. Remember, be the best you can be.

Assessment practice

These features include questions similar to the ones you'll find in your external assessment, so you can get some experience answering them. Each one relates to one or more Assessment Outcomes, as indicated in the top right-hand corner of this feature box. Suggested answers are given at the back of this book. Where Assessment practice features require you to carry out your own research or give individual answers or opinions, however, no answers are provided.

Assessment practice   AO3, AO4

You have been asked to lead a cricket session with a group of women aged over 55. The women have never played cricket before, but are keen to take part because they have watched the Women's Cricket World Cup on television.

1 Write down an aim for this session.

2 State two pieces of information that you would give the group as part of the introduction.

3 Describe what you would include in the warm up for the session.

Getting ready for assessment

This section will help you prepare for external assessment. It gives information about what to expect in the final assessment, as well as revision tips and practical advice on preparing for and sitting exams or a set task. It provides a series of sample questions and answers that you might find, including helpful feedback, or 'verdicts', on the answers and how they could be improved.

Features which link your learning with the workplace

Each unit ends with a 'Work focus' section which links the learning from the unit to particular skills and behaviours that are required in the workplace. There are two parts in each Work focus section.

1. **Hands on** – gives suggestions for tasks you could practise to develop the technical or professional skills you'll need on the job.
2. **Ready for work?** – supports you in developing the all-important transferable skills and behaviours that employers are looking for, such as adaptability, problem solving, communication or teamwork. It will give you pointers for showcasing your skills to a potential employer.

HANDS ON

There are some important occupational skills and competencies that you will need to practise, which relate to this unit. Developing these and practising them could help you to gain employment as a sport and activity leader.

1 **Demonstrate the skills and qualities of a sport and activity leader.**

- Understand the different approaches that a sport and activity leader can use to meet participant needs.

- Listen to people's ideas and take them on board.

- Identify participants' skills and areas of interest to select the best leadership styles to use with them.

2 **Carry out the responsibilities of a sport and activity leader.**

- Be aware of the environment and social setting.

- Plan and deliver appropriate activities.

- Develop participants' knowledge and understanding of sport and physical activities.

3 **Demonstrate how to control an individual or a team to reach a goal.**

- Motivate participants to achieve their full potential.

- Understand the importance and legal requirements of equality and diversity when working with participants.

- Deal with conflict and resolve issues.

Ready for work?

Take this short quiz to find out whether you're ready to work as a sport and activity leader and have a career in the sports sector.

1 What is your time management like?

- [ ] A I always arrive on time, I do not like being late.
- [ ] B I am usually only five minutes late.
- [ ] C I try to be on time but always seem to be half an hour late for things.
- [ ] D I never arrive early.

2 How would you dress to go to work in a leisure centre?

- [ ] A Smart tracksuit bottoms and a polo shirt.
- [ ] B Shorts and a t-shirt.
- [ ] C My best suit (trousers or skirt).
- [ ] D My normal, everyday clothes.

3 When you are given a deadline that puts you under a lot of pressure, what do you do?

- [ ] A Make an action plan and get on with it.
- [ ] B Ask someone for help, I cannot do it on my own.
- [ ] C Tell my boss that I cannot do it.
- [ ] D Complain to everyone that I have too much to do.

4 How do you react to negative feedback?

- [ ] A Look at it as constructive feedback and take it on board.
- [ ] B Listen, but not do anything about it.
- [ ] C React badly and argue.
- [ ] D Ignore it completely.

5 How do you prefer to work?

- [ ] A As part of a team.
- [ ] B On my own.
- [ ] C Being the team leader.
- [ ] D Being in charge of everything, but not doing anything myself.

Your score:

A = 1; B = 2; C = 3; D = 4

If you scored mostly As, you are the dream sport and activity leader.

Mostly Bs, you have got what it takes but you could try a bit harder.

Mostly Cs, you may need to brush up on your interpersonal skills.

Mostly Ds, this is not the role for you. You should look for something else.

1 Leading Sport Safely and Effectively

Having an understanding of the processes that go into planning, leading, communicating and maintaining safe and effective practices is very important in the sports industry.

In this unit, you will learn about participants and groups that sport and activity leaders work with. You will also consider the importance of building positive relationships when leading sport and physical activities. You will learn about the methods used for maintaining health and safety, as well as safeguarding both yourself and participants, and dealing with incidents resulting in injury or illness.

How will I be assessed?

This unit is assessed using an onscreen test, set and marked by Pearson. The test contains different types of question and is worth 60 marks. The test duration is 75 minutes. The assessment is available on demand. The first assessment is available in January 2018.

Sample assessment materials will be available to help centres prepare learners for assessment.

This unit is assessed under supervised conditions.

Assessment outcomes

AO1 Demonstrate knowledge of the principles, responsibilities and procedures a sport and activity leader carries out when leading sport and physical activities safely and effectively for different types of participants

AO2 Demonstrate understanding of considerations, implications and importance of the role, responsibilities and procedures a sport and activity leader carries out when applied to leading sport and physical activities safely and effectively for different types of participants

AO3 Analyse and interpret information relating to the sport and activity leader role when leading sport and physical activities safely and effectively for different types of participants

AO4 Make connections, use and integrate knowledge of the responsibilities and procedures a sport and activity leader carries out and the requirements they need to meet when leading sport and physical activities safely and effectively for different types of participants

A Leading different participants and groups

A1 Sport and physical activity participants

When you start to think about how you will plan and lead sport and physical activity sessions, you need to consider the diverse groups of **PARTICIPANTS** (the people who are taking part in the activity) and how you will support their different needs. As a **SPORT AND ACTIVITY LEADER** (the person responsible for leading the participants in the activity) you will work in very different environments, including sports halls, gyms, studios and outside activity areas. You will need to be able to adapt your communication styles and behaviours to meet their individual needs.

Diverse groups of participants

The **DIVERSE GROUPS OF PARTICIPANTS** you will encounter will all have different needs or requirements that have to be identified and met. These groups can be defined by specific characteristics they share. These characteristics might be physical, social, psychological, health-related, skill-related or developmental. They are summarised in Table 1.1.

Table 1.1: Examples of characteristics for diverse groups of participants

Participant groups	Characteristics					
	Physical	Social	Psychological	Health-related	Skill-related	Developmental
People with disabilities	Possible restrictions due to the nature of the disability, including movement, visibility, hearing.	May lack confidence because of inexperience and lack of support available to them.	Possible self-doubt over ability – participants might think they cannot take part in activities or will not be good enough.	Possible restrictions due to the nature of the disability.	Participants will have different skill abilities and expectations depending on their disability.	May be differences in developmental ability due to the nature of the disability.
Older adults (over 50)	A decrease in muscle mass and possible illnesses and injuries may lead to restrictions in movement and accessibility.	Lack of role models could deter participants from taking part.	It may be a long time since they last took part in sport and physical activities and they may lack confidence in their ability.	May be restrictions due to illness and injuries.	Participants may have different skills and abilities due to their previous experiences in sport and physical activities.	Possible restrictions due to existing illnesses and injuries.

Table 1.1: (continued)

Participant groups	Characteristics					
	Physical	Social	Psychological	Health-related	Skill-related	Developmental
Adults	Different levels of ability depending on previous and current participation in sport and physical activities.	Might want to be part of team or pursue individual activities depending on their preference.	May not have participated in activities since school and might be nervous of trying something new or have had bad experiences in the past.	May have existing injuries or illnesses or be prone to injuries due to the demands made by the sport or physical activity.	Different levels of ability due to previous and existing participation in sport and physical activities.	Depends on the individual's existing level of knowledge of the activity.
Children and young people (5–18)	Still growing so will not be as strong as an adult; consideration must be given to the type of activity, equipment and clothing needed.	May enjoy being part of a large group and want to take part in team activities so that they can be with friends.	Might be worried because the activities are new to them; or might be fearless and not behave sensibly when learning new skills.	Because they are growing there will be activities that are unsuitable or the intensity of the activity may need to be lowered.	As they grow older skill level will increase; skills and activities need to be adapted to match the children's age.	Skills, equipment and rules need to be adapted to meet the developmental stage of the participants.
Pre-schoool children (under 5)	Activities and skills will need adapting as young children are still growing and developing and will lack mobility, strength and coordination.	Will probably need an adult to participate with them to help them take part and to reassure them.	Most activities will be new for them. They will be nervous and excited and will need extra reassurance from the activity leader.	Because they are growing there will be activities that are unsuitable or intensities that need to be lowered.	As they grow older their skill level will increase. Skills and activities need to be adapted to match the children's age.	Participants will need an adult to assist them with activities. Skills will need to be broken down and developed to match the children's ability.
Pregnant women	Participants might have difficulty standing or lying down for long periods of time and may have restricted movements.	Participants may begin participating in activities to meet new friends in similar circumstances to themselves.	May have concerns and fears about taking part in certain activities, not wanting to hurt their unborn child.	They may have pre-existing injuries or illnesses related to their pregnancy that restricts their participation.	They might be restricted due to their pregnancy, body shape and ability to carry out certain activities.	Participants may need assistance with some activities to allow them to participate.

Diverse needs of participants

As a sport activity leader you need to understand the **DIVERSE NEEDS** of different groups of participants. These include: different needs between the groups, the factors that influence them, the aims of activities and expected outcomes related to these needs.

Link it up

This will also be important when you come to completing the synoptic task in Unit 8.

What if...?

Christopher is a sport and activity leader working at a leisure centre. He has been asked to lead a new exercise session for adults. In total, 12 men and eight women have signed up for the session. Two of the women are pregnant and four of the men are aged over 50.

The exercise session will last for 45 minutes and will take place in the centre's aerobics studio.

1 What characteristics are specific to the participants in the group?

2 What does Christopher need to consider about the needs of the participants?

You can meet the needs of diverse groups of participants by thinking about the type of activity you will lead and the physical, social, educational and health requirements for it.

Type of activity

- You can adapt an activity to suit the needs of the group you are leading. For example, it is not always appropriate to use the full national governing body's (NGB) rules for a sport or activity. Sometimes the rules can be adapted or reduced. For example, when leading a volleyball session with children aged 7–8 years, instead of losing a point when the ball bounces, you could allow the ball to bounce once, or even twice, before returning it.
- The size of the equipment you use in the activity should always be appropriate for the age and ability of the participants.
- The size of the activity/playing area can be reduced or adapted to meet the ability level of the participant.

Physical

- Sports and physical activities need to be adapted to meet the physical needs of participants for their age, development, ability and the type of activity. Adaptations should be made for children who have disabilities or learning difficulties (SEND – Special Educational Needs and Disability).
- As children get older, their physical strength, speed and flexibility increase; these then begin to decrease in adults over 35 years old. Activities can be adapted to meet the life stage of the participants.
- As children grow from babies into young adults, bones and muscles become stronger and they are able to take part in activities that require more advanced skills.
- When you take part in physical activity your ability increases; the more frequently you train, the better your ability becomes.
- Participants with SEND, physical disabilities or impairments have a range of abilities and may be at different levels of development; this will depend on the nature of their disability.
- The activity type can be changed depending on the participant; some activities may be unsuitable altogether and some can be adapted. For example, full-contact rugby union would be unsuitable for pregnant women and young children, but could be adapted for young children by removing the contact and instead playing tag-rugby.

Social

- As children grow older they develop socially. Babies do not interact with each other but as toddlers they play with each other and learn social skills.

- Some participants may be self-conscious and may not want to participate in certain activities that involve specific clothing or equipment, or that highlight certain aspects of their ability level. It might be appropriate to issue the same clothing or equipment to all participants so that everyone looks the same, or you might ask participants to bring their own items of equipment, for example, tennis rackets or swim hats.

Educational

- As children grow they develop their knowledge. When participants take on a new sport or activity they learn more about it every time they participate. Activities can be scaled to reflect this development.
- Taking part in a sports activity regularly will result in improvements in skill level (fundamental movement skills and techniques). The more you practise the better you get.
- Some behaviours are learned as we grow older and this can be helped by participation in sports and physical activities. Behaviours are the ways in which people react to situations and events. **LEARNED BEHAVIOURS** are the reactions people apply to specific situations that they repeat each time they encounter that situation. A simple example is a player stopping when the referee blows the whistle. Learned behaviours for participants in sport and activity sessions include self-confidence, competitiveness and fear.

Medical/health

- Participants can have specific medical or health conditions that can affect their level of involvement in different activities. For example, people who suffer from hay fever might be able to participate more and at a higher level on days when the pollen count is low, and might have to stop participating completely when the pollen count is high.

Assessment practice   **AO1**

> William is 56 years old and has been playing tennis for five years. He suffers from asthma and enjoys playing sports on his own.
>
> Identify two characteristics of participant groups that he might have as an older adult.

Key considerations to meet the needs of different groups

To be a successful sport and activity leader you need to think about the methods you will use to meet the requirements of different participants and what the expected outcomes of using these methods will be for the different groups. These key considerations are summarised in Table 1.2.

Table 1.2: Key considerations for meeting the needs of different groups

Factors to consider to meet participants' needs	Factors affecting methods you can use to meet participants' needs
Environment	Facilities: Are they inside or outside? Do they have protection from the weather (e.g. sun shades and rain covers)? Do they have adaptations for participants with disabilities (e.g. ramps, hand rails)?
	Settings: What surrounds participants (e.g. windows, nets, walls with padding)? What time of day is the activity?
	Sport and physical activity environments: Will it take place in a sports hall, fitness studio, gym, pool, outside area (e.g. playing fields, multi-use games areas, grass pitches)?

Equipment can be easily adapted to meet the needs of much younger players; for example, using a T-ball base when playing softball makes it easier to hit the ball.

Rules

These can be altered to make the game accessible to all participants. New rules can be introduced or fewer rules can be used to suit the age and ability of the group.

For example, for an adult group playing cricket, the full NGB rules can be used, with an umpire present to make sure they are followed. In a small game of cricket in a sports hall for a group of visually impaired young adults, the rules can be adapted. You might not allow a totally blind batsman to be stumped, for example, or you might allow a fielder who is totally blind to make a catch after the ball has bounced once. These rule changes mean the participants can all play the game successfully.

The playing area or environment

This can be adapted to enable all participants to take part in any weather or at any time of day or night. For example, the playing area used for a hockey team to train could be an outside artificial pitch with floodlights or an indoor sports hall.

Sometimes equipment, clothing or footwear will need to be changed depending on the playing area. For example, for indoor hockey it would not be appropriate to wear moulded boots in the sports hall.

Practise

Select a sport or physical activity of your choice.

1　For your activity, identify two equipment adaptations you would make so the activity is accessible for a group of four-year-old children.

2　For the same activity, describe how you would adapt the playing area or environment for a group of adults aged over 60.

Staffing numbers

You will need to decide this according to the number and ability of the participants to ensure the activity is safe.

You must follow your organisation's rules and guidance for staffing numbers. Usually, when working with children, one member of staff is needed for every ten children. These rules change depending on the type of activity, the participants' ability and their age.

Participant numbers

This will also need to be adapted depending on the activity, ability and age of the participants. You must follow your organisation's rules and guidance for participant numbers.

For example, if you have fewer participants than anticipated, you could play three-a-side basketball rather than full teams of five. You could also play activities for longer or play lots of different games for shorter periods.

Advantages/disadvantages of adapting sport and physical activities

There will always be advantages and disadvantages when adapting sport and physical activities. You will not always be able to meet everyone's needs. Some participants might find an activity too easy because you have lowered the intensity so that a beginner can join in. Or it might be too expensive for an organisation to buy specialist equipment or employ extra staff, meaning activities cannot be timetabled as often as participants would like.

Assessment practice	A01, A02

Select a sport or physical activity of your choice.

Suggest adaptations you could make so that a group of adults aged 30–65 years old could take part in the activity together. Now list the advantages and disadvantages to the adaptations you have suggested.

Adapting facilities to allow inclusivity for all

In a sport and physical activity environment there are a variety of different FACILITIES that participants can use. A facility is the place used for the specific activity. Facilities help to make the sport and physical activity easier and more enjoyable. They may include: car parks, toilets, changing rooms, sports halls, gyms, pools, cafés and equipment shops.

Facilities can be adapted to allow inclusivity by making them ACCESSIBLE TO ALL. This means making it possible for everyone to access both the facilities and the activities. Added ramps, hand rails and easily accessible parking and changing facilities will all increase levels of inclusivity.

Staff training raises awareness of how activities, the environment, facilities and equipment can be adapted to promote inclusivity. Specialist equipment can be fitted to enable disabled participants to fully take part. For example, providing lifts, incorporating specialist gym equipment and the installation of pool harnesses, hoists and ladders.

By adapting facilities, a participant may be better able to reach their EXPECTED OUTCOMES. Expected outcomes are the effects you expect to see from an instruction or event. For example, when teaching someone to kick a football, the expected outcome is that they will be able to move the ball along the ground successfully with their foot.

Adapting facilities can also create **POTENTIAL CONSEQUENCES**. These are possible outcomes of an instruction or event; for example, a potential consequence of leading a football session outside is that it might rain.

When an organisation looks to adapt a facility they need to consider these factors. For example, if a leisure centre had an upstairs gym, stairs would be suitable for many users, but for those participants with limited mobility, this might mean they could not use the gym. If the centre added a lift, it would solve the problem, however, the centre would need both the space and the finances to install a lift.

Skills and knowledge check

- [ ] What is meant by the term 'participants'?
- [ ] Can you describe the specific characteristics of young adults as a participant group?
- [ ] Can you identify three diverse needs of participants?
- [ ] Can you describe how age can affect a participant's ability?

- ○ When planning or leading a sport or physical activity, I understand that different participants and groups have specific needs that need to be met. I can use different methods to meet the needs of participants and individuals.
- ○ I know why it is important to meet the needs of different participants.
- ○ I have practised leading different participants and groups.

  If you have been unable to give positive responses to any of the questions or statements above, please go back and review the section.

B Leading sport and physical activities safely and effectively

B1 Planning safe and effective sport and physical activities for diverse individuals and groups

Different types of participants have different needs. It is important to plan safe and effective activities using appropriate methods that meet each participant's needs and fulfil the aims of the session.

Planning a safe and effective activity session for diverse participants and groups

A safe and effective plan for a sport and physical activity session, which meets the needs of diverse participants and groups, will make sure that:

- all the participants' needs are identified and the sport and physical activities meet these needs
- safe techniques and demonstrations are integral to the session and also meet the participants' specific needs. For example, when teaching a forward roll, demonstrate the safe technique that involves touching the chin to the chest when performing the roll. Ensure all participants hear and see the correct technique being demonstrated
- all the resources and equipment are appropriate for the activity and the participants
- appropriate safety requirements and procedures are in place and are being followed
- a **CONTINGENCY PLAN** is in place. This is a back-up plan so, if things don't go to plan, you have an alternative course of action. A contingency plan will include how to respond to incidents and emergencies and how to deal with unforeseen circumstances. For example, a contingency plan for a hockey session might include using the sports hall if it is raining heavily, instead of playing outside on the artificial turf. It might also include ensuring you have the phone number of a contact person (another sports leader) who you can call if you need help.

What if...?

Simon works as a sport and activity leader at a local leisure centre. He leads football sessions for children aged 12 years old on the artificial turf outside.

Simon is planning for his football session, which will take place at 5.00 p.m. on a Monday after the children finish school. Simon must ensure that his plan is safe, effective and meets the needs of the children.

1 Identify the possible needs of the children in the group.

2 Describe how Simon could make a demonstration of dribbling a football through cones safe and effective.

3 Explain the safety requirements and procedures that Simon should follow for the session to run safely.

4 Describe two things Simon could include in his contingency plan for the session.

Sport and activity leader preparation for activity sessions

Before leading a sport or physical activity, you will need to prepare for the session. This preparation means that the session will run safely and effectively and will meet the needs of the participants. As a leader, you need to understand the methods you can use to adapt a session appropriately. You need to understand the importance of preparation and what the consequences of poor preparation will be.

Appropriate activity plans

These should include what the aims of the session are and include an introduction, a warm up activity, the main activity and a cool down. An outline is given in Figure 1.1.

Preparing for activity sessions

Before leading a sport and physical activity session you must follow certain procedures to make sure all equipment is appropriate, safe and set up correctly. As part of your role as leader, you are responsible for:

- carrying out equipment checks. For example, have the badminton posts been put up correctly? Are the nets at the correct height?
- setting up the equipment correctly. You may have to deal with both **COMPLEX EQUIPMENT** – which may consist of many components and be very heavy or unwieldy – or **SIMPLE EQUIPMENT** – which is easily moved and set up. For example, has the trampoline, which is a complex piece of equipment, been put up correctly and are the more simple pieces of kit, the crash mats, in the right place?
- preparing participants for the session. For example, are all participants ready for exercise? Are they wearing appropriate clothing? Have they removed any jewellery or accessories that might be hazardous?

Setting up all equipment correctly is an important health and safety consideration.

Preparing participants for the session

As a sport and activity leader, you must fully prepare participants before a session starts. This will include:

- welcoming participants, establishing the participants' consent to take part in all parts of the session and their fitness to participate
- introducing the activity, explaining to the participants the aims of the session and how they will be met
- ensuring appropriate clothing and footwear are worn. This will be checked and, if it is not suitable, the participants will be asked to change or will not be allowed to participate
- setting ground rules. Sport and activity leaders will describe their expectations for the behaviour and conduct they expect from the participants. This could be how to use certain equipment, particular game rules that will be followed during the session or where participants can go in the facility.

Time spent preparing participants at the start of a session is vital to ensuring the success of the session.

Outcomes of effective planning and preparation

Effective and safe planning brings many benefits to the session, both for the participants and the sport and activity leader. These benefits include:

- For the activity session: The activity session is scheduled at a particular time and will include aims, introduction, warm up, main activity and cool down. The session itself can benefit from effective planning because it will run smoothly, the aims will be met and all the activities will be completed. The session will start and end on time and the correct equipment and facility will be used for the activity
- For the participants: If the session has been planned to meet the needs of each of the individual participants, they will all be able to take part in the session and feel part of the group. They will finish with a sense of accomplishment, having achieved what they wanted during the session
- For the sport and activity leader: When the session is well planned and meets the aims and needs of the participants, it is more likely that the session leader will enjoy it as well. If the leader can follow their plan and knows what they need to do to adapt to the needs of the participants when unforeseen circumstances arise, they will find it easier to deal with issues as they arise and will be more confident as they run the session.

Consequences of poor planning and preparation

Failing to plan is planning to fail!

As a sport and physical activity leader, you need to understand the potential outcomes of poor planning and preparation, and how this will affect the session, both for the participants and you. These disadvantages include:

- For the activity session: If the session is not properly planned there might not be an aim for the session, so no aims can be met. Without planning, the correct equipment might be missing or not available, meaning the activity cannot run effectively. The right facility might not have been chosen, or the time or day that the activity is taking place might not be appropriate
- For the participants: Without planning and preparation, the participants' needs cannot be met because the session will not have been adapted to meet these needs. If the participants cannot take part in the session fully they will be unhappy and may want to end the session early or do something else
- For the sport and activity leader: If the session goes badly because it has not been planned properly the leader may not know what to do. They will feel stressed and this may damage their confidence.

Practise

Think of a time when you took part in a sport or physical activity session that was very well planned. Then think of another session where the planning was poor.

1 How did you feel during each of these sessions?

2 Did you learn more during the sport or physical activity when the session was well planned or poorly planned? In what way?

B2 Leading safe and effective sport and physical activities

Best practice

Sport and physical activity leaders need to understand the importance of following **BEST PRACTICE** (the standard and most effective way to carry out a task or how to follow instructions) when leading safe and effective sessions in a variety of settings. They need to know how best practice is achieved and the factors that affect it.

Best practice can be demonstrated by:

- leadership and professionalism: Acting professionally shows respect to participants and your colleagues. By leading an activity you are in a position of responsibility, you are a role model and need to act as one
- use of communication: Being able to use different methods to communicate will allow you to work with different participants. Sometimes you will need to use signals, for example, pointing where to go, and on other occasions you will need to use a whistle to control an activity
- use of appropriate activities, techniques and demonstrations: You must use activities that are suitable for the age and ability of the group or participants and, when leading, you must always show participants the correct techniques and use clear demonstrations. If you fail to select an appropriate activity, use an incorrect technique or use a poor demonstration, participants can become injured or will learn incorrectly

- session management, including timings, use of resources and changeovers: It is important that sessions are run smoothly, that leaders and equipment are in the right place at the right time and participants have the equipment they need for the session to go ahead
- encouraging inclusivity: Activities should be adapted so that they are inclusive. You may change the rules, the equipment and/or the timings of an activity so that it encourages, or allows, more people to take part
- maintaining and encouraging effective working relationships: As a professional leader you will work with other colleagues and members of the public. You must be able to work well with different groups or individuals at all times and keep these relationships positive
- responding to changes: Being adaptable and able to react and respond to situations is important. Leaders must be able to take positive action to make sure participants are kept safe and can carry out their activity
- reviewing session plans and using reflective practice: To become a better leader you must look back at the success of your sessions. You should identify strengths and areas for improvement in your leadership techniques and use these to improve your future sessions
- participant engagement: Participants must feel that they are part of the session. This can be achieved by asking questions, giving responsibilities to others or using different people for demonstrations. If participants are engaged, they will want to join in more and will feel happier about the session.

What if...?

Mitchell is a sport and activity leader. He works at a health club leading a range of fitness activity classes. It is very important that he follows best practice. The health club has a very good reputation with its customers and they expect a high standard from their activity leaders.

1 Describe how Mitchell can use best practice to encourage inclusivity at the health club.

2 Explain why Mitchell must review his session plans after each activity he leads.

3 Analyse the benefits of following best practice for Mitchell, the health club and the participants in his activity sessions.

The advantages of using best practice are that all participants will be safe, be able to join in, and they will enjoy the session. It increases the chances that they will want to come back for more sessions.

However, there are sometimes disadvantages to using best practice. These could include having to spend more time planning and preparing for your session. Time is a precious resource. Mastering a new activity takes a long time, but to lead an activity competently you will need to learn all the skills and techniques required for that activity, and practise them so that you can teach it to others and check their technique.

Implementing best practice in your session will make it more enjoyable for participants – and increase the chances of them returning.

Assessment practice　　　　　　　　　　　**AO2**

Choose one group of participants and give an example of how you could use best practice in communication to meet the needs of this group of participants.

Importance of best practice in delivery

By understanding the importance of best practice for delivering sport and physical activity sessions, sport and physical activity leaders can meet the expectations of all participants and prevent any negative consequences.

Negative consequences of failing to follow best practice can affect the sport and activity leader, the participants and the organisation.

- You could ultimately lose your job if you do not follow best practice. For example, not checking equipment properly could cause an accident, or adapting the intensity of an activity incorrectly could cause injury.
- Participants will not want to take part in activities that are not suitable for them. If they are not happy and feel unsafe they will not return for more sessions.
- The organisation may suffer reputationally if it does not follow best practice. It can be closed down if it does not follow legislation relating to equal opportunities and inclusion. If participants' needs have not been met, or if they have not been properly included in a session, they will most likely look elsewhere to practise their sport and it is unlikely that they will recommend the organisation to others.

B3 Forming relationships that create a positive impression

When working in sport and physical activity environments, it is important that you form positive relationships with participants and create a positive impression of yourself.

Creating a positive impression is good for you, as a sport and physical activity leader, and the organisation you work for. It lets participants know that you are professional, reliable and will provide a good service. Of course, this benefits the business as happy participants and customers will return. This means increased sales in sport and activity classes and sessions.

Forming effective working relationships

Professional relationships are formed when people work on tasks together or towards a common goal. These relationships include those you form with other members of staff and the relationships you build as a sport and activity leader with participants in your session.

Effective working relationships with participants will develop if you demonstrate respect and create a mutually trusting environment. It is important that you communicate effectively with the participants in your session, sharing goals, motivating each other and working together to achieve those goals.

Benefits of effective working relationships

- Participants will receive an improved experience and become more motivated. They will adhere to rules and be more likely to follow training guidance. They will be more focused and engaged and feel like they are receiving a personalised service.
- The sport and activity leader will develop a good reputation. In the trusting environment that is created, they will become more confident, lead sessions more successfully and their enjoyment of delivering the sessions will also be enhanced.
- The organisation will gain an increase in sales because more people will want to participate in activities. The reputation of the organisation will improve in the community because it has met the needs of the individuals.

Barriers to effective working relationships

Sometimes sport and physical activity leaders experience barriers to forming positive working relationships. A barrier is something that stops positive relationships from being formed, and could include:

- a lack of communication between you and your manager over your scheduled working hours
- your pay is lower than that of your colleagues and you think this is unfair
- time of day could be a barrier because you never get to see some members of staff as they are on different shifts
- participants' behaviours and attitudes or those of the sport and activity leader. The leader should always act professionally and should try their best to resolve any issues to improve their working relationships.

Practise

Sam is a sport and activity leader working in a local leisure centre. She usually leads badminton sessions but the football leader is ill and she has been asked to take over the session.

Describe how positive working relationships could affect Sam's ability to lead the group and how this might affect the organisation's reputation.

Promoting the organisation to participants

One of the roles of the sport and physical activity leader is to promote the organisation to the participants. The most common methods used to do this are:

- behaving professionally. Remember you are at work and that first impressions count. You should speak clearly and be welcoming to participants
- presenting a professional appearance. You must make sure that your clothes are clean and appropriate for the work you are doing. For

example, swimwear would be acceptable if you were leading a water-based activity, but not if you were leading football on the artificial turf

- being responsive to participants' needs. You need to listen to participants and be able to adapt to any issues they may have and resolve any problems before they arise. For example, if a participant has lost their tennis racket, you could lend them one. If they need to leave your session early, you could remind them five minutes before they are due to leave
- meeting participants' needs and expectations. You will have an aim for every session you lead. You must make sure that this aim is communicated at the start of the session and assessed at the end of the session. Take a hockey session where your aim is to introduce Indian dribbling to a group of six-year-olds. At the end of the session most will be able to complete the skill, some will be better and others may find it difficult: certainly no-one will be Olympic standard at Indian dribbling after one session
- recommending services and their benefits. You should know the services and facilities within the organisation you work for. If you have a participant who always brings their son to watch when they do an aerobics session, you could recommend a children's activity class for their son or that they try the centre's crèche (depending on the child's age)
- responding to positive and negative customer feedback. You should take on board suggestions, compliments and complaints. Keep doing what customers say you are doing well and try to improve areas in which you could do better.

The outcomes of effective promotion

Effective promotion can be beneficial all round, for participants, for the sport and activity leader and for the organisation. If participants learn more about the different activities offered by the centre, they are more likely to try them or recommend them to a friend or family member. If the sport and activity leader has met the participants' needs by promoting the organisation they will feel confident and happy. When the organisation is promoted in this way, it will become more successful and may be able to offer the same activities more often, as well as being able to expand and introduce new ones.

Skills and knowledge check

- ☐ Can you describe what a contingency plan is?
- ☐ Give two examples of safe and effective planning.
- ☐ Identify the five different parts an appropriate activity plan needs to include.
- ☐ What is meant by 'appropriate dress' for a leader and participants?
- ☐ Can you describe an example of best practice that could be used by a leader delivering a ball skills session to a group of five-year-old children?
- ☐ Can you identify one benefit of a positive working relationship for a participant and one benefit for the sport and activity leader?
- ☐ Describe how effective promotion can benefit an organisation.

- ◯ I have practised planning and preparing safe and effective sport and physical activity sessions.

    If you have been unable to give positive responses to any of the questions or statements above, please go back and review the section.

C Health, safety and safeguarding in the sport and physical activity environment

C1 Maintaining health and safety in the sport and physical activity environment

In your work as a sport and physical activity leader you have an important role in maintaining health and safety in different environments, including sports halls, gyms, studios, outside activity areas and public areas of a sport and physical activity facility. Both you (as sport and activity leader) and your **EMPLOYER** (the organisation) have responsibility for health and safety. Together, you work to keep yourselves and the participants safe.

Sport and activity leader responsibilities

As sport and activity leader, you are responsible for:
- working in a way that ensures the safety of yourself, any other staff or sport and activity leaders and the participants
- actively identifying any **HEALTH AND SAFETY HAZARDS** and working to remove or reduce these (health and safety hazards are hazards or threats caused by objects, facilities or people that will or might cause an accident or incident that is harmful to people's safety)
- dealing with, or reporting, any **HEALTH AND SAFETY ISSUES** promptly and to the correct authority (health and safety issues are concerns about hazards and potential hazards relating to maintaining health and safety)
- following the organisation's procedures relating to **HEALTH AND SAFETY LEGISLATION**. All organisations will have their own procedures, which they will expect sport and activity leaders they are working with to follow.

Employer responsibilities

Your employer (the organisation you work for) is responsible for:
- creating a **HEALTH AND SAFETY POLICY** (a set of rules and instructions that cover all processes and procedures relating to health and safety within an organisation) that is followed and communicated to all staff. This policy will cover all processes and procedures in the organisation and needs to be clearly understood by all employees
- providing a **SAFE WORKING ENVIRONMENT** (employers have to make the place of work safe and must minimise and remove all risks and hazards where people work). All the activities, facilities and equipment must be checked for safety. Depending upon the nature of the activity, these checks will often need to be conducted every time a session begins
- ensuring that any **RISK ASSESSMENTS** (reviews of health and safety that look at the participants and their environment ahead of the planned

activity) are completed and are recorded and that personnel responsible for health and safety, such as duty managers or other key health and safety personnel, are recruited and put in place

- producing appropriate procedures for the day-to-day operation of the organisation. These will need to cover what to do in the event of an emergency – such as a fire or a flood – and are for reporting any accidents or injuries that may occur
- delivering staff training. Training will cover every part of the employee's work, including health and safety training and safeguarding children and/or vulnerable adults. Initial training, when a new employee starts at a facility, is known as induction training
- ensuring that employees follow all the manufacturer's instructions for equipment or facilities that are used in the organisation
- complying with health and safety legislation and regulations relevant to the organisation.

What if...?

Alexi has just started work as a sport and activity leader at a large sports centre. Alexi knows that she has a very important role in maintaining health and safety in the different environments she will work in, including the sports hall, gym, aerobics studio and artificial turf.

- Describe two of Alexi's responsibilities for health and safety while at work in the sport and physical activity environments.

- Identify two ways that the employer will ensure that Alexi is up to date with health and safety policies as a new member of staff.

- Explain the employer's role in maintaining health and safety for Alexi and the participants at the sports centre.

Health and safety legislation

Legislation is law. It provides specific rules that need to be followed to ensure the health and safety of all. The Health and Safety at Work Act was made law in 1974. This Act states that employers must make all workplaces safe and without any risks to health, that all equipment and machinery is safe and that procedures for their use are followed correctly. Employers have to provide welfare facilities, information and training about health and safety. As an employee, legislation also provides rules that you have to adhere to. This means that you have to cooperate with your employer on health and safety issues and take care of yourself and others around you.

In an organisation such as a leisure centre there will be further legislation that employers have to comply with to keep everyone safe. Key pieces of legislation are shown in Table 1.3.

Table 1.3: Key legislation for employers

Legislation	What the legislation aims to do	How the legislation impacts on people
Management of Health and Safety at Work Regulations 1999	Makes all workplaces safe and without any risks to health. Ensures that all equipment and machinery is safe and that procedures for their use are followed correctly. Makes employers provide welfare facilities, information and training about health and safety.	Employers have to follow the legislation and use it in their organisation. Employees have to make sure they work safely at all times and are protected by the legislation. Participants are kept safe because all employees are working safely.

Table 1.3: *(continued)*

Legislation	What the legislation aims to do	How the legislation impacts on people
Health and Safety (First-Aid) Regulations 1981	Ensures that first-aid provision is in place for all. First-aid provision includes first-aid kits and fully trained first aiders who know how to respond to accidents and medical emergencies.	Employers must provide adequate and appropriate equipment, facilities and personnel to ensure their employees receive immediate attention if they are injured or taken ill at work. Participants and employees will have first-aid provision whenever they need it.
Control of Substances Hazardous to Health Regulations (COSHH) 2002	Makes sure that rules are in place for the use, storage and disposal of controlled substances or substances hazardous to health. These substances include chemicals such as bleach and other cleaning products.	Employers have to follow COSHH procedures for working with and disposing of controlled substances. Employees will need regular training and the use of protective clothing. Employees and participants will be safe from hazardous substances.
Children Act 2004	Allows children to be healthy and to remain safe in their environments. Helps children to enjoy life. Helps make a positive contribution to the lives of children. Helps to achieve economic stability for children's futures.	Children will be safe when participating in activities and when at the organisation. Any person who works with children will need to be checked by the Disclosure and Barring Service (DBS) to make sure that they are safe to work with children.

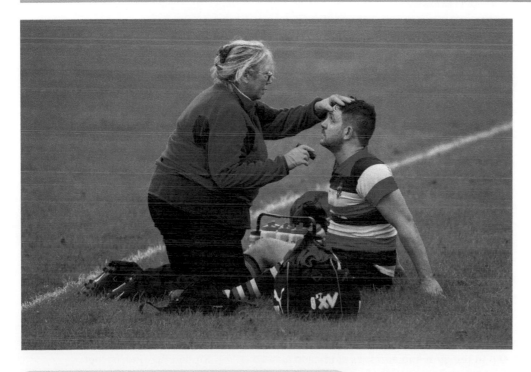

As part of your role as a sport and physical activity leader you need to be aware of legislation and how it impacts your day-to-day duties, such as administering first aid.

Consequences for employers and employees of non-compliance with legislation

If employees (staff, including you in your work as a sport and activity leader for an organisation) and employers (the organisation that you work for as a sport and activity leader) do not follow health and safety policies and procedures there are serious issues that could impact on you, the organisation and participants.

- *Legal consequences*: It is a legal requirement to follow or comply with legislation. If this does not happen employers or employees, depending on the situation and the severity, can be fined or be sent to prison.

- *Business consequences:* If legislation is not followed by an organisation then it cannot stay in business. If legislation is not followed and an incident occurs the business can be sued, which can lead to the organisation having to pay a fine or ultimately being shut down. If corners are cut and legislation is not followed correctly the organisation could gain a poor reputation, causing staff and participants to stop going there.
- *Increased health and safety risks:* Health and safety legislation is in place to reduce the likelihood of injuries and accidents occurring. If the legislation is not followed there is a much higher risk of participants and staff having accidents during participating or working in sport and physical activities.

Assessment practice	AO1, AO2

1. Name two pieces of legislation that you and your employer must follow when working in a leisure centre.

2. Choose one piece of legislation. Describe a consequence for an employer of non-compliance with this legislation.

C2 Hazards in the sport and physical activity environment

When working as a sport and physical activity leader you need to understand what the potential hazards are in the environment in which your activity is taking place, and what their potential consequences are. You must know how to respond to any incident appropriately and also how to minimise the risk of anything adverse happening.

Specific hazards in a sport and physical activity environment

Facility

Certain hazards are present in the facility where the sport or physical activity is taking place. Some of these hazards are summarised in Table 1.4.

Table 1.4: Facility hazards in a sport and physical activity environment

	Hazard	Example
Surfaces ⚠	Surfaces for activities must be appropriate for the type of activity and must be free from hazards. The surface should be carpeted in the gym and aerobics studios to absorb impact; the surface in the sports hall is smooth and vinyl or wooden to allow people and equipment to move around freely. Any hazards on the surface must be checked and removed.	Water spillages Uneven surfaces Ripped flooring/carpet Type of flooring inappropriate for activity
Cleanliness and tidiness ⚠	Cleanliness and tidiness must be maintained to minimise risk. When an activity is completed the equipment must be put away and any larger pieces, e.g. benches, must be moved to the sides of the area.	Equipment left out from a previous session Dirty equipment or clothing An unclean environment
Equipment ⚠	Equipment must be checked before it is used by participants to ensure that it is free from defective parts, damage or broken fixtures and fittings. For example, in a table tennis session any broken or torn nets must be replaced and table tennis balls that are dented should be taken away and new ones used.	Broken equipment Missing pieces of equipment

Equipment left lying around may seem harmless but can present a serious hazard.

Participants

Participants can also create hazards. Some of these hazards are summarised in Table 1.5.

Table 1.5: Participant hazards in a sport and physical activity environment

	Hazard	Example
Behaviour ⚠	Participants can cause a hazard to themselves and others. They need to demonstrate a positive attitude and awareness to risk and behave in a sensible and appropriate manner. For example, all participants must listen to the sport and physical activity leader and follow their instructions. If they cannot do this they will be asked to leave.	Inappropriate use of equipment A lack of understanding of how to use equipment Not listening or following instructions
Clothing, including footwear, jewellery and personal equipment ⚠	This must be appropriate for the activity. Some sports and physical activities are more physically demanding than others. Activities that involve physical contact have stricter rules for clothing, equipment and jewellery than those with no contact. For example, to play netball you must trim your fingernails and remove all jewellery because they could cause an injury to you or another player. To play table tennis you should remove loose jewellery, which could get in the way, but you could keep your watch on because it is unlikely to cause an injury to you or another participant.	Incorrect clothing or footwear Wearing jewellery during a contact sport session Using a mobile phone during a physical activity
Fitness level/ experience/ability/ skill level ⚠	If participants work at an intensity that is too high, they may get an injury. For example, in a spinning class, if a participant works at a high intensity for the whole session, they might become fatigued and slip on the bike causing an injury to themselves.	Lack of knowledge of the equipment or the rules Poor technique

Activity-based

Some hazards relate to the particular sport or physical activity that is taking place. These hazards are summarised in Table 1.6.

Table 1.6: Activity-based hazards in a sport and physical activity environment

	Hazard	Example
Activity space	The size and type of space must be appropriate for the activity. There must also be sufficient access for all participants. Participants must be able to play the sport or activity safely and get in and out of the activity area easily. For example, when playing basketball, the sports hall or outside court must have enough space around it for participants to run past the lines of the court safely, without running into walls or other equipment.	Too little space Too much space No clear access routes
Activity session components for participants	Activity session components for participants must be of an appropriate type, time and intensity for all participants. For example, before playing 45 minutes of football, participants must take part in a warm up to prepare their body for the intensive exercise they are about to do to reduce the risk of tearing a muscle.	Fatigue Injury Loss of concentration
Techniques	Techniques that the sport and activity leader use and demonstrate must be relevant to the age and ability of the participants. If participants try to do something beyond their ability they are at risk of injury. For example, before using a trampoline, participants need to be shown and taught how to stop so that once on the trampoline they can safely stop and not fall off, to avoid possibly causing an injury.	Incorrect techniques Injuries from over-stretching or over-reaching to carry out a technique
Equipment	Equipment for participants must be the correct size and type for the participant and appropriate for them and the activity they are participating in. For example, a small child participating in volleyball would use a large, soft foam ball to prevent them from being injured by being hit with a smaller, hard leather ball.	Equipment that is too big or too small Using the wrong equipment for a sport

Responding to hazards in a sport and physical environment

You need to know how to respond to any hazards that occur or are present during a sport and physical activity.

You must be able to follow procedures when responding to hazards in different sport and physical activity contexts. These can be summarised as follows.

- Assess the level of the identified hazard and the appropriate action to be taken.
- Take appropriate action to reduce the hazard.
- Know when to report the hazard to relevant colleagues, and know who the relevant colleague is.
- Understand the advantages and disadvantages of different responses to hazards.

Practise

1 Identify the hazards relating to the facility, participants and activity that you would look for before beginning a hockey training session.

2 How would you deal with each of these hazards?

Assessment practice · AO1, AO3

Look at the photographs below.

Can you identify the potential risks caused by the hazards in each photo?

What would you do to respond to each hazard?

C3 Safeguarding children and vulnerable adults

SAFEGUARDING means protecting people's health and well-being and allowing them to live free from harm, abuse and neglect. Safeguarding aims to keep people safe. The sport and activity leader's responsibility is to safeguard children, vulnerable adults (those with learning difficulties or disabilities) and themselves from abuse, neglect and suspicion (of neglect or abuse).

NEGLECT is failing to meet a child's basic needs. This might mean that a child is left hungry or dirty, without appropriate clothing, supervision, medical or health care and shelter. Neglect can be putting a child in danger or not protecting them from physical or emotional harm. Neglect is very dangerous and can cause serious damage or even death.

ABUSE is an action by another person that causes significant harm. It can be physical, sexual or emotional, but can also be from a lack of love, care and attention.

It is important that all children and vulnerable adults can participate in sport and physical activities safely and feel secure and free from harm, so they can play and learn without fear. It is crucial that you, as a sport and activity leader, protect yourself by not putting yourself in a position of suspected abuse or neglect by following **SAFEGUARDING PROCEDURES** (steps you must follow to safeguard yourself and others as well as understanding what to do if you suspect a safeguarding issue).

Safeguarding yourself

You will safeguard yourself by:

- following staff ratios for working with groups of adults and children. These ratios mean that there are enough adults to supervise children's activities and, for adults, it means that there are enough leaders to help teach and demonstrate skills and activities. When working with children, it is recommended that there are a minimum of two adults present at all times. Up until the age of 18, participants should be classed as children for these working ratios. The following are commonly used staff to children ratios:
  - 0–2 years: 1 adult to 3 children
  - 2–3 years: 1 adult to 4 children
  - 4–8 years: 1 adult to 6 children
  - 9–12 years: 1 adult to 8 children
  - 13–18 years: 1 adult to 10 children
- regularly taking part in safeguarding awareness training so that you are up to date with the organisation's current procedures and policies
- always following the centre's **CODES OF CONDUCT** (a set of rules, which could be written or unwritten, that dictate how people should behave in certain situations). Figure 1.2 shows an example of a code of conduct.

Code of conduct

- Display consistently high standards of behaviour and appearance.
- Make sure all activities are appropriate to the age, ability and experience of those taking part.
- Always be enthusiastic.
- Use varied teaching methods.
- Hold appropriate valid qualifications and insurance cover.
- Always report any incidents or accidents according to the centre's procedures.
- Attend meetings and courses as appropriate.
- Demonstrate **PROFESSIONAL CONDUCT** at all times (professional conduct is the standards and behaviours you must follow in the workplace). For example, you will not do anything to discriminate against anyone; you would not give participants your mobile phone number; you would always show respect to others.

Figure 1.2: Sample code of conduct produced by a leisure centre for its employees.

The centre or organisation you work for as a sport and physical activity leader will need you to complete a **DISCLOSURE AND BARRING SERVICE (DBS)** check. The DBS help employers make safer recruitment decisions and prevent unsuitable people from working with vulnerable groups, including children. The DBS will check personal and criminal records and will prevent people with certain histories from working with children or in specific roles.

What if...?

Felix is a sport and activity leader in a small leisure centre. He is planning a gym tots session for a group of 12 three-year-olds. Felix must ensure that he follows procedures to safeguard the children and himself.

1 What staff to children ratio should Felix use for a gym tots session with 12 three-year-olds?

2 Identify the organisation that carries out checks on people to make sure that they are safe to work with children.

3 Describe two examples of professional conduct that Felix must display to safeguard the children and himself.

4 Explain the purpose of safeguarding procedures for Felix, the children and the leisure centre.

The sport and activity leader's role in safeguarding

As a sport and activity leader you are responsible for safeguarding the participants in your activity session and reporting any signs of abuse or neglect you see. Remember the following points.

- Be aware of signs of abuse/neglect. If you see any signs of abuse or suspect the abuse or neglect of a child or vulnerable adult you must speak to the safeguarding officer or person in charge of safeguarding at your centre. Do not speak to the child or vulnerable adult and do not discuss this with anyone else. Signs of abuse and neglect include: becoming withdrawn; suddenly behaving differently; anxiety; aggression; obsessive behaviour; self-harming.
- Understand the importance of information sharing (how much information to share, who to share the information with, and when you should share the information).
- If someone tells you that they have been abused, you must tell them that you must refer this to your safeguarding officer. Do not tell them you can keep it a secret. You must refer the person to the safeguarding officer. Do not tell anyone else what has happened because this is confidential between you, the person involved and the safeguarding officer.
- Know the organisation's REFERRAL PROCEDURES (when to refer, how to refer and the role of the designated safeguarding officer). Referral is the process of handing over something to someone else for them to review or take further action. If you suspect abuse or neglect of a child or vulnerable adult you must contact the safeguarding officer or person responsible for safeguarding in your organisation and complete the referral process. This process will probably include you writing a brief report that includes what you saw or heard and the circumstances surrounding it and the details of your concerns and suspicions. The safeguarding officer will then follow up your referral and will look into the situation. Do not speak to the child or vulnerable adult and do not discuss this with anyone else.

What if...?

Sport and activity leaders have an important role in reporting signs of abuse and neglect. Jemma works as a sport and activity leader in a primary school where she delivers mini-sports sessions to the young children. Jemma notices that one of the children has become very withdrawn and is not joining in with the activities like she used to. When Jemma asks the child if she is okay, she says that her Mum hit her.

1 What should Jemma say to the child who may have been abused?

2 Who should Jemma refer this issue to?

3 Why is it important that Jemma does not speak to anyone else about what the child said?

Safeguarding risks in a sport and physical activity environment

There are ways of ensuring that safeguarding is central to the activities you lead. At your organisation you may become aware of the following risks.

- *Inadequate staff training*: If staff are unaware of safeguarding they might not notice a participant showing signs of abuse or neglect. Without training staff may not conduct themselves in a professional manner or follow the codes of conduct, thereby putting themselves in danger of suspicion of abuse.
- *Facilities and environments*: Toilets, changing rooms and activity areas can be possible areas for safeguarding issues. To prevent safeguarding issues occurring, these areas should be secured and checked regularly by staff to ensure that participants are safe at all times.
- *Inadequate supervision by a responsible adult*: This can lead to safeguarding issues if the adult does not follow professional and organisational codes of conduct. Participants must be supervised at all times and know that a responsible adult is there for them throughout their time within the organisation.
- *Inappropriate behaviour*: Participants and sport and physical activity leaders must show respect and follow the codes of conduct at all times. Failure to do so can lead to a safeguarding issue.

Skills and knowledge check

☐ Identify one role of the employee (the sport and activity leader) in maintaining health and safety in the workplace and one role of the employer (the organisation).

☐ State two pieces of legislation you will follow when working as a sport and physical activity leader.

☐ Describe a legal consequence for the organisation in the case of non-compliance with health and safety legislation.

☐ Name two types of facility hazard, two types of participant hazard and two types of activity-based hazard you would aim to reduce when working as a sport and physical activity leader.

○ I know how to respond to a hazard to minimise the risk to myself and others.

○ I know what to do if I see possible signs of abuse towards a participant during a sport session.

○ I understand my role in safeguarding.

○ I know how to keep myself and others safe from abuse, neglect or suspicion.

If you have been unable to give positive responses to any of the questions or statements above, please go back and review the section.

D Emergencies and injuries in sport and physical activity leadership

D1 Common incidents, injuries and illnesses

As a sport and physical activity leader you need to be able to recognise the signs, symptoms and severity of common incidents, injuries and illnesses that may happen during your activity session. Unless you are a qualified first aider you cannot give any treatment. In the case of an incident, you must notify the person in charge of accidents and incidents and follow the organisation's procedures for dealing with emergencies.

Common incidents include:

- accidents – slips, trips, falls, sport-related injuries
- minor injuries and illnesses
- severe injuries and illnesses.

Minor injuries and illnesses

The types of minor injury or illness you are most likely to encounter are detailed in Table 1.7.

Table 1.7: Minor injuries and illness: signs and symptoms

Minor injury or illness	Signs	Symptoms
Strains and sprains	Swelling, bruising and tenderness around a joint or in a muscle	Pain around the affected area Difficulty moving the affected body part
Bruising	Swelling and discolouration	Pain
Cuts and grazes	Swelling and redness There will be bleeding if the skin has been cut	Pain
Blisters	Swelling and redness Possible bleeding if the blister has broken	Pain

Getting ready for assessment

The assessment is an onscreen test. The test is in two sections. Section A is a series of short answer questions, some of which are multiple choice questions. Section B includes a longer question worth up to four marks. There are three types of question in the test:

- multiple choice questions

- short answer questions worth 1–2 marks

- longer answer questions worth up to 4 marks.

The external assessment (onscreen test) is taken under specified conditions, then marked by Pearson and a grade will be awarded. You are permitted to re-sit the external assessment for this unit once during your programme by taking a new assessment (onscreen test).

Preparing for the test

Make sure you have revised all the key topics within the unit content.

To help plan your revision, it is very useful to know what type of learner you are. Which of the following sounds like it would be most helpful to you?

	Visual learner	Auditory learner	Kinaesthetic learner
What it means	Need to see something or picture it in order to learn it	Need to hear something to learn it	Learn better when physical activity is involved: learn by doing
How can you prepare for the test most effectively?	• Colour code information on your notes • Make short flash cards (so you can picture the notes) • Use diagrams, mind-maps and flowcharts • Use sticky notes to leave visible reminders for yourself	• Read information aloud, then repeat it in your own words • Use word games or mnemonics to help • Use different ways of saying things – different stresses or voices for different things • Record short revision notes to listen to on your phone or computer	• Revise your notes while walking – use different locations for different subjects • Try to connect actions with particular parts of a sequence you need to learn • Record your notes and listen to them while doing chores, exercising, etc – associate the tasks with the learning

Remember

- **Do not start revision too late:** Cramming information is very stressful and does not work.

- **Plan a revision timetable:** Schedule each topic you need to revise and try to spend a small time more often on each of them. Coming back to each topic several times will help you to reinforce the key facts in your memory.

- **Take regular breaks:** Short bursts of 30–40 minutes are more effective than long hours – remember most people's concentration lapses after an hour and they need a break.

- **Allow yourself rest:** Do not fill all your time with revision – you could schedule one evening off a week, or book in a revision holiday, during which you take a few days away from revision.

- **Take care of yourself:** Stay healthy, rested and eat properly – this will help you to perform at your best. The less stressed you are, the easier you will find it to learn.

Sample questions and answers

Question 1

Joanna is a sport and activity leader. She has been working at a local leisure centre. Joanna's manager has asked her to lead a new activity session for a group of 8-year-old children. The session will have ten children and will take place in the main sports hall.

Joanna will need to plan adaptations into the activity to meet the needs of the 8-year-old children in the group.

The activity Joanna wants to adapt is a 50-minute-long tennis game that she has used with adults. She has adapted the equipment to use larger rackets and soft balls and is planning to simplify the rules.

1 a) Identify two other adaptations Joanna would need to make so that this activity is suitable for the 8-year-olds. (2 marks)

Sample answer

Joanna can decrease the time the children take part in the activity and she could allow the ball to bounce several times before they return the ball.

Verdict

The answer demonstrates a good knowledge of how to adapt activities to meet the needs of individuals and groups. Joanna could also have identified that reducing the size of playing area would make the game more accessible for the 8-year-olds.

At the start of the session, Joanna must ensure that the children are fully prepared and ready to take part in the tennis session. Joanna starts by welcoming the children and checking that they are wearing appropriate clothing and footwear.

1 b) State two other ways that Joanna should prepare the children to take part in the tennis session. (2 marks)

Sample answer

Joanna introduces herself to the group and tells them what they will be doing in the session. She checks that the children are all fit to participate by asking their parents and carers.

Verdict

The answer demonstrates a good understanding of the procedures Joanna must follow at the start of a session. Although the learner has not mentioned that Joanna should set the ground rules for the activity, they have shown their knowledge of establishing fitness and introducing the activity to prepare participants for activity.

During the session, one of the 8-year-old children is being naughty. He does not listen to what Joanna asks him to do and is not following instructions. Joanna decides to ignore the child's behaviour.

1 c) Explain how Joanna's action, ignoring the naughty child, may impact on the other children in the group. (2 marks)

Sample answer

Joanna ignores the naughty child's behaviour because it is naughty and the child is not following the ground rules for the session. The other children are not being naughty, just one of them.

Verdict

The learner's answer does not answer the question. They have pulled out key parts of the question and re-written them without explaining how Joanna's action may impact on the other children in the group. The learner could explain that the session could be spoilt for the other children because Joanna ignores the naughty boy's behaviour, and the rest of the group may not have as much fun because the group are not able to participate as well in the session. Or the learner might explain that the other children will not get the best out of the session because the aims of the session may not be met due to the naughty child's behaviour.

1 d) Explain one reason why ignoring the naughty child is inappropriate for Joanna's practice in leading activities. (2 marks)

Sample answer

Joanna is not taking responsibility or demonstrating the practice of an effective leader. By ignoring the naughty child, she is not being fair to the other children.

Verdict

The learner's answer shows a good understanding of the role of a leader. The learner could also include in their response that Joanna is not helping the naughty child by failing to challenge their poor behaviour.

Question 2

Petre is a sport and activity leader who works in a large sports centre. He has been asked to lead an indoor hockey competition for the local secondary school. There will be 28 schoolchildren aged 12–13 years old taking part in the competition, which will be held in the sports hall.

Petre's manager has told him to make sure that he follows all of the appropriate health and safety procedures for leading a hockey competition for children. As a sport and activity leader, this is Petre's responsibility.

2 a) State two health and safety responsibilities that Petre has when leading the hockey competition. (2 marks)

Sample answer

Petre has a responsibility to follow the sports centre's health and safety procedures and he must work in a way that ensures safety for the participants and himself.

Verdict

This answer is sound and shows a good understanding of the sport and activity leader's responsibility for health and safety. The learner could also state that Petre has a responsibility to identify any possible health and safety hazards and issues.

Petre has to make sure that the sports centre is safe for the children to take part in the hockey competition.

2 b) Identify two equipment-based hazards that Petre would need to check to ensure that health and safety is maintained. (2 marks)

Sample answer

Petre should check that the hockey sticks and goalposts are not damaged.

Verdict

The answer demonstrates a good knowledge of hazards, but the question is worth two marks so the learner should identify two separate equipment-based hazards. The learner could identify that there must be no equipment left on the playing area, as this could be a tripping hazard.

During the hockey competition one of the children hits another, accidentally, on the head with a hockey stick when they both went in low for a tackle. Petre is the sport and activity leader but is not a qualified first aider.

2 c) Explain two actions that Petre should take and the consequences each action could have. (4 marks)

Sample answer

Petre must reassure the group and the injured children, this will keep everyone calm and prevent any further injuries. Petre should call for the first aider to come to the sports hall to deal with the injured child because he cannot give any first aid. This will make sure that the child receives the best first aid care and will not be at risk from further injury or pain.

Verdict

The learner's answer is very thorough and explains two actions that the sport and activity leader must follow when an incident occurs during a sport or physical activity session.

At the end of the hockey competition Petre hands out feedback cards to the children and tutors who attended the activity.

2 d) Analyse the benefits to Petre, the sport and activity leader, and the organisation, the leisure centre, of responding to positive and negative customer feedback.
(4 marks)

Sample answer

Petre should collect the feedback cards from the customers (tutors and children) and sort them into positive comments and negative feedback. If Petre has received positive comments, that means he is doing a good job and should keep doing the things the customers have commented on. He should take on board any negative comments and try to address them. For example, if he had a comment that said he needed to include a wider variety of activities in his sessions, he could add this to his aims for the next session and put more types of activities into his session. When Petre receives positive feedback it reassures him and makes him feel like he is doing a good job. It will give the leisure centre a good reputation and help to promote the business's reputation. When Petre receives negative feedback it might make him try harder and work on his leadership and organisation skills so that he can improve his performance. For the leisure centre, negative feedback needs to be resolved and they will work with the staff, as a team, to resolve the issues. If the centre does not do this, they could get a bad reputation and lose business, as customers will go elsewhere.

Verdict

The learner shows a good understanding of how to respond to customer feedback. They have analysed the benefits of customer feedback for the sport and activity leader and the organisation.

WORK FOCUS

HANDS ON

There are some important skills and competencies that you will need to practise, which relate to this unit. Developing these and practising them could help you to gain employment as a sport and physical activity leader.

1 Adapt a sport or physical activity to meet the needs of a specific individual or group.

You need to know the requirements of the individual or group and adapt the activity to suit them.

You should be aware of the participants' age, ability and experience.

2 Show you can lead safely and effectively at all times.

You can do this by making sure you have a session plan that includes a contingency plan.

3 Use appropriate verbal communication with colleagues and participants in the work environment; this will help you to form positive relationships.

You can communicate with people using language, gestures and signals, and by listening.

4 Maintain health and safety by identifying hazards and following the organisation's procedures for reporting them.

You can do this by being vigilant when working in different sport and physical activity environments.

You can make sure you know who to report broken equipment or hazards to and the procedure to follow.

5 Show you can safeguard yourself, children and vulnerable adults.

You will do this by following the organisation's codes of conduct.

You will follow the appropriate staff-to-participant ratios when leading sport and physical activities.

6 Demonstrate that you can identify common incidents, injuries and illnesses and respond to them appropriately.

You can do this by knowing the signs and symptoms of injuries and illnesses.

Ready for work?

Hannah is going to be a sport and activity leader at a leisure centre in her local town. Today is her first day in her new job. She starts work at 8.00 a.m. and has been told to report to the duty manager at the reception desk. She will lead her first session at 9.00 a.m. This is due to be badminton for a group of over-50s.

1 What time should Hannah aim to arrive at the leisure centre on her first day?

2 Name two things Hannah should do when she meets the duty manager for the first time.

3 What would you suggest Hannah wears for her first day at work?

2 Working in Sport and Activity Leadership

Sport and activity leaders are involved in the development and delivery of activities that support sport and physical activity initiatives.

In this unit, you will investigate common types of sport and physical activity initiatives and the benefits and barriers to sports participation for different people. You will consider ways to overcome the barriers to participation, compare the skills, qualities and responsibilities that engage different types of participants and support the aims of a sport and physical activity initiative. Finally, you will explore the issues and considerations arising from activities planned to address the requirements and needs of different initiatives and participants.

How will I be assessed?

This unit is assessed using a task that is set and marked by Pearson. All final outcomes will be submitted in a format specified by Pearson. The assessment is available in four windows each year on a quarterly basis. The first assessment is available in January 2018.

Sample assessment materials will be available to help centres prepare learners for assessment.

Assessment outcomes

AO1 Demonstrate knowledge and understanding of the skills and qualities of a sport and activity leader and the requirements of different sport and physical activities, initiatives and needs of different groups of sports participants

AO2 Apply knowledge and understanding of the skills and qualities of a sport and activity leader and the requirements of different sport and physical activities, initiatives and needs of different groups of sports participants to familiar and unfamiliar contexts

AO3 Be able to suggest and justify an activity and the benefits it brings to the participants through analysis and interpretation of a scenario

AO4 Make connections between different pieces of information to justify the qualities, skills and attributes of a sport and activity leader for two different groups of sports participants

A Sports initiatives and provision of sport in the UK

A1 Sports and physical activities

When working as a leader delivering different types of sport and physical activities, you must be aware of what the aim of the activity is, and also understand the requirements for leading it, as well as considering any potential problems that could arise. A good leader will identify these and be able to adapt sessions to meet different criteria and the needs of the different participants.

Types of activities and their characteristics

Sport and physical activities have specific characteristics and these impact on each other. For example, the duration of an activity will depend on the type of activity it is, and this will also affect the staffing number required. The main characteristics of activities you need to consider are:

- the activity type
- staffing
- duration
- specialist equipment
- accessibility.

There are several different types of activities you need to consider.

Classes

CLASSES are timetabled activities, which happen at the same time every day or every week. The type of sport or physical activity is set and will always be the same in terms of age, ability and gender of the participants/group. The staff required to run the activity will be the same each session, as will the equipment and the duration. Participants know when the class is running and what to expect. Classes are often pre-paid by participants and need to be booked in advance to secure a place in the class. For example, a leisure centre might timetable a 60-minute yoga class for adults, for which there will be one yoga tutor who will supply yoga mats. The class will take place in the yoga studio and will need to be accessible for all adults.

Drop-in sessions

Depending on the facility, any timetabled class could be run as a **DROP-IN SESSION**, or just selected ones. Drop-in sessions give participants an opportunity to try a sport or physical activity and to come at a time that suits them. The duration and activity type will be known in advance but the staffing, equipment and accessibility requirements may change depending on how many participants turn up. For example, a local football coach might offer an under-9 football session on Tuesdays 4.00 p.m.–5.00 p.m.; the session will be accessible to children of this age and their parents and the coach will provide bibs, footballs and cones.

Taster sessions

TASTER SESSIONS might be added to a timetable to introduce groups of new participants to a sport or physical activity, or they might be offered to existing participants to try a sport or physical activity they have not done before. The activity type and duration will be known in advance and appropriate staffing can be provided. However, unless participants have booked to try the taster session in advance the equipment requirements and accessibility will be unknown and staffing will need to be flexible to meet these needs. For example, an outdoor centre might offer an archery taster session for two hours on Saturday and Sunday mornings. Archery equipment, staff numbers and accessibility needs will be confirmed once participant numbers and needs have been specified.

Tournaments and competitions

TOURNAMENTS AND COMPETITIONS are run by centres, gyms and sport and physical activity clubs to allow participants or groups to compete. This type of activity will be planned in advance and participants will apply to enter the tournament or competition. All characteristic requirements will be known in advance. For example, a leisure centre might run an adults' badminton competition, catering for 20 adults on a Saturday morning 10.00 a.m.–2.00 p.m. The centre will need to provide badminton equipment, and ensure that accessibility and staffing provision reflect the number and ability of the adults.

Activity days

ACTIVITY DAYS are usually one-off events that are targeted at a specific age, gender or ability. They often include a variety of sport and physical activities and can be used to introduce participants to a new facility. The staffing, equipment, duration and accessibility requirements need to be confirmed before the activity day takes place, and participant numbers will need to be restricted to ensure the requirements of the event are met appropriately. For example, a new leisure centre might offer a children's activity day, to include a range of sports and physical activities, staff and equipment plus accessibility to meet the requirements of the activity types and participants.

Summer camps and holiday activities

SUMMER CAMPS AND HOLIDAY ACTIVITIES are usually aimed at children and take place during school holidays. They might run in a leisure centre, youth club or school. For example, a gym might offer a gymnastics summer camp for 30 children aged 5–11. They will provide equipment for all gymnastic activities, as well as four members of staff (one adult for every ten children, and one extra member of staff). The facility will need to offer access to children of all abilities along with their parents.

Practise

1   Suggest an activity type for a group of older people who have never tried playing racket sports.

2   Consider the staffing, duration and specialist equipment requirements for a gymnastic session for two-year-olds.

Aims of sport and physical activities

As a sport and activity leader, you will set out an aim you wish to achieve in every session you lead, but remember participants also have their own aims when taking part. A session will be more successful if the aims of the leader and the participant are the same.

* Sometimes the aim of a session is simply for fun and enjoyment. This could be a sport or physical activity session where participants either go with their friends or attend in order to make new friends. The session structure will be relaxed and the participants might have control over

what they do within the session and for how long. As a leader in this type of session, your role may be more advisory and supervisory than coach and leader. Examples of this are fun swim sessions, adult drop-in badminton and under-10s sessions on a climbing wall.

- Adults will often take part in sport and physical activities to improve their fitness. This type of activity is led by a sport and physical activity leader or specialist tutor, for example, a spinning or pilates tutor. Participants might choose to join a gym and attend aerobics or circuit training classes. These aim to improve health and physical fitness. Adults might also take part for weight maintenance or to lose weight.

- Another aim of sport and physical activities is improving specific skills. Sessions with this aim will be led by a sport and physical activity leader (or specialist tutor, for example, a swimming tutor) who will teach and coach participants and enable them to improve their ability. These sessions are often aimed at children, but can be adult-only, where adults can learn new skills or develop existing ones. Examples of this type of session are swimming lessons, netball team training and athletics coaching sessions.

The aim of an activity session might be fun and enjoyment, or to improve fitness, but it can also be run to improve specific skills.

Requirements for planning sport and physical activities

Before planning sport and physical activities, you need to know what type of activity you are going to lead and what its aims are. When this has been confirmed, you will need to plan in order to meet the specific requirements of the activity and the needs of the participant. You must consider the following planning requirements for each different sport and physical activity you lead: facilities, equipment and clothing, planning and contingency planning, timings, number of participants, and first aid and health and safety provision. These are shown with examples in Table 2.1.

Table 2.1: Planning for different sport and physical activities

Planning requirement	Example for an under-three gym tots session	Example for an under-21 rugby training session
Facilities specific to the sport or physical activity: Includes gym, sports hall, artificial turf, tennis courts, climbing wall, pool and changing rooms, showers.	Indoor sports hall or gymnasium with a padded floor or matted area. Changing facilities and toilets for children and parents. Car parking for parents.	Sports field or artificial turf. Changing rooms, toilets and car parking for the rugby players.
Equipment and clothing required for the sport or physical activity: Includes specialist equipment and clothing, which may be provided by the centre or the participant.	Padded, soft gym equipment and mats. Participants should wear loose-fitting clothing and remove shoes and socks.	Goalposts, rugby balls, cones, bibs. Participants must wear gumshields, sports clothing and trainers/rugby boots depending on the training surface.
Planning and contingency planning: This must be in place for all activities before they take place and will include a risk assessment and contingency plan, so that all potential risks and hazards are identified and minimised.	Planning and contingency planning will identify any risks and hazards related to the gym equipment, the age and ability of the children.	Planning and contingency planning will identify risks and hazards associated with playing rugby, the use of goalposts, rugby boots, playing surface, the age, ability and level of intensity of the sport.
Timings: These will vary depending on the sport or physical activity type and the participant age and ability.	Due to the age of the children the session will be 30 mins–1 hour.	The session is two hours.
Number of participants: This should be known before sessions take place and will be determined by the number of staff allocated. It will vary depending on the activity type and the participant age and ability.	Children aged under three require one adult for every four children. If parents stay in the session they can be counted as 'adults' in the session.	The participants are over 18, the recommended staff ratio is one adult to 30 participants. Due to potential risks associated with playing rugby there would also be an additional member of staff for every session.
First aid and health and safety provision: This must be organised for all sports and physical activities. If the leader is not a qualified first aider, they will require an additional member of staff who is trained and qualified.	The recommended requirement for first aid provision is one qualified first aider for every 30 participants. There will need to be a large first aid kit, a specified meeting point and a fire marshal on duty.	

Practise

1 Identify three planning requirements a sport and activity leader must consider before leading an indoor football session for 16-year-olds.

2 Suggest how the timings for the indoor football session would need to be adapted to meet the needs of 16-year-olds, adults over 60 and children under four years old.

3 Justify the facility demands required to meet the needs of 16-year-olds, adults over 60 and children under four years old.

Factors to consider when planning sport and physical activities

All sport and physical activity plans need to identify clear aims, the roles and responsibilities of leaders, participant needs, content of the session, **HEALTH AND SAFETY ISSUES** (potential hazards and risks that may cause injury or illness), and **EQUALITY AND DIVERSITY ISSUES** (these aim to eliminate discrimination, harassment and victimisation, and to advance equality of opportunity and foster good relations between different parts of the community).

Link it up

For more on SMART targets, go to Unit 5.

- The aims of the sport or physical activity must be clear. The outcomes for the session will have SMART (Specific, Measurable, Achievable, Realistic, Time-bound) targets that are understood by the sport and activity leaders and the participants. The leader must use effective promotion and awareness of the activity and initiative to participants.
- The sport and physical activity leader and participants have **ROLES AND RESPONSIBILITIES**. The leader needs to select appropriate methods of communication, behaviours, personal qualities and leadership styles. The participants must also display appropriate behaviours, personal qualities and methods of communication.
- **PARTICIPANT NEEDS** must be identified and understood to engage and motivate them. Participants need to understand the benefits of the activity.
- Activity planning allows the sport and physical activity leader to identify the **CONTENT OF THE ACTIVITY**. This includes how the activity will be organised, realistic consideration of cost, logistics and technical competence of the leader and participants. The **APPROPRIATENESS OF THE ACTIVITY** must meet the participants' needs, wants and abilities. The leader must also consider the size of the group, any required adaptations to their selected sport or physical activity and equipment requirements.

Link it up

Go to Unit 1 for more information about equality, diversity and inclusivity, as well as more on health and safety.

- Health, safety and safeguarding risks and considerations must be followed for all sport and physical activities to ensure that everyone is safe and risks and hazards have been identified and minimised. Health and safety legislation will be followed within the organisation by the employer and all employees to keep the workplace safe.
- Equality, diversity and inclusivity have to be maintained to ensure all participants and staff feel valued and included. Equality and diversity legislation is in place throughout the organisation to make sure that no one is excluded or treated unfairly.

Assessment practice   AO1, AO2

Michael is a sport and physical activity leader at a sports centre. He has been asked to lead a new adult-only volleyball session on Thursday afternoons in the sports hall from 2.00 p.m. to 3.30 p.m. Michael needs to plan for the volleyball session and must consider factors to meet the needs of the activity and the participants.

1 Identify an aim for Michael's adult volleyball session.

2 Describe two roles and responsibilities Michael has as the leader of the session.

3 What does Michael need to think about to make sure the session is accessible to all of the adults? How can he put his thoughts into action?

4 Identify two pieces of legislation that must be considered and followed when planning the session.

A2 Sport and physical activity initiatives

Aims of sport and physical activity initiatives

INITIATIVES are ideas that have been made into a programme, event or scheme, which help to promote something and raise awareness of it. Sport and physical activity initiatives are used to promote and increase participation to make sports more popular and to help people to enjoy participating in them. Sport and physical activity initiatives can be targeted to the whole population or to a specific group. They might be aimed at a specific age, gender, ability level or activity.

Initiatives can be aimed at improving physical and mental health. They involve getting people active or increasing how often they take part in physical activity or try new sports. They focus on physical activities and fitness and well-being. Examples of sport and physical activity initiatives include increasing knowledge surrounding the benefits of maintaining good health, reducing obesity and promoting healthy eating – often following government recommendations.

Using initiatives

Organisations, government departments and sporting national governing bodies (NGBs) all use initiatives to promote the benefits of sport and physical activities. For example, the Youth Sport Trust (YST) works with children and young people to increase the awareness of physical education and school sport. Its aim is to give all children a sporting start and to maintain sports opportunities throughout their school life allowing them to achieve their sporting best.

Sport and physical activity initiatives can be used to introduce new sports and physical activities to different groups. This might be because the sport is a new trend and more people want to try it or it might be targeted at a group who do not usually take part in it. For example, a leisure centre might start to offer rock climbing sessions for children aged five to six because they see their older siblings and parents taking part and want to try it. The leisure centre is using the children's climbing session as an initiative to get young children involved in a physical activity that they might not have done before.

Link it up

Go to Unit 7 for more information about initiatives and how they can be used to promote and increase participation in sport and physical activities.

Link it up

Go to Unit 6 for more information about the different national governing bodies for each category of outdoor activities.

Initiatives encourage participants to try an activity they have not done before.

If the numbers participating in a particular sport are dwindling, and fewer and fewer people are taking it up, an initiative could be introduced that aims to increase the number of participants in a sport or physical activity, or its popularity. For example, the national governing body for netball (AENA) runs initiatives that aim to increase the number of older people playing netball by introducing 'walking netball'. This activity can also be played by people of all abilities and ages.

Initiatives are used to promote grassroots involvement and also to set up elite development. Within the sports sector, 'grassroots' is used to describe local level sports clubs that are self-organised, run by community members who take responsibility for their community sport. Grassroots clubs aim to increase participation in sport. The aim of 'elite development' is to help sports people reach their potential in their chosen sport and enable them to compete at the highest level.

Competitive sports need to recruit and nurture new talent and be able to further develop their best performers. UK Athletics, the governing body for athletics, uses initiatives to help advertise itself to youngsters and aims to get them involved in athletics from a very young age. UK Athletics also uses initiatives to help develop talent and facilitate training and opportunities for elite athletes.

Sport and physical activity initiatives are often used by schools, councils and sports centres to try to address social problems in the local area. A local leisure centre might introduce an initiative that allows teenagers to use the centre's facilities for free or for a very small cost. Part of the initiative may involve a special programme of activities, tailored to teenagers' interests. By offering the teenagers sports and physical activities, they have somewhere to go and something to do, and this helps to keep young people out of trouble and gives them a purpose and opportunity to mix with their friends.

What if...?

Harrison is a sport and activity leader at a local leisure centre. A new activities manager has joined the staff, and has asked Harrison to introduce a new sport or physical activity to a specific group. Harrison has selected walking football for the sports activity and the group at whom he will aim the activity is adults aged over 60 years old.

Harrison has been told that he needs to consider: cost, staffing, timing, equipment and adaptations when planning how to introduce his new sports activity.

1 Describe the staffing and equipment needs Harrison must consider.

2 Harrison has chosen to run his activity for adults aged over 60; explain why he must consider costing when he plans this sports activity.

3 Describe any adaptations you think Harrison might need to make to the sports hall to carry out his selected sports activity.

Link it up

Go to Unit 5 for more information about employment opportunities offered by providers in different sectors, to include private, public and voluntary sectors.

A3 Sport and physical activity provision

Characteristics and benefits of different types of sport and physical activity provision

Sports facilities are provided by three sectors: local government, private businesses and voluntary organisations. They all provide sport and physical activity environments to be used for leisure and competition. Each sector has different characteristics and benefits for participants and employees, as shown in Table 2.2.

Table 2.2: Characteristics and benefits of different types of sport and physical activity provision

Sector	Facilities	Benefits	Examples
Public	Facilities are open to the general public – that is, everyone. They provide a service for the local community and offer activities that target specific groups. The facilities are usually adequate, although they do not normally have the newest or most expensive equipment. They are funded by the government and/or local authorities. Tax payers pay towards these facilities when they pay their taxes. The public pay directly through admission fees or for classes when using the facility. The facility does not run to make money and is usually subsidised by the local council, so makes a loss overall. Activities are offered to encourage people to participate.	They are easily accessible for everyone, and are reasonably priced – there are concessions for people on reduced incomes and the activities and events offered are community orientated.	Examples include: local authority leisure centres, local authority swimming pools, local parks and playing fields.
Private	This type of facility is exclusive and open only to members. They usually serve people with a higher disposable income. Their focus is less on specific target groups and more on delivering high-quality service and facilities. These facilities are funded through memberships and by the owner's financial input. The facility is a business and the aim is to make money for the owners. They will programme sports, activities and events that make money.	These facilities provide additional choice for people to take part in sport and physical activities and may be sport specific, e.g. a golf or tennis club. They will have the latest equipment and facilities and are able to start or respond quickly to new trends. There will be membership schemes and incentives that encourage new members to join.	Examples include stadiums for football, rugby, private sports clubs (tennis, cricket and golf), private health clubs and professional sports clubs.
Voluntary	Facilities and clubs are run by members or committees on a voluntary basis, sometimes owned by members or a charity trust. These clubs/organisations do not receive funding from local government or through membership fees. They can apply for grants from the National Lottery and the government to improve or develop their facilities. They may hold fundraising events and ask for sponsors to provide money to support their facility. They may also get money from sports players who pay a subscription fee each time they use the facility or play a match. This money helps to cover the cost of transport, washing kit, paying for equipment and the cost of entering competitions.	They are open to all, serve the local community, and exist for their members and users. They are not focused on making a profit, and often work in partnership with public/private sector to use facilities and for sponsorship.	Voluntary sector provisions create links within the community and the sport's national governing body, promoting grassroots developments and elite participation. They are accessible, affordable to all and sport focused. Examples include Sunday league sports teams and local sports clubs.

Public facilities offer sports to the whole community.

Private facilities can offer more in terms of luxury and choice.

Voluntary clubs and organisations bring opportunities to all parts of the community.

What if...?

Troy has recently completed a BTEC Technical Diploma for Sport and Activity Leaders. He has been looking at different jobs available in his area. He has seen two jobs he would like to apply for as a sport and activity leader: one in a private gym and another in a public leisure centre.

Troy needs to decide which sector he wants to work in. He needs to consider the benefits to him and his career of either workplace and the opportunities available to him.

Troy enjoys meeting new people, he likes working in different environments and leading a range of sports and activities. Troy wants to become a fitness instructor and aims to become a manager in the next five years.

Using your knowledge of the public and private sectors:

1 Describe the benefits to Troy of working in either the private or public sector as a sport and activity leader.

2 Explain which job you think Troy would be best suited to.

Skills and knowledge check

- [ ] What is a sport and physical activity initiative?
- [ ] Can you describe the aims and requirements of delivering sport and physical activities?
- [ ] Can you identify three different aims of sport and physical activity initiatives?
- [ ] Describe how you could introduce a new sport or physical activity to a specific group.

- ○ I understand how an initiative can be used to improve physical and mental health, fitness and well-being.
- ○ I can explain the different sectors who provide sport and physical activity facilities.
- ○ I know why it is important to offer sports facilities for all.

  If you have been unable to give positive responses to any of the questions or statements above, please go back and review the section.

B Sports participants, their needs and barriers to participation

B1 Sports participants and their needs

Many people face **BARRIERS TO PARTICIPATION**. These are particular needs preventing them from participating regularly in sport and physical activities. Barriers may be due to work or school/college commitments, money, childcare issues or other issues.

It is important to encourage inclusiveness in sport and physical activity, regardless of an individual's gender, race, culture, language, disability, religion, health, economic and social status, age or sexual orientation. You should always aim to reduce any barriers you identify that prevent participation.

Link it up

Go to Unit 7 for more information about the factors that influence participation in sport and physical activity for different groups.

Types of activity participants

Activity participants, or people who take part in activities, have specific characteristics and needs that are related to their age, gender, ability, families and cultural background. It is important to be able to recognise these characteristics to meet their needs and reduce any potential barriers to participation.

- *Pre-school children (under five)* are still growing physically, mentally and socially. They will need to be supervised by their parents and may not want to take part in activities without a parent present. Parents are responsible for pre-school children, have to give their consent for the children to take part in activities and will have to pay for their activities. Before children start school they can participate in activities during the day and at weekends.
- *Young people (under 18)* will be at different stages of physical, mental and social development. As young people get older they become more confident, more physically able and keen to take part in activities with their friends and without parental supervision. They become more independent and no longer need as much help and support from their parents – they can often make their own way to attend activities. When young people reach 16 or 18 years of age, depending on the organisation's rules, they can give their own consent to take part in activities and do not require parental permission. Some young people may have part-time jobs and be able to pay for their own sports and activity sessions. Because young people attend school or college, they are unable to attend activities during the day and mainly take part after school or at weekends.
- *Adults* in this context include participants aged over 18 and under 50 years of age. They have developed physically, mentally and socially but may have had different experiences with sport and physical activities in their past that affects their participation. Adults who work may not be able to take part in activities because of work commitments. Adults with children will need childcare to look after their children. Adults who do not work may have difficulty affording the cost of participating.

Age is no barrier to participating in sports and activities.

- *Older people*, aged over 50 years of age, will include a wide range of participants. Some will be working full-time, some may have retired or be working part-time, some might have physical restrictions due to injury or illness and some may face financial difficulties. Activities offered for this participant type need to take these different factors into consideration.
- *Women* are a different participant type because the category can include pregnant women, women aged over 18 and over 50, women who work full-time, part-time, are retired or look after their children. Women might have difficulty finding childcare to attend activity sessions and may be on a reduced income.
- *People with disabilities* include those with physical and mental impairments. Their individual requirements will depend on their ability and restrictions. People with disabilities often need extra space, this might be in the car park, changing rooms, showers and activity area. Leisure centres will often build ramps, handrails and put lifts in instead of stairs to increase accessibility in and around the facility. This participant type includes people who may work full-time, part-time, are retired, are unemployed and have children to care for.
- *Parents and babies* are a participant type made up of one or two adults and one or more babies. The parent can be mum or dad and the baby, aged under one, will be totally reliant on their parent. Parents and babies will require activities that can be adaptable, because the participants will need to leave and re-join at unknown times due to feeding and changing the baby. They will often require more space for parking and well-equipped changing facilities. The parents may work full-time, part-time, be on maternity leave or unemployed. Activities are usually timetabled during the day and at weekends.
- *Black and minority ethnic group (BME)* participants include people of all ages, abilities, men and women. This participant type belongs to a specific ethnicity group. Their cultural background may influence their choice of activity, clothing and availability.
- *Unemployed people* who do not work will have a limited income and may find it difficult to afford equipment, specialist clothing and the cost of taking part in sport and physical activities.

Link it up

These considerations will also be important when you come to completing the synoptic task in Unit 8.

Leisure centres and sports facilities will offer concessions or different pricing structures to participant types who have restricted or limited incomes. These pricing structures aim to make taking part in sport and physical activities more accessible so that everyone can take part.

Concessions or lower prices are often available to participants who are in full-time education (students), unemployed, retired or over 60 years old, families and children.

Practise

1 Compare the needs of participants with disabilities to those of parents with babies.

2 For a type of activity participant of your choice, justify how a leisure centre can meet their needs and become more accessible for them.

Factors that influence the needs of different participants

All participants have needs and, as a sport and activity leader, you need to think about these needs when you plan your sessions. The factors that influence planning of activities for different types of participants include: age, gender, ability, families and cultural background. These are explained further in Table 2.3.

Table 2.3: Factors that influence planning of activities for different types of participants

Factors	Explanation	Example
Age	Staff to children ratio decreases as children get older and are more capable of looking after themselves. Babies and very young children will need their parents with them during activities. Older children will require more adults (leaders or assistants) to help them during their activities. Adults will require minimal assistance and will require fewer staff during activities.	The suggested ratio for indoor football sessions for children aged three to four years old could be one member of staff for every ten children. For children aged 14–16 years old the ratio could change to one member of staff for every 20, while for adults, it is one member of staff for every 30 adults.
Gender	Men, women, boys and girls will require changing facilities for them to get ready for activities. Members of staff should reflect the gender taking part in the activity, but it is not essential for a woman to lead a mainly female activity.	Gym sessions that are promoted as women-only must be taken by female leaders.
Ability	If the participants have a lower level of ability they will need more staff/leaders to help them. If the activity is more physically demanding it will also need more staff.	A beginner's basketball session needs more staff to help the participants than an over-18s team training session. Participants using the climbing wall would be limited to a smaller number so that the leader can give more help to each individual.
Families	Changing facilities need to be larger to enable the whole family to be together. Families will need activities programmed that allow them to take part at the same time, although their ability and ages will differ.	Family swim time requires mixed changing rooms so that parents and children can change together. The pool needs lifeguards who will be aware of the mixed age and ability level in the pool.
Cultural background	Clothing, activity types and language spoken may need to be adapted for people of cultural backgrounds.	A member of staff who speaks a commonly used language within the local community can help translate. Activities can be programmed that have been requested by the community.

Planning considerations related to participants

As a sport and physical activity leader, you must plan any sessions you lead with the needs of both individuals and the whole group in mind. To do this, you must take on board specific considerations, for example, the environment the activity will take place in, the psychological, physical, social and educational needs of the participants, and any medical and health issues they might have.

- *Environmental*: The environment is the area in which the sport or physical activity takes place. The environment can be inside or outside and can include playing fields, artificial turf, the gym, sports hall – anywhere that is used for sport and physical activities. This also includes the sports facility itself, the leisure centre, the car park,

Link it up

Go to Unit 1 and Unit 7 to learn more about sport and physical activity participants.

changing rooms and pool. You need to consider what information you need to know about the environment. How accessible is it? Are the buildings and facilities appropriate for the activity and the participants? What are the transport links within the area and is there appropriate parking?

Get to know your working environment – an open-air pitch will have different considerations to an indoor gym.

- *Psychological*: Do any participants lack confidence? Does anyone have a fear of injury, or think they lack a particular skill and ability? Is anyone worried or anxious about taking part and meeting new people, or do they have a negative attitude towards participating?
- *Physical*: You need to be aware of the participants' ability levels. Are they beginners, advanced, young children, adults or competitive sports players?
- *Social*: Participants may think they have barriers to participating, or may have strong opinions and stereotypes (thoughts or beliefs) that prevent them from participating. Likewise, they may worry that other people will have prejudices about, and stereotype, them. For example, young women may feel that they cannot take part in boxing because they may feel there is a perception that boxing is not a sport for women and that it is wrong for women to do it.
- *Educational*: You must be aware of the different levels of training participants have experienced in different sports and physical activities. In an activity where the equipment or activity itself may be more dangerous and involve physical contact, you need to make sure the participants receive more training and are all at an appropriate level of understanding before they take part.
- *Medical/health*: It is very important that you are aware of any medical conditions, physical injuries and disabilities participants may have. It is also the responsibility of the participant to share this information with you, so that they are safe and you can plan for them to be safe and prevent further injury or accidents.

Assessment practice   **AO1, AO2**

Emma is a sport and physical activity leader. She works at a health club and leads a range of activities in different environments, including adults' circuit training in the exercise studio and children's football play sessions in the main hall.

Emma plans all of her activity sessions before she leads them. She has to consider how to meet the needs of the participants and promote inclusion.

1 Identify the environmental considerations Emma must consider when planning a children's football session in the sports hall.

2 Describe how Emma can include social considerations into her planning when she plans an adults' circuit training session.

B2 Benefits of participation in sport and physical activity

Participation in sport and physical activities has many benefits for the participants. It improves health and well-being, allows time to relax and de-stress, and provides a place to meet new friends. Participation has four key benefits: physical, psychological, social and economic. These benefits often overlap. For example, the physical benefit of improving fitness will also make the participant feel better, which is a psychological benefit.

Physical benefits

Taking part in regular physical activity can help to prevent or reduce the risk of disease and can help to manage certain medical conditions, such as diabetes and high blood pressure. Doing at least 30 minutes of exercise most days of the week can lower blood pressure and make the heart stronger. A stronger heart can pump more blood with less effort. High blood pressure can be reduced to safer levels by regular physical activity. The best types of exercise for lowering blood pressure are walking, jogging, cycling, swimming or dancing. Strength training can also help reduce blood pressure, for example, using fixed weights in the gym.

Taking part in sports and physical activities will also help with weight maintenance and can help people to lose weight, gain more muscle and improve their physical fitness.

Psychological benefits

Exercising and taking part in physical activities can have a positive impact on your psychological health and can reduce depression and stress, while improving self-confidence. Exercise releases feel-good brain chemicals called endorphins. These chemicals may ease depression by reducing toxic chemicals that attack the immune system and increasing body temperature, which can have a calming effect.

Social benefits

Taking part in physical activities encourages social interaction: you meet people, work as a team and learn to cooperate with others. It will help to improve your social skills, make you feel less isolated and can help to enhance your self-esteem and confidence.

An important benefit of group activity is the social opportunities it offers.

Economic benefits

There are benefits to the community, both locally and nationally, when people participate in physical activity. It creates employment, it gives jobs to people working in the sector and helps support businesses within the sport, leisure, health and fitness sector. By keeping active and maintaining health and fitness levels, people will be less likely to suffer with long-term illnesses and diseases such as type 2 diabetes and heart disease. In turn, this reduces the stress on the National Health Service (NHS) and helps to reduce the cost of treating patients, allowing the NHS to focus its budget elsewhere. You are also less likely to need time off work due to sickness if you are fit and healthy. This is another benefit to the economy, as it saves money on businesses having to pay for temporary and cover staff.

Practise

Participation in sport and physical activities benefits its participants. It helps them to keep fit and active, gives them a hobby or interest and somewhere to meet and make new friends.

1 State two benefits of participation in physical activity for the participant.

2 Explain how the benefit of participants taking part in sport and physical activities can benefit the community.

B3 Factors and barriers that affect participation in sport and physical activity

There are many factors that can become barriers and influence your participation in sport and physical activities. You can read about them in Table 2.4.

Table 2.4: Factors affecting participation

Factor	How it affects participation	Examples
Social	Peer and family pressures, portrayal of young people and the use of role models.	A young person might want to take part in boxing, but their family do not think it is safe and will not let them. The media sometimes show young people as being lazy and unmotivated. This image could actually make young people become lazy, or at least lower their motivation for participating. On the other hand, it could make young people try to prove that this image is wrong and do the opposite.
Economic	The cost of participation, recession, level of unemployment and income.	Some activities are free to take part in, for example, jogging and walking. Some sports require very expensive specialist equipment and clothing, for example, skiing. If you have a low income or are unemployed there may be sports and physical activities that you just cannot afford to try.
Access to provision	Location of the facility/ sports environment, choice of activities available, information, appropriate buildings and transportation.	In a large town or city there are many sports and activity facilities. These usually have bus routes, car parks and even stations nearby to enable people to get to them easily. There is a lot of choice and information about where to go for different activities. In a small village there may not be a sports centre, although there might be a park or playing fields. This lack of provision means that the choice of activities can be very limited. Unless there are good transportation links into the town or city, the sports available to these people can only be those that use the park and playing fields.
Historical	Gender imbalance (male-dominated sports) and the popularity of certain sports and activities.	Historically men have participated and competed in football and rugby, our nation's favourite sports. Men also dominate most other popular sports, for example, golf, boxing, snooker and cricket. Recently we have seen more and more women participating and competing in sports and activities, making them even more popular. One such example is women's football.
Educational	Poor attitudes to PE, lack of personal skills, lack of facilities or choice of sport, and lack of funding and government direction on which sports are taught in schools can mean that some sports are never accessible to young people.	School is where most people learn about sport and physical education. The government decides the type of sport and activities schools must teach and the individual school's provision dictates which they can deliver. For example, if a school has a pool it can offer swimming lessons; if it has large playing fields it can offer rugby, hockey and football. Due to limitations in school provision and funding, some sports are never offered and young people never have access to try them, for example, fencing, pole vaulting, lacrosse or water polo.
Fashion/trend	Media coverage and success/ decline of different sports, the impact of sports people as role models on the popularity of sport and physical activities.	The media can make sports popular or make interest in a sport decline. If a sport or activity is fashionable, the media will pay it more attention. For example, when there is a trend for taking part in extreme and outdoor activities, more people are keen to participate in rock climbing and military assault courses.

Table 2.4: *(continued)*

Factor	How it affects participation	Examples
Sports legacy of major sporting events	Inspires participation in sport and physical activities and provides role models.	Following a major sports event people feel motivated to take up sports activities. They may see a new role model and want to participate in their sport, for example, Louis Smith in gymnastics or Hannah Cockroft in wheelchair athletics. When an event is hosted, facilities are built; this legacy can be used after the event by local people. Having a new sports facility can make people more keen to take up and continue participating in sports.
People with disability and ability level	Lack of early experiences in sport, limited opportunities and programmes for participation, lack of training and competition, lack of accessible facilities and limited accessible transportation.	Provision needs to include a range of sport and physical activities but also the availability of equipment and coaches to meet all ability levels (from beginner to elite level). There is often a lack of sports provision and competition suitable for people with disabilities. Facilities need to become more accessible and offer activities and competitions that are open to all ability levels.
Cultural background	Cultural preferences or familiarity with different sport and physical activities, cultural attitudes towards participating in different physical activity and sports.	Different cultures will have sports and activities they are familiar with or favour over others. For example, in Britain the most popular sport is football, in India it is cricket and in the USA it is American football. Kabaddi is the national sport of Bangladesh, yet it is not well known in the UK.
Role of the media	Increased or decreased spectator attendance, better-informed supporters, personalities and role models are promoted through their sporting success, certain sports get exposure and others do not.	If sports and activities are on television, people will watch and take part. This can make the sport/activity more popular. The reverse is also true, if a sport/activity is never shown on television it does not gain an audience and people do not know about it, so will not try it. Since the Tour de France came to the UK, there has been more media attention on cycling, which has helped people to become aware of the sport and has created more opportunities for them to participate.

Assessment practice A03

Jason is a sport and activity leader working in a local sports centre. He has been asked to develop a new activity to help encourage teenagers to participate more regularly in sports activities. The activity can use any equipment and facilities Jason would have available in the sports centre. The activity should last 1 to 2 hours.

1 Identify two barriers to participation facing teenagers.

2 Suggest an activity Jason could introduce to a group of teenagers to help increase their participation.

3 Explain how your chosen activity has met the needs of teenagers and how it has helped to reduce the factors affecting their participation in sports activities.

B4 Overcoming barriers to participation in sport and physical activities

Sport and activity leaders will use different methods to overcome barriers to enable everyone to participate. Barriers can affect individuals and groups, so the method used by the leader to reduce the barrier needs to be appropriate and adaptable.

Methods to overcome barriers

- *Raise awareness of opportunities available to people*: Advertising, putting up posters, producing leaflets and making a website to show what facilities and sports/activities are available, where and when.
- *Promote equality and diversity in all activities*: A 'sport for all' attitude should be adopted. Where possible all sports and physical activities should be made accessible to all. No-one should be discriminated against or treated unfairly.
- *Promote the positive impacts of participation for people*: If people understand the benefits of participating in sport and physical activities they are more likely to take part. Positive effects include weight management and improved physical, social and psychological health. The positive benefits could be displayed on posters and on activity session information so that people can clearly see the physical benefits linked to participation in specific activities.
- *Use examples of positive role models to promote sport, avoiding stereotypes*: Seeing a famous person take part in sport can make people want to participate. Famous sports people make sports more popular. Using a role model who takes part in a sport that is less well known can make it more popular.
- *Comply with organisational policies and legal requirements*: By following the organisational and legal requirements and policies you will make activities fair and accessible for all. By following the legal requirements for equality and diversity, activities will be made accessible, meaning discriminatory or unfair treatment will not be tolerated.
- *Use staff training to help raise awareness of different opportunities*: Regular staff training keeps everyone up to date on organisational and legal procedures, policies and requirements. Staff training can be used to promote opportunities for participants in the local area and can focus on getting people to participate in activities they enjoy.
- *Report/challenge any instances of discriminatory behaviour that you encounter*: As a sport and activity leader you must be intolerant of any discriminatory behaviour. Anyone who behaves unfairly or discriminates against others must be challenged and their behaviour reported to your supervisor/manager.

Assessment practice   **AO2, AO3**

The manager of the leisure centre where you work as a sport and activity leader has noticed that there are very few older people participating in aerobics and circuit training sessions.

1 Identify two barriers to participation that may affect older people.

2 Suggest a method to overcome each barrier to participation you have identified for older people.

3 Justify how the methods to overcome barriers you have suggested would help older people to participate in aerobics and circuit training sessions.

Adapting facilities to allow for greater inclusivity

Facilities and environments may need adapting to ensure they are accessible for all participants. Staff training will be needed to ensure that everyone is aware of how to achieve this, and how to use specialist equipment.

Methods of adapting activities to meet the needs of different participants

Activities can be adapted to meet the needs of different participants by making changes to the rules or the equipment or the time taken to carry out the activity. If you understand the different ways to adapt an activity you can make almost any sport or physical activity inclusive. Most adaptations take minimal time to implement and just need some ideas and good planning.

The following methods can be used to adapt activities to meet the needs of different participants.

- *Size of activity/playing area*: This can be reduced or increased depending on the participants' age, ability and the number taking part.
- *Rule changes*: Younger children and beginners will need fewer rules to enable them to take part in the sport or physical activity. Rules regarding contact will change according to the participants' age and ability to ensure their safety.
- *Equipment*: Must be appropriate for the sport or physical activity. It can be adapted for individuals depending on their age, ability and size.
- *Time*: Sports and activities can be shortened to make them appropriate for younger children and beginners. Time can be split to make more, shorter segments and extended as participants become more able and familiar with the skills and demands of the activity.
- *Intensity of activity*: Must be appropriate for the ability of the participants. Working at a level above your ability can cause injury and accidents.
- *Staffing numbers*: These must meet the requirements for the age, ability and type of activity, to ensure all participants and staff remain safe.
- *Participant numbers*: The number of people in an activity or in a group should be adapted to meet the needs and ages of the participants and the demands of the activity.

Table 2.5 shows how indoor five-a-side football can be adapted for adults and visually impaired participants.

Table 2.5: Adapting five-a-side football for adults and visually impaired participants

Five-a-side indoor football: adaptation	Adults	Visually impaired participants
Activity/playing area	Main sports hall, an area with a level, uncarpeted surface.	Main sports hall, an area with a level, uncarpeted surface. The area could be cordoned off, by using nets or curtains, to prevent the ball going too far from the playing area.
Rule changes	Indoor five-a-side rules should be used, e.g. no offside, only the goalkeeper can touch the ball in the semi-circle, no heading the ball.	Blind football rules should be used, e.g. the goalkeeper is sighted, the football contains a bell, no offside rule, players must shout 'voy' before tackling another.
Equipment	Indoor goals. Size five indoor ball.	A football that contains a bell. Indoor goals.
Time	Two 25-minute halves with a five-minute half-time break.	Two 25-minute halves with a ten-minute half-time break.
Intensity of activity	Moderate intensity, determined by the participants.	Moderate intensity, determined by the participants.
Staffing numbers	One leader or referee.	One leader or referee; players can have guides to help direct them.
Participant numbers	Teams of five with up to three substitutes.	Teams of five with up to four substitutes.

What if...?

Taylor is a new activity leader in a large sport and leisure centre. She has experience of leading gymnastics for children aged 11–14 years old. Her manager has asked her to lead a new gymnastics session for three-year-olds.

Taylor usually leads gymnastics sessions in the gymnasium, the session is one hour, there is space for up to 20 participants and there are always two other assistants in the session to support her.

Explain how Taylor would adapt the gymnastics session to make it suitable for a group of 20 three-year-old children.

Taylor must consider the following.

- Rule changes (rules for gymnastics and Taylor's own rules for the session)
- Equipment
- Time
- Intensity of activity
- Staffing numbers

Skills and knowledge check

☐ Can you describe the different types of activity participants?

☐ Can you identify three factors that influence the needs of different participants?

☐ Describe the benefits of participation in sport and physical activities.

☐ When planning or leading a sport or physical activity, what are the planning considerations related to participants' needs?

○ I understand the importance of encouraging inclusiveness in sport and physical activity.

○ I can use different initiatives and activities to specifically encourage the benefits of participation in sport and physical activities.

○ I know the factors and barriers that affect participation in sport and physical activity.

○ I have practised using methods to overcome barriers to sport and physical activity.

If you have been unable to give positive responses to any of the questions or statements above, please go back and review the section.

C The skills, qualities and responsibilities of a sport and activity leader

Sport and physical activity leaders use different approaches to meet the needs of different types of participants and groups.

Link it up

Go to Unit 3 to learn more about developing an effective leadership style and Unit 4 for information about the roles, responsibilities and qualities of a coach, and specialist coaching skills to improve performance.

C1 The skills and qualities of a sport and activity leader

In order to be an effective sport and activity leader, you will need to have certain skills and qualities (see Figure 2.1 on page 66). For example, a good leader will be able to change the way they communicate so that they can be understood clearly by both a group of three-year-old rugby tots and by an adult of 65 who is using the gym for the first time.

Key skills of a sport and activity leader

Good communication skills are vital for effective leadership. Communication may require tailoring depending on the intended audience. It is very much a two-way process. The leader must be prepared to listen to clients or colleagues in order to confirm understanding, and provide additional communication where needed to ensure the participant understands. Non-verbal communication can be used to emphasise key points, e.g. hand gestures, facial expressions. The leader can also check their reception by looking for tell-tale signs of misunderstanding, i.e. facial expressions, body language.

Other key skills include:

- *organisation skills*: These are key to using all available resources and ensuring the best use of time and effort. A leader must be able to forward-plan, identify participants' needs and draw on appropriate resources in a timely manner.
- *being approachable and personable*: Leaders need to foster team spirit and, in order to do so, they must convey an attitude of being open and honest. This will put people at ease and make them feel that they can ask questions, suggest ideas and generally understand the leader's aims and processes. Good leaders need to be able to find common ground in individuals and utilise it to build rapport.
- *being authoritative*: Good leaders must display effective direction and control in order to manage activities. They must be able to establish boundaries so that participants and colleagues understand who is controlling events and who is setting direction. Failure to do so can result in divisive personalities causing disruption to planned events.
- *motivating others*: Leaders have to be able to motivate. Words of encouragement and the setting of goals are often needed in order to get buy-in from participants during activities. Establishing points of success can be used in order to demonstrate achievements and convince people to keep going.

Effective leaders are good communicators.

- *demonstrating*: Conveying instructions and ensuring understanding is fundamental to achieving successful activities. Participants must be able to quickly understand the purpose and/or methods of a session in order to make best use of the time available and get the most out of an activity.
- *problem-solving*: Being a leader inevitably carries the responsibility of having to solve problems when they arise. Problems can take many

different forms and a leader must be able to draw upon experience and resources available to find ways either to resolve issues or circumnavigate them to find a workable solution. A leader must be able to fully evaluate an issue and understand its implications in order to decide upon the best course of action to pursue.

- *being knowledgeable*: A leader by definition should be of a level that has experience and knowledge of sports activities, games and training equipment. The leader must know the rules of activities, how to deliver them effectively and, importantly, how to do this safely.
- *understanding*: Leaders must have an understanding of the mental and physical needs of the participants. It is important to be able to gain useful insight into the needs of clients. Evaluation is a key skill-set necessary to understand what a person wants, what frame of mind they are in and what they can safely undertake due to any known physical restrictions, medical conditions or areas of concern that a client may have.
- *having confidence*: A leader must have confidence and self-belief and be able to demonstrate control and clear direction. To encourage others to follow them, the leader must believe in their decisions and must gain the trust and support of participants and the group. A leader must be self-assured.

Key qualities

Professional appearance

Enthusiastic

Committed

Patient

Understands others' needs

Consistent

Diplomatic

Proactive

Ethical

Leads by example

Collaborator

Works under pressure

Responsive

Key skills

Communicator

Organised

Approachable and personable

Authoritative

Motivational

Good demonstrator

Problem solver

Knowledgeable

Understanding

Confident

Additional skills

Understands activity structuring

Uses target setting

Uses appropriate language

Collects effective feedback

Carries out evaluations

Additional qualities

Can use different leadership styles

Outgoing personality

Attentive

Visionary

Ambitious

Experienced

Persistent

Empathetic

Figure 2.1: Skills and qualities of an effective leader.

Additional skills

A good leader can use additional skills to meet the needs of participants. They will know how to structure activities, they will use **TARGET SETTING** (a process of gathering and analysing information that can then be used to set challenges for improvement to be made), they can use language to make the message clear to all participants. A good leader will use methods to collect effective **FEEDBACK** (when information about someone's performance of a task is used as a basis for improvement) from their participants and will evaluate their performance alongside the feedback to improve their future planning and performance.

Feedback can be collected by handing out questionnaires for participants to complete, by producing an online form, by carrying out an interview or by simply asking, 'How do you think the session went?' or 'Is there anything you would like me to do differently?'

Assessment practice	AO2, AO4

Luke is a sport and activity leader. He is leading a badminton session for adults aged over 60.

1 Identify two key skills and two additional skills that would be relevant for Luke to use when working with the adults.

2 Consider how Luke would adapt the two key skills identified in question 1 when he leads badminton sessions with adults aged over 60 and teenage girls.

Qualities of a sport and activity leader

Link it up

Go to Unit 3 for more information about how to give effective feedback.

Go to Unit 5 to learn more about how to review performance in sport activity leader roles and action planning to develop skills needed for sport and activity leader roles.

Qualities of a good sport and activity leader are summarised in Figure 2.2. A sport and activity leader should be easily recognisable so that they stand out from the group. They should be dressed appropriately for the applicable activity so that they can be easily identifiable and easy to follow.

Throughout any session the leader needs to exude enthusiasm for the activity and a commitment to their participants. This can be achieved through maintaining positive energy levels and maintaining tempo.

Leaders must have patience and understanding of the needs of others. A leader needs to understand the varying abilities and levels within a group. Not all participants will be able to perform at the highest level, and a degree of understanding will need to be employed to support and encourage those of a lesser ability or who are less proficient so that everyone feels accommodated.

A high standard of delivery must be maintained at all times. The leader must be consistent in what they do and what they say. Participants need to know that the rules will be the same and what is expected from them, and that the leader will remain constant.

Sport and activity leaders need to show diplomacy at all times. This means they need to be aware of others' feelings and preferences and ensure that no-one is treated unfairly or ignored. The leader will need to treat participants differently to ensure that they are all treated fairly.

Leaders must demonstrate proactivity. They need to be ready for what is happening next and should think about what they can do to meet the needs of participants before the need arises.

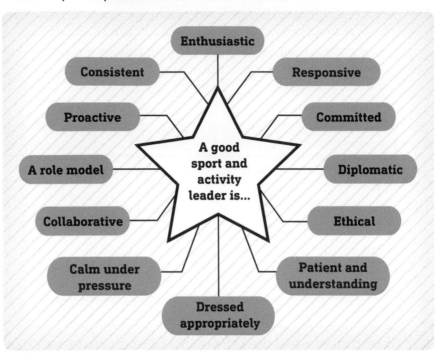

Figure 2.2: Qualities of a good sport and activity leader.

A leader must be ethical, they need to behave in a positive and respectful manner. The leader should follow their own morals and principles, but also those of the organisation they work for and those of the participants.

Leaders set a good example, they lead by example. Leaders should treat everyone fairly and expect participants to do the same.

Working as part of a team is crucial for a leader. They need to be a collaborator. Although the leader may be 'in charge' they have to work with others, they need to be able to listen and take on ideas and advice from others.

The ability to work under pressure is vital for a leader. Meeting the needs of participants changes due to the type of participant – their age, ability and the activity. No two days will be the same and the leader needs to be able to work to tight deadlines and be able to adapt to changing circumstances immediately. The leader needs to demonstrate responsiveness to keep participants and themselves safe and to ensure all legal requirements are followed.

Additional qualities of a sport and activity leader

A good leader will be able to change their leadership style to suit the needs of the participants or the group. For example, command style is more suitable for younger children who need to be told where to go and when; with older adults it would be appropriate to use a more relaxed approach where the adults can have some input into making decisions. Additionally, an effective leader will have an outgoing personality, be attentive to others' needs and have vision. A good leader is ambitious, persistent and has experience of working with others and of the activities they are delivering.

Practise

1 State three key skills a sport and activity leader must have.

2 State three qualities a sport and physical activity leader must possess.

3 Explain why it is useful for a leader to have additional skills and additional qualities.

What if...?

Paulo is a sport and physical activity leader. On Mondays he leads the following sessions:

9.00–10.00 a.m.	Over-60s badminton in the sports hall
10.30–11.15 a.m.	Circuit training in the aerobics studio
11.30–12.30 p.m.	Adults' table tennis in the sports hall
12.45–1.15 p.m.	Covering the gym while the instructor is at lunch
2.30–3.30 p.m.	Trampolining for pre-schoolers in the sports hall
4.00–5.00 p.m.	U16s five-a-side football on the artificial turf

1 Identify three different participant types Paulo will work with on a Monday at the sports centre.

2 Describe how Paulo will use communication with the different participants during over-60s badminton and pre-schooler trampolining.

3 Analyse how Paulo uses his skills and qualities throughout the day in his role as a sport and physical activity leader.

C2 The responsibilities of a sport and activity leader

Sport and activity leaders have responsibilities for themselves, the participants, the group and for meeting the legal requirements for safeguarding, equality and diversity and health and safety. The leader must know how to meet these responsibilities and adapt to meet the needs of the different participants and requirements of the activities and initiatives.

What if...?

Logan is a sport and activity leader working in a large leisure centre. He has responsibilities for himself, the participants, the group and for meeting legal requirements.

1 Identify two legal requirements Logan is responsible for.

2 Describe how Logan uses his leader responsibilities to keep the participants and the group safe at all times.

3 Suggest how Logan can adapt a badminton activity to meet the needs of participants with different levels of ability.

Responsibilities of the sport and activity leader

A sport and activity leader must:

- conduct themselves in a professional and ethical way at all times
- be vigilant to health, safety and safeguarding risks and dangers
- create the right conditions for session aims to be achieved
- have knowledge of the activity and of the participants' needs
- be aware of the environment and social setting
- know how to plan and deliver appropriate activities to meet session aims and the participants' specific needs
- develop participants' knowledge and understanding of sport and physical activities
- demonstrate an ability to control individuals or groups to reach a goal
- motivate participants to achieve their full potential
- understand the importance and legal requirements of equality and diversity when working with participants
- deal with conflict and resolve issues.

Skills and knowledge check

☐ What is meant by verbal and non-verbal communication?

☐ Can you describe the mental and physical needs of the participants?

☐ Can you identify three qualities of a sport and activity leader?

☐ Describe the responsibilities of a sport and activity leader.

○ When planning or leading a sport or physical activity I understand the importance and legal requirements of equality and diversity when working with participants.

○ I can use different methods to motivate participants to achieve their full potential.

○ I know why it is important to deal with conflict and resolve issues.

○ I have practised planning and delivering appropriate activities to meet session aims and participants' specific needs.

If you have been unable to give positive responses to any of the questions or statements above, please go back and review the section.

Getting ready for assessment

Sitting the test

Listen to, and read carefully, any instructions you are given. Lots of marks are often lost because people do not read questions properly and then do not complete their answers correctly.

Most questions contain command words or terms. Understanding what these words mean will help you understand what the question is asking you to do.

Command words or terms	Definition
Compare	Estimate, measure, or note the similarity or dissimilarity between two things or concepts.
Consider	Think carefully (about something), typically before making a decision.
Justification	Give reasons or evidence to: • support an opinion and/or decision • prove something right or reasonable. For example, 'Justify how overcoming...'
Relevance	Importance to the matter at hand.
Scenario	Includes details of initiative and participant details/needs.
Suggest	Put forward for consideration a detailed description of proposed activities.

Remember, the number of marks can relate to the number of answers you may be expected to give – if a question asks for two examples, do not only give one. Similarly, do not offer more information than the question needs.

Planning your time is an important part of succeeding on a test. Work out what you need to answer and then organise your time.

If you finish early, use the time to re-read your answers and make any corrections – this could really help make your answers even better and could make a big difference to your final mark.

- Revise all the key areas and topics of the unit content – draw up a checklist to make sure you do not forget anything.

- Arrive in good time so you are not in a panic.

- Read each question carefully before you answer it to make sure you understand what you have to do.

- Remember you cannot lose marks for a wrong answer, but you cannot gain any marks for a blank space!

Sample answers with comments

The set task may be completed over two days, within a period timetabled by Pearson.

The set task must be carried out under supervised conditions. The set task can take place over more than one supervised session.

Set Task

- You are required to suggest an activity that meets the aims of a sport and physical activity initiative and the needs of a selected group of participants in a scenario.

- You will need to consider key information, such as the context of the scenario, the main aim(s) of the initiative and the needs of the participants, including any barriers to participation.

- You will justify how the activity is designed to meet the initiative's aims and overcomes the identified barriers to participation. You will explain the benefits that the participants will gain from the activity.

- You will compare and justify the leadership skills, qualities and responsibilities that need to be demonstrated to successfully deliver the activity to two different groups of participants that may have very different needs.

- You must complete all sub-tasks in the set task.

- You will provide answers in response to the structured prompts in this task and answer booklet.

Scenario

You are working as a sport and activity leader employed by a private leisure centre in a small town. The centre manager is keen to engage older people into participating at the centre. There are very few over-50s using the centre. The manager is going to introduce an initiative to increase participation of over-50s at the centre.

The leisure centre is in the centre of town, it has on-site parking and has a bus stop outside.

Aims of sport and physical activity initiative

The leisure centre manager has introduced a sport and physical activity initiative with two aims.

1 Increase the participation of over-50s men and women in sport and physical activities.

2 Provide social opportunities for over-50s men and women to interact with each other and make new friends.

You have been asked to suggest an activity for the over-50s that will achieve the aims of the initiative.

You have been given use of some activity areas in the leisure centre and access to a range of equipment.

Activity area

Sports hall (equivalent to the size of four badminton courts)

Four indoor tennis courts

Aerobics/yoga studio

Equipment

A large number and variety of rackets, shuttles and balls for tennis and badminton.

A number of yoga mats.

Four badminton nets, but only five badminton posts.

Four netball posts with nets.

The leisure centre is new and has a café, sports shop and male and female changing rooms.

You have been given use of the centre facilities from 9.00 a.m.–11.00 a.m. and 1.00 p.m.–3.00 p.m. only.

The leisure centre is in the centre of town. There are several direct bus routes between the different areas of the town and the leisure centre.

Sub-task 1

Aims of the initiative:

1 increase the participation of over-50s in sport and physical activities

2 provide social opportunities for over-50s men and women to interact with each other and make new friends.

Suggest an activity that is suitable to meet the aims of the initiative and engage this group. Provide justification for why you have suggested the activity.

In your answer you must make reference to:

- the requirements of the activity, including the equipment, timings and facilities available

- participants and their needs

- barriers to participation and how these can be overcome.

(Total for Sub-task 1 = 20 marks)

Sample answer

Suggested activity

Racket skills

Equipment

Tennis rackets

Tennis balls

Badminton rackets

Shuttlecocks

Cones

Timings

9.00 a.m.–11.00 a.m. Mondays and Wednesdays

1.00 p.m.–3.00 p.m. Tuesdays and Thursdays

Facilities

Four badminton courts

Four tennis courts

The café

Male and female changing rooms

Participants and their needs

Men and women aged over 50 years old

Working or retired

Physical restrictions due to injury or illness

Possible financial restrictions

Age, gender and cultural background

Barriers to participation and how these can be overcome

Social – peer and family pressures, role models, portrayal of older people

Economic – cost of participation, income

Access to provision – location, activity choice, information, transportation

Fashion/trend – media coverage and success of different sports/sports people

Justification of suggested activity

The activity I suggest for the over-50s men and women is racket skills. I have allowed two hours for the session. I plan to have the group play badminton-type games for the first 45 minutes, including a round robin tournament so that everyone can play each other. Then there would be a 30-minute break in the café where the group can have a drink and something to eat and get to know one another. The last 45 mins will be tennis-based activities with some doubles tennis games at the end.

I will have a range of rackets, balls and shuttles so that they suit the individuals' ability. The activities will be of a medium intensity level, so that everyone can join in and there will be an option to lower or increase the intensity if needed.

To overcome the barriers to participation, I would offer a low price for the racket skills session and this price would include a drink and snack in the café. I will put posters up around the centre to advertise the new session and will try to see if I can get a local tennis player to come in and show some skills in a session.

Verdict

This answer is sound and shows a good understanding of the aims of the new initiative. The learner could include more explanation about the participants' needs and how these relate to the scenario. The learner has justified their selection of activity with their given requirements. They have made clear links to the information in the scenario and the aims of the initiative.

The learner has given some explanation of how to overcome the barriers to participation, which are related to the scenario and show good knowledge of the selected group.

Sub-task 2

The initiative aims to bring benefits to the participants who take part in the suggested activity.

What are the benefits that the participants will gain from the activity?

In your answer you must make reference to:

- benefits of participation that the initiative intends participants to receive
- how the suggested activity will bring about the intended benefits of participation.

(Total for Sub-task 2 = 8 marks)

Sample answer

What benefits the initiative is intended to provide

The benefits of participation for the over-50s are physical, psychological and social:

Physical – they will be active and will get health and well-being benefits, such as reduced risk of illness and disease. It can also help them to lose weight and get fit.

Psychological – it can have a positive impact on their psychological health. Exercise can reduce depression and stress and improve their self-confidence.

Social – by taking part in physical activities, they will meet new people and make new friends.

How the suggested activity will bring about the benefits

The over-50s will get the physical benefits because they are being given different types of physical activity within the racket skills session. The psychological benefits will come from being active and joining in with other people. The social benefits will come from the over-50s mixing together while playing racket sports and during their time in the café when they can relax and make new friends.

Verdict

The answer is sound and shows a good understanding of the benefits of participation in sport and physical activities. The learner has demonstrated an in-depth understanding of the benefits for the over-50s of participation.

The learner has provided sound links to the scenario and explained how they will bring about the benefits to the over-50s of participating in their selected activity.

Sub-task 3

A group of new parents and babies have been asking about participating in an activity similar to the one you suggested in Sub-task 1. You have been asked to deliver a session to this group.

Your leadership skills, qualities and responsibilities as a sport and activity leader would be different when delivering to:

- a group of over-50s men and women
- a group of new parents and babies.

Justify how your leadership skills, qualities and responsibilities would change to ensure success of the session with a group of over-50s men and women and the group of new parents and babies.

(Total for Sub-task 3 = 12 marks)

Sample answer

The leader needs skills, qualities and responsibilities for the two different groups.

For both groups:

Skills: communication, organisation, approachable and personable

Additional skills: understands activity structuring, can use appropriate language

Qualities: professional appearance, enthusiastic, committed

Additional qualities: good personality; attentive and visionary

For the over-50s:

Skills: authoritative, motivational

Additional skills: collects effective feedback, carries out evaluations

Qualities: patient, understands others' needs

Additional qualities: persistent and empathetic

For the new parents and babies:

Skills: good demonstrator, problem solver

Additional skills: uses target setting

Qualities: works under pressure, responsive

Additional qualities: ambitious and experienced

The leader needs to adapt their skills and qualities when working with the two different groups. Lots of these skills and qualities will be the same, such as communication, organisation, attentiveness. The leader may need to adapt these for each group, which might be achieved by using different words or phrases or using verbal and non-verbal cues.

Verdict

The learner has identified the skills, qualities and responsibilities needed for the two different groups and has provided some description of these.

The learner has not included links and connections showing how the skills, qualities and responsibilities identified meet the needs of the participants and their proposed activity. The learner has identified these requirements but needs to expand on them further to fulfil this task.

The learner has provided a basic comparison of skills, qualities and responsibilities required to deliver to different participant groups.

WORK FOCUS

HANDS ON

There are some important occupational skills and competencies that you will need to practise, which relate to this unit. Developing these and practising them could help you to gain employment as a sport and activity leader.

1 Demonstrate the skills and qualities of a sport and activity leader.

- Understand the different approaches that a sport and activity leader can use to meet participant needs.

- Listen to people's ideas and take them on board.

- Identify participants' skills and areas of interest to select the best leadership styles to use with them.

2 Carry out the responsibilities of a sport and activity leader.

- Be aware of the environment and social setting.

- Plan and deliver appropriate activities.

- Develop participants' knowledge and understanding of sport and physical activities.

3 Demonstrate how to control an individual or a team to reach a goal.

- Motivate participants to achieve their full potential.

- Understand the importance and legal requirements of equality and diversity when working with participants.

- Deal with conflict and resolve issues.

Ready for work?

Take this short quiz to find out whether you're ready to work as a sport and activity leader and have a career in the sports sector.

1 What is your time management like?

- [ ] A I always arrive on time, I do not like being late.
- [ ] B I am usually only five minutes late.
- [ ] C I try to be on time but always seem to be half an hour late for things.
- [ ] D I never arrive early.

2 How would you dress to go to work in a leisure centre?

- [ ] A Smart tracksuit bottoms and a polo shirt.
- [ ] B Shorts and a t-shirt.
- [ ] C My best suit (trousers or skirt).
- [ ] D My normal, everyday clothes.

3 When you are given a deadline that puts you under a lot of pressure, what do you do?

- [ ] A Make an action plan and get on with it.
- [ ] B Ask someone for help, I cannot do it on my own.
- [ ] C Tell my boss that I cannot do it.
- [ ] D Complain to everyone that I have too much to do.

4 How do you react to negative feedback?

- [ ] A Look at it as constructive feedback and take it on board.
- [ ] B Listen, but not do anything about it.
- [ ] C React badly and argue.
- [ ] D Ignore it completely.

5 How do you prefer to work?

- [ ] A As part of a team.
- [ ] B On my own.
- [ ] C Being the team leader.
- [ ] D Being in charge of everything, but not doing anything myself.

Your score:

A = 1; B = 2; C = 3; D = 4

If you scored mostly As, you are the dream sport and activity leader.

Mostly Bs, you have got what it takes but you could try a bit harder.

Mostly Cs, you may need to brush up on your interpersonal skills.

Mostly Ds, this is not the role for you. You should look for something else.

3 Leading Sport and Physical Activity

Inspiring. Motivating. Exceptional. These are just some words used to describe some of the best leaders working in sport today. All sports require good leaders who can support and encourage the people around them. Your role as a sport and activity leader is to develop and improve the performance of each person in your team or group. In order to be successful, you need a range of skills and qualities to stand out from the crowd.

Every year more people of all ages take part in sport and physical activity. This means the demand for sport and activity leaders is growing. Employers require organised candidates with excellent time management skills and a good attitude. In this unit, you will learn how to effectively plan and lead sport and physical activity sessions for others. Be prepared to learn a lot about yourself and to push yourself outside your comfort zone. This unit will help you to gain the skills and qualities employers are looking for. A positive, honest and flexible attitude is required as after you have led your sessions you will need to review them.

How will I be assessed?

This unit will be assessed through a series of assignments set by your tutor. You will be expected to plan, deliver and review a sport activity session. You will design your own session plan that will include: aims, objectives, equipment, timings and a range of activities appropriate to your group or participants. Closely following this plan, you will lead a session demonstrating your sport leadership skills. After your session has finished you will review your own strengths and areas for development.

Your assessment could be in the form of:

- a session plan taking into account health and safety and the requirements of your group
- observation of you delivering your session
- visual evidence of you delivering your session (video or photographs)
- a review of your session and an action plan.

Assessment criteria

Pass	Merit	Distinction
Learning aim A: Plan a sport or physical activity		
A.P1 Produce a session plan with appropriate content for identified participants.	**A.M1** Produce a detailed session plan with effective content for identified participants.	**A.D1** Produce a comprehensive session plan with justified and effective content for identified participants, describing key factors to be considered.
Learning aim B: Lead a sport or physical activity		
B.P2 Lead a sport or physical activity session for five or more participants, demonstrating basic sport and activity leadership skills (the main content must be at least 10 minutes).	**B.M2** Lead a sport or physical activity session for five or more participants, demonstrating a range of appropriate sport and activity leadership skills (the main content must be at least 10 minutes).	**B.D2** Lead a sport or physical activity session for five or more participants, demonstrating a range of relevant and effective sport and activity leadership skills (the main content must be at least 10 minutes).
Learning aim C: Review leadership of a sport or physical activity		
C.P3 Identify own strengths and areas for improvement and list at least one way to improve performance.	**C.M3** Describe own strengths and areas for improvement and outline ways to improve performance.	**C.D3** Analyse own strengths and areas for improvement and comprehensively plan ways to improve performance.

A Plan a sport or physical activity

A1 Planning activity sessions

All successful sport or activity sessions start from a detailed plan. If you are well prepared and organised you will be ready to deliver a fun and educational session. Good preparation will help you to be equipped to deal with any last-minute changes such as bad weather, a change in the number of **PARTICIPANTS** or a lack of equipment.

In this section you will learn how to plan a range of different sports and activity sessions. You will consider the health and safety considerations of the session you plan to lead, and learn about different types of session and their structure and how to tailor the individual components of a session to meet the needs of your participants.

Practise

In small groups discuss and make notes on the following points:

- what sort of activity sessions have you been involved in?
- what was good about these sessions?
- what could be improved in these sessions?

Requirements of those taking part

Each session plan must suit the group you are leading. It must be aimed specifically at the requirements of those taking part. It is important to think clearly about what is best for the participants. Having a detailed plan often gives participants confidence in their activity leader. However, remember plans might need to change in response to events or different situations.

Every individual that enters a sport or activity session has different requirements and expectations. Some of these include:

- age
- gender
- medical history
- previous experience
- ability level.

The more information you can gather and learn about the participants, the more chance you have of planning a session that offers fun and learning to the group. This chapter will look closely at all of these requirements.

Participants need to be the focus of your session.

Importance of planning

Planning a session is absolutely vital. Planning enables you to work out how you will achieve your session aims and objectives. You are also much more likely to get the best out of all the individuals in your session. A well-planned session, which moves efficiently from one activity to the next, is more likely to focus each individual and keep him or her engaged. This often means the leader will get a higher level of respect and the group will learn more, therefore improving performance.

A poorly planned session will most likely result in a chaotic and non-productive learning environment. In this instance 'failing to plan' really is 'planning to fail'. Imagine walking into a session with ten participants and having absolutely no idea what you are going to deliver. Not only is this a poor service, but it also denies the group the best possible chance of learning and achieving. Individuals will become disengaged and may even withdraw their participation.

It is clear that the planning process is a fundamental part of a leader's role. Planning a session is a step-by-step process. It is important to gather as much information as possible before you begin planning (see Figure 3.1).

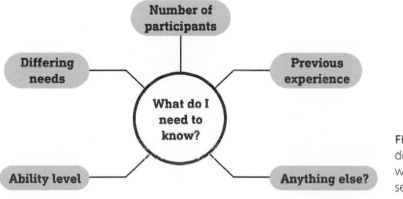

Figure 3.1: What do I need to know when planning a session?

A good leader will have **PLANNING TEMPLATES** ready to write new ideas on, and they will complete these well in advance of their session. Templates are useful as they provide you with prompts as to what you need to consider and include. Many sports centres and organisations have their own templates, so make sure you are using the correct one for where you are working or volunteering. This is also a way of sharing ideas and making good contacts, who may be able to help you with future opportunities.

When delivering your actual session it is really important you are flexible. It is likely you will have to adjust your plan before or during your session. There are many reasons you might have to do this. For example, there might be a last-minute change to the venue or the equipment you have available. Whatever adjustments you make, the most important thing is ensuring you are delivering a safe and active session. It is very important that all of your participants are involved in all activities.

What if...?

You are leading a tennis session for eight to ten-year-olds after they have finished school. Everyone in the group is a beginner and you are expecting 12 participants. You are planning to use the whole sports hall, which has four tennis courts in total. You are planning to do a lot of pair work in your session.

You turn up 45 minutes before your session to prepare and get the equipment ready. You meet one of the tutors and she tells you some things have changed.

1 You now only have nine participants as three are off sick today.

2 One of the other tutors needs to use some of the sports hall during your session due to bad weather. She is going to take one of your tennis courts.

Discuss with your partner how you are going to adjust your session following these changes.

Planning for different groups

Sport and activity leaders work with many different people, including: children, teenagers, the elderly, individuals with special needs and people from different cultural and backgrounds. When you plan a session you need to take into account the different needs of the individuals. These needs will be reflected in your session aims and objectives, as well as your chosen activities, equipment and style of leadership.

Age

Working with children

Age is often an important factor when you are planning your session. There are psychological, emotional and physiological differences between children and adults and these must be taken into account. Children often need to be reminded to do basic things such as taking plenty of fluids on a regular basis to ensure they are hydrated. You will need to take this into account in your planning.

In the same way, children are often not aware of their limitations. This can be both positive and negative.
- It can be a positive because they are often willing to try activities and skills without fear.
- It can be a negative as children are not as aware of health and safety as adults.

This makes it even more important that you are constantly focused on their health and safety. Take, for example, a warm up activity for a tennis session where participants are asked to run in different directions using the court lines. Children are more likely to bump into one another due to their excitement and focus levels. However, an adult is more likely to be aware of where they are and less likely to run into someone. Make sure you take this into account when planning the aims and objectives for your session and adapt it accordingly. You might choose to create a larger area across multiple courts for children. This is compared to your adult session where you only use one court or a smaller space.

Coaching children is very different to coaching adults.

Working with teenagers

As a child turns into a teenager there are other factors to consider. Teenagers' bodies change and develop at different rates. There may also be differences between males and females, as shown in Figures 3.2 and 3.3.

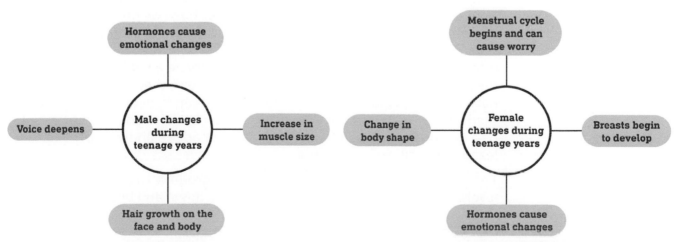

Figure 3.2: Male changes during teenage years

Figure 3.3: Female changes during teenage years

Everyone is an individual and we all change and develop at different rates. As a sport and activity leader you need to be aware of the physical, psychological and emotional changes and stresses placed on a teenager's body. Never focus on a particular change or difference. Support every individual in your group and understand that they might be going through a new and often worrying time. Finally, teenagers often struggle with coordination in their early adolescent years. This is a really important point when planning sessions for this age group as this will affect your expectations, as well as the session aims and objectives. Giving positive feedback to individuals and encouraging them to try again if they fail will help to set them at ease and enjoy your session.

Supporting young people in their sporting activities is a rewarding experience for sport and physical activity leaders.

Working with the elderly

Activity and sport is becoming increasingly popular with the elderly population. This is due to the numerous and widely publicised health benefits of taking exercise. The elderly population is often a rewarding population to work with. They can sometimes have varying needs and it is important you are aware of any health concerns that may prevent them from taking part in certain activities. You will need to find out this information by asking the participants to complete a health questionnaire. If you are working in a leisure centre environment, they may well already have each participant's details on file and you can familiarise yourself with them. Be aware that often this age group can be referred to a leisure centre by a doctor or hospital. Make sure you ask for advice and support before leading a session of this nature.

There are frequently participants in this age group with varying fitness levels. As your body ages it can start to break down and become prone to medical conditions, for example, high blood pressure, diabetes and joint problems. It is important you get as much information as possible before planning your session to ensure your aims and objectives are suitable for all of your participants.

Experience

You also need to take into account the experience of your participants. You could have a group of complete beginners or you might have two individuals in your session that are highly experienced and play for their county or country. As a sport and activity leader you need to make sure everyone in your group is learning and enjoying the session. An effective leader will make sure this is reflected in their aims and objectives. If you have participants that are much more experienced you will need to have progression activities planned to keep them interested and engaged.

What if...?

You are leading an after-school netball session for 11 to 12-year-olds. You have been told that everyone in the session is a beginner. When you arrive at your session two of the participants mention to you that they play for a local club. You have planned to teach the group how to execute a chest pass.

Discuss with your group how you are going to progress the activity to ensure the two club netball players are engaged.

The age of your participants will affect your session's aims and objectives.

Health and safety considerations

A key responsibility of a sport or activity leader is managing the health and safety of everyone in the session. Health and safety considerations are important before, during and after all sessions. Assistant coaches and leaders will also need to make sure they prioritise health and safety. If you are ever unsure about anything or you see something that you think is unsafe you must tell someone immediately.

Due to the nature of sport, accidents and injuries do happen. If you have played a lot of sport and taken part in activity sessions you will be aware of this. It is usually down to the nature of the sport itself, not a lack of health and safety care from the leader. Every sports coach and leader must ensure they safeguard their participants as far as reasonably possible. This level of care begins with the completion of a RISK ASSESSMENT. (A risk assessment is a written document that identifies and aims to reduce the hazards that have the ability to cause potential harm to participants.)

Practise

Reflect on your own sporting and activity experience. Note down your answers to the following questions. Present these answers to a small group or the rest of your class.

- Have you ever been injured while participating in sport?
- How did this injury happen?
- Could it have been prevented?

Risk assessments

Every sport and activity facility has to have a risk assessment by law. (A **RISK** is the likelihood of someone being harmed by a hazard. A **HAZARD** is something that is identified as having the potential to cause this harm.)

The risk assessment is a written document that aims to identify such risks in order to prevent accidents or injuries, as well as safeguard the staff and participants to ensure their health and safety. The purpose of a risk assessment is to:

- identify hazards, for example, a wet sports hall floor, a weight left out where someone might trip over it, or damaged equipment
- give a risk rating; see below for a step-by-step guide for working out a risk rating
- state the measures that can be taken to minimise the risk, for example, all equipment to be checked prior to the session.

When completing a risk assessment and considering the health and safety of a session, a sport or activity leader needs to take into account the location, varying activities, equipment and participants. They need to work out the severity of the risk – this is how dangerous it will be. They also need to work out the likelihood of harm being caused – this is how likely the hazard is to cause harm. This can be calculated as follows.

STEP-BY-STEP: | **HOW TO WORK OUT A RISK RATING**

☐ It is important to follow a step-by-step approach when completing a risk assessment.

STEP 1

☐ Identify a hazard.

☐ Walk around and visit the area you are risk assessing. Make a note of all of the things that might cause potential harm to someone.

STEP 2

☐ Identify who is at risk.

☐ You will need to identify who in the session is at risk of being injured or harmed from the hazard. Once you know who is at risk you can minimise the chance of the risk occurring.

STEP 3

☐ For each hazard consider how likely it is to cause harm. Think about the chance of this happening. Use the key below to give each hazard a likelihood rating.

Likelihood:

1 – Unlikely

2 – Quite likely

3 – Very likely

STEP 4

☐ For each hazard consider how dangerous it could be. Think about how severe and how much damage it could cause. Use the key below to give each hazard a severity rating.

Severity:

1 – Minor injury

2 – Injury requiring medical assistance

3 – Major injury

STEP 5

☐ Once you have got your likelihood and severity rating for each hazard you now need to work out the risk rating. To do this you need to complete the calculation below.

☐ Likelihood x Severity = Risk Rating

STEP 6

☐ The total of this calculation will give you a risk rating. The risk rating will tell you the level of the risk. Use the key below to work out the risk rating.

Low: 3 or below

Medium: 4–6

High: 7–9

STEP 7

☐ Finally, you need to identify the measures you are going to put in place to minimise and reduce the level of risk. This will make the environment as safe as possible for your participants.

REMEMBER

☐ The assessment of risks should be carried out on a regular basis and written down. The person who has overall responsibility for the risk assessment will sign and date their name.

Figure 3.4 shows a sample risk assessment form completed by a sport and activity leader for a basketball session. Remember to look back at the above guide to calculating a risk rating if you need further explanation of some of the terms or figures.

Risk Assessors Name: *Danielle Budhu*				Date: *13.6.16*		
Name of Activity: *Basketball*				Location: *Sports Hall, New College.*		
Hazard	**Who is at risk?**	**Likelihood (0-3)**	**Severity (0-3)**	**Risk Rating**	**Risk Level (H/M/L)**	**Measures to minimise risk**
Wet sports hall floor	*Leader and participants*	*2*	*2*	*4*	*M*	• *Leader to check the sports hall for hazards before the session.* • *Code of conduct issued to staff and the group to include cleaning up of drinks.* • *Regular cleaning checks of the sports hall.*

Figure 3.4: An example of a risk assessment

Planning for outdoor sessions

If you are planning an outdoor session remember that the weather and location can be a deciding factor that can impact on the health and safety of your group. Cold or wet weather may mean you need to move your session location or adapt it to ensure all your participants are kept warm. It is not just cold or wet weather you need to consider. On a very hot day you will need to have regular drinks breaks and consider the intensity of your activities.

Encourage the participants to communicate how they are feeling and ask them to inform you if they are feeling unwell at any time. Remember, when planning a session always have a **CONTINGENCY PLAN** for varying weather conditions.

Planning the structure of your sessions

When planning the structure of your session, you need to consider your chosen activities and how these impact on **HEALTH AND SAFETY ISSUES**. Make sure you have allocated enough space for the activity to be completed correctly and in a safe manner. Activities need to challenge each individual but not push them too hard. Pushing too hard may lead to an increased chance of injury.

Planning for participants' medical needs

Before working with any group, a sport and activity leader must be aware of any medical conditions. Depending where you are working, this information may have already been gathered. Make sure you remind your superior to give you this information and ask about their first aid procedures. It is vital you are aware of this information. You may need to check with the participants before the session that they have any appropriate medication with them. For example, a participant suffering from asthma may need to carry an inhaler.

Many sport and activity leaders are first aid qualified so they can be ready to act if needed. This might be a qualification you think about pursuing in the near future.

Link it up

Go to Unit 6 to learn more about planning for outdoor sessions.

What if...?

Julie needs your help. She hasn't been coaching football long and asks your advice. She is planning a football session for ten participants who are aged between 11 and 12 years old. Her session plan is designed for an outdoor session on the school field. Overnight the weather has been cold and raining and her manager has told her she will have to move the session inside. Julie is not sure what to do or how to adapt her session. She needs your help.

Write an email to Julie giving her some suggestions and advice about ways she can change her session to suit the new location.

Different types of sessions and their structure

Sport and activity leaders need to be aware that different types of sessions will follow different structures. The structure you choose will depend on your environment and your participants.

- *Formal coaching sessions* are often very structured and are particularly good with children and beginners. For this type of session you will need a clear plan with contingencies in place. For example, a netball coach who is teaching young children will need to have a detailed session plan. The plan will need to follow a logical order with the coach being in control of the session design at all times.

- *Unstructured sessions* are often used with groups or individuals that have been participating in the activity for a long time, such as an elite level athlete. The leader gives the learners some freedom. For example, a football manager working with a Premier League team might allow the players to structure their own warm up. The football players will be experienced and will have participated in numerous sessions over the previous years. They are likely to have a high level of knowledge on how their body feels and when it is ready to perform at its highest level. The manager will need to build up trust with the athletes and take a flexible approach.
- *Cooperative activities* are where the leader works with someone else (this could be another leader or a member of the group) to fulfil their session aims and objectives. For example, two tennis coaches at the same academy might work together and share their ideas when leading a session on the backhand.

Experienced athletes will benefit from unstructured sessions where they are free to apply their high level of knowledge and understanding of their own physical fitness.

Different types of sessions and their content

Every sport and activity session is made up of three different COMPONENTS. (A component is an individual part of the session: usually warm up, main content and skill development, cool down and plenary.)

Any session you create will follow this structure. Of course, the content of the sessions will vary depending on your participants, activity and available equipment.

Warm ups

The warm up component signifies the beginning of the session and aims to prepare the body and mind for exercise. The warm up reduces the chance of the participants getting injured. This part of the session should take 10 minutes approximately and consists of three main parts:

- *pulse raiser*: This increases the heart rate and raises body temperature
- *stretching*: Main muscles and joints are mobilised using movements similar to those of the activity
- *practice*: Basic rehearsal of some of the activities that are required in the sport.

When planning an effective warm up, you need to think about all participants. For example, a warm up for an under-16 basketball session might include a **CONDITIONED GAME** of 'stuck in the mud'. (A conditioned game is where the rules are changed to work on a particular skill.) If there are varying abilities within the group, you can stop the session and 'release' some people, making it easier for some people to get away. After this the group would complete stretching exercises followed by a series of passing drills.

Practise

Write detailed warm up plans that include all three components – pulse raiser, stretching and practice – for the following sessions:

1 over-60s walking football

2 teenage local swimming club

3 after school under-13 netball club

4 adult wheelchair basketball.

Main content and skill development

The main content of the session includes a wide variety of activities and is normally 40 minutes in length. The main content of the session will depend on the aims and objectives set by the activity leader. If the leader wants the group to work on a technical element of the game, then a skills development session might be followed by a game situation. Each of these is likely to last 20 minutes each, giving a total of 40 minutes for the main content. For example, if the main aim of a beginners' hockey session is to learn the technique of a push pass, the leader is likely to spend 20 minutes on this, followed by a conditioned game where a team has to complete a number of push passes before attempting to score a goal.

However, if the main aim of a session is to develop **MUSCULAR ENDURANCE** the leader might set up a 40-minute circuit session. (Muscular endurance is the ability for one muscle or a group of muscles to keep working for a long period of time without getting tired.) The session could include a variety of exercises, such as press-ups, lunges and burpees, specifically aimed at increasing this aspect of fitness.

What if...?

You are working at a leisure centre. A personal trainer has asked for your help in designing a circuit session for a group of adults. The adults exercise on a regular basis and are used to working out in the gym.

Design a 40-minute circuit session for this group of adults.

Cool down

The cool down takes place at the end of the session and aims to help the body recover from exercise. It is really important that, as a leader, you leave plenty of time for all the participants to cool down. The cool down normally lasts for 10–15 minutes. It consists of an activity to lower the heart rate followed by STATIC STRETCHING (this is stretching muscles when the body is at rest).

Practise

During a circuit session you are leading, you notice one participant leaves early and does not complete the cool down.

Design a poster to display in the gym informing people of the benefits of a cool down. Give examples of appropriate cool downs that participants can complete after using the gym.

Session aims and objectives

All sport and physical activity sessions should have clear overall aims and objectives. These should be agreed before the session and written on the session plan.

The AIM is the main goal you want your participants to achieve by the end of the session. It is often best to keep this to one sentence and keep it simple. Think of your participants walking out the door at the end of the session. What is the main thing you want them to learn and take away with them? After you have planned your aim you need to work out how you are going to achieve it. This is where setting clear objectives will help you. The OBJECTIVE is how you are going to achieve your aim.

For example, a sport and activity leader is planning their first hockey session for a group of young children who are all beginners. The leader needs to decide what they would like the participants to achieve before leaving their session. The aim of the session could be for all of the participants to be able to complete a push pass. With this in mind, the leader will need to think about how they are going to help the participants achieve this aim. The leader knows that the group has either no or limited knowledge of a push pass technique. Therefore, the objective of the session might be to introduce, demonstrate and deliver the key coaching points for the push pass in hockey.

Figure 3.5 shows what part of a session plan might look like for a beginners' badminton session for 10 to 11-year-olds.

Date and Time: 8 March 2017 3.30–4.30pm	Number of participants: 12	Aim of my session: For everyone to learn and execute a basic forehand lift in badminton.
Age of participants: 10–11 years old	Ability level: Beginner (participants have had two previous sessions).	Objectives of my session: Introduce, demonstrate and deliver the key coaching points of the forehand lift in badminton.

Figure 3.5: A sample extract from a session plan

A sport and activity leader working with more experienced players will need to have different aims and objectives. For example, a leader who is coaching a group of Sunday-league-level female footballers needs to have a different set of aims and objectives to one leading a group of female academy players. They might aim to develop players' confidence in 1 v 1 battles. The objective of the session could be to demonstrate and deliver the main coaching points, for example, by encouraging individuals to attack positively in different situations. Whether you are planning a session for experienced athletes or beginners it is important that the participants always have fun.

Practise

In pairs, create the aims and objectives of a session for the following groups of participants:

1 beginners' tennis for females only

2 professional hockey players

3 members of a local athletics club training for a half marathon.

Session considerations

There are numerous aspects to take into account when planning a session. As a sport and activity leader it is your responsibility to organise all components of the session. You need to be highly organised to ensure your session runs smoothly and your participants want to return week on week. Before the session you will need to:

Link it up

Look back at Unit 1 to read about health and safety considerations in more detail.

- ensure you have booked the facility where the session is taking place and be aware of how much space you have
- decide what equipment you will need
- plan your time accordingly
- organise all the equipment before your participants arrive
- find out how many participants you are expecting and have a register ready
- be aware of any health and safety considerations
- return all of the equipment back to where you found it.

Be prepared to adjust the amount of equipment needed for your session or to adapt timings. This is where your organisation skills will be really tested. For example, you may need different equipment for different components of the session, including warm up, main activity and cool down.

What if...?

You have a part-time job at a sports centre and have been asked to help the sports coach prepare for their session. You will be helping with a badminton session for 12 participants aged 10–11.

Make a list of all the equipment you will need to prepare. Remember to consider all three components of the session.

Leadership approaches

Leaders in sports and activities all have different styles. The way you choose to manage a group will affect their learning experience. You might choose to adopt different styles for certain situations and different groups. To be successful, a leader will recognise when to quickly change styles to suit the individual needs of their group. A more experienced leader will tend to favour one or two leadership styles. This is likely to reflect their personality and experience.

There are three main types of leadership approaches:

AUTOCRATIC – This type of leader tells the players what they want them to do. They make all of the decisions and have complete control.

DEMOCRATIC – This type of leader involves players in all decisions. Everyone is given the opportunity to share their opinion.

LAISSEZ-FAIRE – This type of leader steps back and lets the group make decisions for themselves. The group has a lot of freedom.

Link it up

These leadership styles are also covered in Unit 4 in relation to successful sports coaching.

Table 3.1: Advantages and disadvantages of leadership approaches

Leadership approaches	Advantages	Disadvantages
Autocratic	• Effective when teaching young children basic skills • Good for large numbers in a group	• Group is not self-sufficient • Lack of two-way communication between leader and group
Democratic	• The group is involved in decision making • Effective two-way communication between the leader and the group	• Decisions might take a long time • If the group is large it is difficult to listen to everyone's opinion
Laissez-faire	• Encourages the group to take control • The group are not restricted or dictated to	• Does not work with a young or inexperienced group • Lack of direction

What if...?

The photo shows Andy Murray with his former coach Amélie Mauresmo. Answer the questions below:

1 What type of leadership style is Amélie Mauresmo adopting in this photo?

2 Give examples of other situations where Amélie Mauresmo might use other leadership styles in her coaching.

3 Describe situations where you have experienced autocratic, democratic and laissez-faire leadership.

4 Explain which approach you prefer, giving reasons for your answer.

Everyone has to practise their own **VERBAL COMMUNICATION** skills (expressing yourself through language and sound) and **NON-VERBAL COMMUNICATION** skills (expressing yourself without words, using body language, facial expressions and gestures). Sport and activity leaders will need to use different communication methods at different points of the game. For example, a Premier League football manager will need to use non-verbal communication in noisy stadiums to tell their players where to position themselves.

Communication is a two-way process. As well as giving information, it is equally important for a sport and activity leader to be able to receive it. Listening to the participant's feelings and experiences will make a sport and activity leader more aware of individual needs. Using this information can help improve the outcomes of future activity sessions.

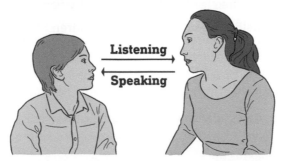

Figure 3.7: Communication is a two-way process

Good communication is vital when delivering instructions. A football manager might only have a few seconds to instruct the player to perform a particular task. If the player does not receive or understand this information a goal could be scored and the game potentially lost. The player and manager need to understand each other and have a shared purpose in terms of their ideas and the goals they want to achieve.

Effective communication builds **RAPPORT** (good rapport is a positive working relationship between the leader and the group). It is important to remember that rapport does not just happen. It can take days, weeks and months to develop. In the football example above, the player and manager may build their relationship while training and sharing conversation. Without a rapport, a player might choose to ignore an instruction or perform the task differently. If a leader cannot communicate well it can often hinder their relationship with a participant.

Football manager Pep Guardiola using verbal and non-verbal communication.

Session instruction and delivery

Good communication skills are essential as you deliver your session. During the session introduction, you should aim to inform the participants about what they can expect from the session, and also what is expected of them. As leader, you will be a role model for the group, so it is vital to build rapport and engage the participants immediately. A reminder of the structure of a sport or physical activity session can be seen in Figure 3.8.

Elements of the introduction will be revisited in the **SESSION PLENARY**. (The session plenary takes place at the end of the session and is where a coach will recap what was learnt in the session.) A plenary can be the summary of the key points that participants have covered during the session, as well as a chance to ask the participants their opinions. With a more experienced group, an appropriate question could be: 'How important will this learning be to you?' With a beginners group a more suitable question might be: 'Which aspect of the session did you most enjoy and why?'

By asking questions and listening, you will gain valuable information about the learning that has taken place in the session. It will also help you think of how best to prepare for the next session. It might be the case that participants did not grasp a skill as quickly as you had hoped, therefore you can plan to review this before the next session.

Figure 3.8: Structure of a session

Being a good leader is not just about having excellent technical knowledge of the sport. It is about understanding your group, creating trust and gaining respect. A leader's instructions need to be communicated correctly and the session needs to inspire your group. Spending time planning and producing contingency plans (back-up plans), will mean the delivery of your session follows a logical order and flows well.

Positioning when leading a group

The physical position of a leader when coaching a session can often make a huge difference to its success. For example, if a session takes place outside on a sunny day, always ensure the group are not facing the sun when you are delivering instructions. In the same way, if there is something that will distract the participants in the same area, make sure you face that distraction. This will guarantee that the group listen and focus on their session and not on something else.

Motivating participants

Good activity leaders will have a high degree of **MOTIVATION** and will be able to inspire others. (Motivation is the drive within you to achieve your goals.) Motivated activity leaders will: plan their session in advance, show a desire and passion for their activity and delivery, and look to improve themselves at all opportunities. A motivated leader will do everything they can to uplift and make a positive impact on every individual in their session. Naturally, over time this can build a rapport between the participant and leader. This positive relationship helps an individual to trust the leader and increase their learning opportunities.

Participants who are motivated are much more likely to enjoy the session and thus improve. However, being prepared for participants with low motivation is important. Quite often something will have happened before they arrive at the session that has impacted on their motivation levels. It is vital not to take it personally. There are many tools you can use to increase someone's motivation levels:

- set them a target or a goal
- reward them for achieving something
- give praise for good performance
- remind them of a previous time they were motivated
- give useful feedback.

Practise

In pairs, discuss and make notes on a sports situation where you have both been highly motivated.

- How did you feel when you were motivated?

- What were you trying to achieve?

- Who else had an influence on your motivation levels?

England Women's Head Coach Mark Sampson is thrown in the air to celebrate beating Germany 1-0 to finish third in the 2015 FIFA Women's World Cup.

What if...?

A rugby coach has been working with the same group of girls for a year. Last season they finished second in the league and the coach is now getting her players ready for the season ahead. She is pushing her players physically and mentally for the games ahead.

She has noticed that a lot of the players are not very motivated and often moan that they are not enjoying her sessions.

The rugby coach has asked on social media for some tips to increase her players' motivation levels. You see this request and offer to help.

Produce a leaflet or poster to send to the coach offering tips and advice on how to increase a player's motivation levels.

Providing effective feedback

Providing effective **FEEDBACK** to individuals in your group is essential. Leaders must give feedback during and after the sports or activity session. As a leader, you need to make sure feedback is appropriate for the players' ability and experience level. What you say needs to be specific to each player and include their strengths as well as areas for development. Feedback needs to be simple and avoid complicated technical language, especially if you are working with children or inexperienced individuals. For example, at the end of a beginners' football match the leader might say to a defender: 'I really like the way you used your head to defend corners today. It really helped the team clear the ball out of the danger area.'

Feedback should not only come from the leader. The individual should be encouraged to reflect on their own performance, giving their own strengths and areas for development. To check their understanding, ask questions. It is a good idea to write the questions and responses down to be recapped at the start of the next session.

Creating a safe and inclusive environment

Health and safety is the most important responsibility of a sport or activity leader. Earlier you looked at the importance of a risk assessment and the need to ensure this is completed before the session. Go back to Learning aim A to look again at the health and safety considerations of a session. This will also give you information on risk assessments and the responsibilities of a sport and activity leader for keeping all participants safe during a session.

Throughout the session a leader will continuously be checking on health and safety. If you are not first aid trained, it is your job to make sure someone is available during your session who can act on any form of injury or accident. They must have the appropriate equipment and resources too.

Each session needs to be inclusive. This means each individual is included in all aspects of the session and everyone learns at their own rate. A sport and activity leader needs to ensure the session is aimed at the whole group and is delivered with appropriate language for everyone to understand. If one learner is at a much higher ability then progress them through activities to ensure they are learning. Each session must be enjoyable, with the leader providing positive feedback to encourage learners.

Link it up

Health and safety considerations were also covered in Unit 1.

A kayak coach leading a safe and inclusive session.

with their own ball in a coned-off area, dribbling the ball around the area to avoid other players. Using this same idea, the under-18 players could be invited to do exactly the same but have the threat of opposition players trying to take the ball from them. The visually impaired session could use exactly the same task, however, this time each player is followed by a partner, who directs him or her in the coned area. Additionally, the leader might choose to make the area larger to give more space.

The England blind football team lining up for a penalty shootout.

Skills and knowledge check

☐ Can you describe the key features of verbal and non-verbal communication?

☐ Describe three tools to increase an individual's motivation.

☐ Why is creating an inclusive environment so important?

☐ Give an example of a relay within a football coaching session.

○ I can define the term 'motivation'.

If you have been unable to give positive responses to any of the questions or statements above, please go back and review the section.

C Review leadership of a sport or physical activity

C1 Developing evaluation and self-reflection techniques

As a sport and activity leader you will need to assess your delivery of each session you lead. A good leader will evaluate their strengths and areas for improvement in a session. Reviewing allows you to improve your skills and take these forward into future sessions.

Methods of evaluation and self-evaluation

Sport and activity leaders are often so concerned with making sure they are improving participants' skills and techniques that they can forget to focus on their own evaluation. **SELF-EVALUATION** is where you review your own progress and development by highlighting your strengths and areas for improvement. Self-evaluation involves thinking about what you have done well and what needs to be improved. Self-evaluation should happen on a daily basis. When you play sport you assess your own performance, often without even realising it. You think of what went well in the game and what was less effective. If you have to complete a presentation to the group you assess your presentation skills or if you are meeting new people you might think about how you came across.

Self-evaluation in sport and activity leadership is a skill, but it is not necessarily the first skill you think of when mind mapping skills and qualities of an effective leader. Whatever their level of experience, all sport and activity leaders can learn from every single session they deliver. As a sport and activity leader you will spend time after each session reflecting on your strengths and identifying areas for improvement in both planning and delivering the session.

To help with self-evaluation, you can ask for feedback from participants, observers and tutors. You can use a range of methods to generate feedback. These could include:

- questionnaires
- witness statements or observation records
- using visual media.

Asking for feedback when leading a group is important.

The method you use to collect feedback from participants will be different from the method you use to collect feedback from tutors and observers. For example, you might choose to use a questionnaire to gain feedback from participants. It is often best to ask the participants to complete this anonymously, as this way you are more likely to receive honest feedback.

Practise

Design your own questionnaire to get feedback from participants at the end of a session you have led.

A further method of evaluating a sport and activity leader's performance is to use visual media. By filming a sport or activity session, the recording can be used to review the session and see it from the participants' point of view. You can then assess how effectively you communicated with the participants, and what the participants' responses and engagement levels were. You might even assess how successful your demonstrations were. One benefit of this method is you can watch the recording as many times as you like.

Feedback from tutors or observers can either be FORMATIVE (this is ongoing feedback from an instructor, highlighting strengths and areas for improvement) or SUMMATIVE (this is a formal assessment at the end of a unit).

- Formative feedback focuses on the development of an individual and provides feedback over a period of time. An example of this is your tutor giving you verbal feedback when you are practising leading different sports or activity sessions.
- Summative feedback is a formal assessment at the end of your unit. You will normally be given a grade for your performance and evaluated against national standards. This is likely to be supported by a witness statement or observation record.

Both formative and summative feedback will help a sport and activity leader assess their own performance.

Splitting a review into separate focus areas

In order to review your strengths and areas for improvement, it is often useful to split your review into separate focus areas.

- *Planning and organisation*: Reflecting upon your planning and organisation is often the easiest part of the review. You will already know during your session if you spent an adequate amount of time planning and if your plan met the needs of your group. It is often easy to reflect on whether your organisation before the session was adequate by asking yourself a few simple questions. Were you there in enough time? Was all the equipment set out before the group arrived? The answers to these questions will be obvious.
- *Content of the session*: The content of the session includes the warm up, main content, skill development and cool down. This is a large area to review and you will need to break down each component for evaluation. The participants always need to be at the centre of this review. How appropriate was the activity for the participants? Were there health and safety concerns?
- *Leadership skills*: When reviewing leadership skills you need to assess your own qualities and skills in the delivery of the session. It might help to make a list of all the skills and qualities you believe an effective sport and activity leader should have. Use this list to reflect upon your own abilities. Did I communicate effectively? Was my delivery motivational?
- *Achievements of aims and objectives*: To reflect upon the aims and objectives of the session, pay attention to where the group started and what their skill level was. Compare this to where they finished the session. As a leader it is important to assess the achievement throughout the journey of the whole session. How were the aims and

objectives met or not met in the session? Did you outline the aim of the session in the introduction and, at the end of the session, did the group members reflect on their achievement?

When delivering the session content, try to gather feedback – both verbal and non-verbal – from participants.

An effective leader will not only listen to their own thoughts and opinions but will also consider feedback from their participants. This might be verbal through direct questioning, for example, 'How did you find the session?' Or it might be non-verbal. This can sometimes be more effective as participants, especially adults, might find it difficult to give honest and direct feedback. A leader can look at participants' body language, eye contact, posture and facial expressions for their evaluation. For example, if a participant looks focused and is showing positive body language then they are likely to be learning and enjoying their session. Compare this to a participant that is looking down at the floor and has negative, demotivated body language. They are probably disengaged and have lost motivation.

Practise

Observe two different practical sport or activity sessions in two different sports.

Write feedback to each leader explaining the strengths and areas for development of the activity sessions. Make sure the feedback includes:

- planning and organisation of the session
- appropriateness of the session's content
- demonstrated leadership skills
- how and why the session's aims and objectives were achieved or not achieved.

What if...?

Michael has recently been offered a job at a local leisure centre. He will be leading tennis sessions for young children who all want to learn the basics of the game. Michael has done some voluntary coaching before but this is his first paid job. He wants to be the best he can be and knows that to do this, he needs to learn from every session he delivers.

In the past, Michael has not completed many reviews or evaluations of his sessions and finds this difficult. Michael has asked for your help.

Produce a presentation, poster or leaflet to advise Michael on how he can develop his evaluation and self-reflection techniques.

C2 Writing an action plan

After gathering a range of information from participants and observers across a number of sessions, a leader will look to complete an action plan. Writing an action plan can often bring together ideas and help the leader to ensure they are continually developing. The plan will include both the self-evaluation findings and the information gathered from the participants, as well as feedback from the tutors or observers.

Carrying out a SWOT analysis

A common way of assessing performance is to carry out a **SWOT ANALYSIS**. This can help a leader to develop and contribute to forming an action plan. It is broken down into four areas:

1 Strengths

2 Weaknesses

3 Opportunities

4 Threats.

Strengths and weaknesses

Identifying strengths and weaknesses is a valuable tool. A sport and activity leader needs to have a good understanding of their strengths so they can use these even more and progress them further. It is also important to understand your weaknesses to enable you to improve these. An outstanding sport and activity leader will turn weaknesses into strengths. It is often difficult for you to honestly reflect on your own qualities. This means listening to the feedback from others; learning to not take it personally is incredibly important.

In order to determine your own strengths and weaknesses for a session or number of sessions, ask yourself the following questions.
- Did I communicate effectively for that age range and ability level?
- Do I have a good rapport with the group?
- Can I lead a session independently with confidence?
- Were the activities I chose appropriate?
- Did every learner in the session progress?

How good is your rapport with the participants?

Opportunities and threats

These are aspects that might not be in your control. Opportunities can often occur unexpectedly as a result of hard work. Threats are also equally unpredictable and sometimes you cannot do anything about these. However, being prepared and being aware of what might happen can help you to plan and be the best you can be.

Figure 3.9 shows a sample SWOT analysis created by a sport and activity leader who is assessing their own performance.

Strengths	Weaknesses
• Good verbal and non-verbal communicator • Time management skills • Organised	• My confidence levels • I want to get more qualifications • Self-evaluation is difficult
Opportunities	**Threats**
• Seek out coaching qualifications • Work experience opportunities • Practical and theory lessons at college are helping me to improve	• What will I do at the end of my college course? • Coaching/leading is a popular job • I need money to do qualifications

Figure 3.9: SWOT analysis

Practise

After leading a coaching or activity session with your group, complete a SWOT analysis of your session. Make sure you put at least three bullet points in each of the following boxes: Strengths, Weaknesses, Opportunities and Threats.

Skills and knowledge check

☐ What is summative feedback?

☐ Give an example of formative feedback in a sports coaching session.

☐ A sport and activity leader can split their review into four areas – what are these?

☐ What does SWOT stand for?

○ I can provide a definition of self-evaluation.

○ I am aware of how important it is to gain feedback from the participants in a session.

○ I can produce a SWOT analysis of my own performance.

If you have been unable to give positive responses to any of the questions or statements above, please go back and review the section.

Ready for assessment

For this unit you will need to design and produce an activity plan that can be used for an activity session for five or more participants. You will need to show that you can plan, lead and review a sports or activity session. Your session plan will include all the details relevant to your session and participants. You will show you have considered the resources you will need, the activities you are going to provide and the leadership behaviours you are going to demonstrate.

During the session you will show all the leadership skills, qualities and responsibilities that you have developed throughout the unit.

After the session you will need to review your own performance and produce an action plan that helps you improve for the future.

The more experience of leading activities you can gain before your assessment, the better you will be. Consider work experience and voluntary opportunities. Remember, be the best you can be.

WORK FOCUS

HANDS ON

There are some important occupational skills and experiences that you will need to practise, which relate to this unit and your future career. By developing these now it will help you on your path to work in the sports industry and become a sports or activity leader.

Give two practical ideas or examples for how you could develop the following skills:

1 **Using verbal and non-verbal communication effectively**

2 **Working as part of a team**

3 **Creating a safe and inclusive environment.**

Ready for work?

Take this short quiz to find out if you are ready for work in the role of an assistant sport and activity leader.

1 At work you should:

☐ A follow the employer's dress code

☐ B wear trainers and jeans

☐ C wear your school or college sports kit

☐ D wear anything – it does not matter what I am wearing.

2 At an interview you should:

☐ A talk about the skills and qualities you have in sports and activity leadership

☐ B focus on your weaknesses and how you can beat them

☐ C tell the interviewer about the mistakes you made in your previous session

☐ D refuse to speak about your skills and qualities.

3 At work you should:

☐ A work hard and follow all instructions you are given

☐ B discuss your social life and how it can help your ability to lead

☐ C turn up exactly on time, as being early will look disorganised

☐ D start inappropriate conversations with customers.

4 At an interview you should:

☐ A show examples of risk assessments that you have completed

☐ B show risk assessments that are still being worked on

☐ C explain that you are not willing to let health and safety get in the way when running a session

☐ D explain why parts of health and safety are not part of your role as a sport and activity leader.

How did you do?

You should have all As as your answers. It is important to show everything you have learnt from this section to any future employers. If you have not achieved all A answers then please go back to your tutor and review the section.

4 Coaching Sport

The role of a coach is to inspire an individual or team and improve their performance. It might sound easy but having the appropriate people skills, as well as knowing how athletes learn and improve their performance, requires a lot of work.

Many people can call themselves a coach, which is an easy term to refer to when explaining your role in practical sport. However, to become a successful coach takes much time, dedication and skill. In your sporting career, you may be able to recall a good coach who has been influential in your success, and one who was not so good. These differences may be due to a number of factors, and it is these which will be considered within this unit on sports coaching.

In this unit, you will develop the skills needed to: coach others effectively, plan and deliver coaching sessions, break down and coach skills, and to use specialist techniques to improve sports performance.

How will I be assessed?

This unit will develop your skills to deliver a range of activities to prepare you for work within a sports and activity coaching environment. Your assessments will be practically based in order to reflect your future working career. The assessments will encourage you to apply the skills and knowledge gained throughout this unit in a variety of scenario-based applications. Your tutors will design all your coaching assessments to meet the requirements of the assessment criteria. The assessments they provide could be in the form of observations, assessment of coaching plans prior to an activity session, your communication with participants and your overall professionalism throughout the activity. As part of the assessment, tutors may record evidence using observation records, filmed footage, and/or annotated photographic evidence of the session.

Assessment criteria

Pass	Merit	Distinction
Learning aim A: Demonstrate coaching skills to improve performance		
A.P1 Select and use specialist methods when coaching an appropriate session.	**A.M1** Select and use relevant specialist methods to coach a coherent session.	**A.D1** Select and use justifiable specialist methods when coaching an effective session.
Learning aim B: Communicate clearly to others while coaching		
B.P2 Provide clear and relevant feedback while coaching.	**B.M2** Provide clear and meaningful feedback, targeted towards improving performance while coaching.	**B.D2** Provide relevant and developmental feedback, using professional and/or technical language, targeted towards improving performance while coaching.

A Demonstrate coaching skills to improve performance

A1 Roles, responsibilities and qualities of a coach

Roles of a successful sports coach

An **AMATEUR SPORTS COACH** (someone who offers coaching services on a voluntary basis) often fulfils many roles and responsibilities, which can be overlooked or taken for granted. Their skills and talents are valuable to a coaching group, and their dedicated efforts should be commended. Unlike **PROFESSIONAL SPORTS COACHES** (who are paid to coach), many amateur coaches have limited support from others, and the resources available to them can often be limited too. Therefore, for a coach to be successful, their role may be varied.

A good coach needs to be able to:

- manage their **PARTICIPANTS**, keeping them focused on the activity they are performing so that they meet the aims of the activity session
- act as a role model in order to reinforce good conduct and participant expectations
- provide supportive friendship, meaning they are approachable and encourage positive participation
- train their participants so that they make improvements in their abilities
- motivate their participants in order to encourage them to achieve and create a positive attitude towards success
- act as a good demonstrator of activities so the participants clearly understand what they are required to do.

By performing these roles successfully, the coach has the potential to achieve the desired levels of success.

Practise

Think of a coach or PE tutor who has taken you for a practical coaching activity. Consider the roles they performed and the style of coaching they used. Identify three strengths and three weaknesses of their session(s).

1 Explain what you think their strengths were and why.

2 Explain how you could help them improve any weaknesses you have identified.

Responsibilities of a successful sports coach

As well as performing an important role, a coach also has varied responsibilities that will help to provide a safe, inclusive environment that encourages participation for all.

As a coach, it is important to be positive. Use your role as a motivator to encourage your participants to achieve their aims. **MOTIVATION** will come from effective **COMMUNICATION**, which includes providing the feedback necessary to encourage success. The communication should also encourage **INCLUSIVITY**, whereby you try to involve all the participants, and promote **EQUALITY**, treating all participants as equal.

When you have the opportunity to coach, always consider:

- am I motivating my participants to succeed?
- are all of my participants taking part in the activities equally?
- am I treating all of my participants equally?

If you answer 'No' to any of those questions, ask yourself: 'What could I do to make this a 'Yes'? How could I overcome these barriers?'

Motivating participants to achieve their best is a key coaching responsibility.

You should also consider the safety of your coaching environment. Every coach has a **LEGAL OBLIGATION** (a requirement by law) to ensure that all of the participants who take part in the coaching activity do so in a safe and suitable environment. These are fundamental **HEALTH AND SAFETY OBLIGATIONS** that aim to protect the participant throughout. For example, if participants are under the age of 18, and/or have special support needs, a coach will need to follow strict child protection policies and **SAFEGUARDING** legislation. These policies protect the welfare of a child and/or vulnerable adult by providing strict guidelines on appropriate behaviour and conduct from those in influential positions, such as a sport coach or leader.

Another legal obligation you have as coach is to make sure the environment in which your coaching practice takes place is safe. Before commencing any of your coaching activities, ensure you check your coaching **FACILITY**. Consider whether the facility is suitable for the session, and that the equipment is also suitable. The health and safety of your participants is a priority: you should always do what you can to avoid injury or harm coming to any of your participants. Remember, they attend because they enjoy taking part and want to learn or improve, not to become injured. Take time to ensure you are protecting your participants – and remember this is a legal obligation!

What if...?

You are observing Peter, who is delivering a football activity to a group of under-10s. The group ranges widely in ability. During the session, you have a number of concerns that you feel Peter needs to consider for future coaching sessions. You notice that while Peter is very organised, with appropriate equipment and an accurate coaching plan, he provides very little verbal instruction. He focuses his attention only on helping the male participants, and allows others to stand at the side and chat when they should be taking part.

You have not seen Peter's session plan, however, you feel you should mention the points you have observed.

1 Which roles could he perform better? How could he achieve this?

2 Which responsibilities has he neglected? How could he improve on this?

3 Which qualities could he demonstrate better? How could he achieve this?

Qualities of a successful sports coach

Not everybody is born with the natural gift to coach. It comes to some more easily than others. All coaches have both strengths and weaknesses or areas for improvement. Many of the qualities you display will be linked to the type of leader you are.

Leadership styles

There are many different types of leader, and it is important to understand the type of leader you are. Your leadership style will be more appealing to some participants in your group and less appealing to others. For example, some coaches are very strict and direct, and others may be more relaxed in their approach. Table 4.1 breaks coaching leadership styles into three categories:

Table 4.1: Leadership styles for coaching sport

Leadership style	Personal qualities
Autocratic	Behaves as a dictator, making decisions on their own without discussion with others. Focused on achieving a task, but using only the method they have decided upon.
Democratic	Happy to listen to views of others. Will communicate with participants to gain feedback and ideas, which they will take into account when working towards a task.
Laissez-faire	Withdraws from the leadership process, leaving it to the group to take greater ownership of the decision making. Although they may be the 'leader', the coach's role is limited and they often encourage others to contribute to the activity.

Whichever leadership style you follow, it is important that you show **PATIENCE** (the ability to accept delays or problems without becoming annoyed), **ENTHUSIASM** (having strong excitement or interest about something you enjoy) and **SENSITIVITY** (being able to consider and respond to another's feelings). If your participant is unable to perform a skill, it is important not to laugh or mock them. As a coach, you must recognise that we all learn at a different pace. Motivate participants to achieve greater things, providing them with the belief that they can achieve a task or activity. Do not tell them they are 'rubbish', or walk away to coach someone more talented: be patient and sensitive. Challenge yourself to help them improve and challenge them to do so with a positive attitude. When you start to coach, consider how you could help a participant to make an improvement. What can you do to help? These are just some of the qualities that are part of becoming a good coach.

Link it up

For more on these qualities and attitudes, see Unit 3.

Practise

Identify three different coaches from top-level sporting activities. One should show an autocratic approach to their coaching, one a democratic style, and one a laissez-faire approach.

1 For each coach, explain why you have identified their coaching style in this way and outline how that style has contributed to their success or lack of it.

2 Select the coaching method you feel most reflects your style and explain why you identify with this type of coaching.

Coaching children can require patience and enthusiasm to encourage them to develop success.

A2 Specialist coaching skills to improve performance

Being good at sport will not always make you a good coach. Similarly, being a less talented performer does not mean you will be an unsuccessful coach. There are many factors that can contribute to good coaching. Just as participating in a sports activity involves learning and developing skills, so the same is true in coaching. The more you develop, learn and understand about coaching, the better your performance as a coach.

Coaching skills

Your knowledge of skills for different sports is essential when you are communicating with a participant. Being familiar with the sporting skills needed to achieve success, knowing how to perform skills, understanding how to develop them and when to use them in competitive situations, can significantly contribute to making improvements in your participants' performance. Familiarity with the required skills can help you relate better to a task or activity. You will be more aware of how the movements should be physically performed and this will give you an insight into performing the skills better. You want to help the participants learn how to perform a skill or movement with the minimum outlay of energy and time. Take dribbling in hockey, for example: you want the participant to be able to move the ball smoothly with their stick along the ground, rather than tapping it and frequently losing control.

- **COMPLEX SKILLS**: those that require coordinated movements needing control and concentration. These are more difficult to perform and include movements such as a tennis serve, a basketball lay-up or a gymnastic tumble routine.

Practise

You are completing a work experience placement at a local primary school. The tutor has asked you for some quick activities that you could use to improve the children's simple and complex skills.

1 Select three simple skills and provide some coaching points demonstrating how you could help the children improve their performance.

2 Select three complex skills and provide some coaching points demonstrating how you could help the children improve their performance.

When you coach, it is important to consider how you can develop these types of skills so that they are easy for the participant to understand, yet also challenge them to develop their abilities further. Depending on the type of skill you are aiming to develop, you will need to use the most appropriate method to gain the best results.

Specialist methods

The methods you use for training skills will vary. **WHOLE PRACTICE** is a method in which you try to practise the exercise activity as one. An example of this may be shown with the high jump event. During whole practice, you perform the entire performance from run-up, jump phase, and landing on the crash mat as one whole performance. To assess the success of this performance, you would reflect upon the performance of the activity as a whole.

While this can be useful, it is usually much easier for a participant to understand and improve their performance if you break it down into its smaller components. **PART INSTRUCTION** may be defined as the process in which you take a skill or activity and break it down into smaller individual components. For example, using the high jump performer, the coach could instruct the run-up as one component, the take-off as another and the clearance and landing as the final component.

Once you have worked on your part components, you can then combine all your individual skills – run-up, take-off and landing – together as one whole performance. This process is referred to as **WHOLE-PART-WHOLE INSTRUCTION**.

PART INSTRUCTION refers to the process of breaking a whole performance into component parts and practising them individually. As a participant improves, you can build on the level of difficulty in the skills they are taught. Part instruction is more suitable for new or complex skills, as it allows you to break down the complexity of a skill into its component parts. Your whole performance will only improve if you master the components that make up the skill.

WHOLE-PART-WHOLE is a practice method in which you practise a skill as one, then break it into its smaller components to practice each individually, and finally put the components back together as one complete performance. This method is ideal for developing simple skills, particularly those where only a low level of technical change is necessary to make improvement.

Techniques to improve performance

Whatever method you use to develop skills, it is important you use the most appropriate technique to identify a participant's strengths and areas for improvement. There is a range of techniques you can use and these are shown in Table 4.2.

Table 4.2: Techniques that can be used to assess and develop a sports performance

Technique	How to use it
Observational/ notational analysis	This is where you study a performance through observation and develop ideas or strategies to improve it. You need to have a good understanding of what to do, therefore this technique is only as good as the coach's ability to interpret a performance. As can be seen in Figure 4.2, the process is a cycle of events that helps to gradually improve a performance throughout each rotation.
Effective demonstrations	This is where you show a performer how to complete a skill or task. Good communication skills are essential in order to explain the desired outcome and how to achieve it.
Adapted practices	There are four different types of adapted practice: • Variable practice: Skills or tactics are practised within a range of situations to gradually improve the competitive performance • Distributed practice: Use short rest breaks or vary the practice with the use of another skill, to avoid it becoming too continuous • Fixed practice: Use repetitive drills or practices to develop a skill – this style of practice can often be very rigid • Massed practice: A form of continuous practice without any breaks that is performed until the skill has been developed.
Goal setting	This is where you identify an aim for the participant to be achieved over a period of time, for example, by the end of the session, week, month or year. The goal is entirely down to the coach and participant to decide on but needs to be SMART (Specific, Measurable, Achievable, Realistic, Timed).
Session design	This is when you plan your session, considering how it flows throughout. Your session will comprise one method or a combination of the methods of practice described above. Try to develop skills that can be gradually developed, either in terms of complexity or intensity (either moving to the next stage of the skill or performing the skill quicker/ more frequently/to a higher standard). Do not forget to take account of your equipment requirements as you do not want to spend much of the session moving equipment, as this will reduce the time you can spend on performing the practical activities.
Performance profiling	Not all your participants will be at the same level, nor will they all be best suited to the activity you are planning to practise. Some performers will have specific characteristics that make them more successful in certain events or activities than others. For example, a female who is tall, agile and has good hand-eye coordination may be suited to playing netball. In this case, the performance profile would show potential for greater success in this sporting activity.
Fitness assessment	As mentioned in performance profiling, not everyone is the same when it comes to sport and activity. As a coach you can measure your participants' fitness levels using a range of fitness tests. You can identify areas for improvement, then develop training sessions aimed at practice in this area. This could be achieved using adapted practices, increasing the difficulty of a practice to make the participants work harder than they would normally do in a game or competitive situation.
Modelling	In this technique you encourage a participant to copy the same technique of another individual. The participant will try and model their performance on that of another. It's important to remember the person selected to be the 'model' should be highly skilled in that activity, otherwise the participant can learn bad habits.
Coaching diaries	Using a written diary can help you to track progress in coaching sessions. You can record your session plan, how well it was completed, and the outcomes from its completion. For example, were there improvements in performance? How hard did the participants find the session?
Simulation	This is very similar to adapted practices. Here you aim to practise under competitive situations. Examples could be practising football penalties and scoring.

Practise

You are going to take three different coaching sessions, each for an hour, following one another.

You will be coaching a group of adults, a group of 16 to 20-year-olds, and a group of under-12s. You will use adapted practice methods for each of the coaching sessions.

1   Consider each adaptive practice method and justify its strengths or weaknesses as an effective means of coaching a session.

2   Which method do you think will work best with each group? Why?

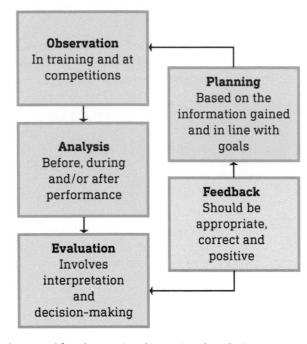

Figure 4.2: Procedure used for observational/notational analysis

Netball goal shooter Louisa Brownfield: height 6ft 3in (191cm). Performance profiling of athletes like this enables a coach to ensure the athletes fulfil their personal potential.

A3 Planning and delivering safe and effective sessions

Planning a coaching session

When planning your coaching session, there are many points you need to consider. These include:

1 do I know the session aims and objectives?

2 will I have enough time to carry out the session?

3 have I planned for the needs and considerations of my participants?

4 is the facility available and suitable for my session?

5 do I know that the equipment will be available and in good condition?

6 can I look after the health and safety needs of my participants?

If you have answered 'No' to any of these questions, you need to decide how you can overcome it before starting your coaching session. Remember, by failing to prepare, you are preparing to fail.

Link it up

For more on planning activities and sessions, go to Unit 1 and Unit 3.

Planning considerations

When establishing your session aims and objectives, you will need to think about the activities you want to perform.

- *Aims and objectives*: What do you want the participants to have achieved by the end of the session? As the coach, how do you want to lead the session? Do you want them to improve a performance or only part of a skill, such as passing a ball?
- *Time*: Consider how many activities you want to perform in a session. Are there too many or too few? How long will they last for? Consider how long it takes to set up equipment during the session. If there is a lot of equipment to move in the session, will this reduce the enjoyment of the participants?
- *Participant considerations*: Do the participants have any special needs. Think about the performance profiling, fitness level, participant age, gender, or any disabilities your participants may have. If there are any specific needs, how will you support them?
- *Facility*: Consider what playing surface is available to you. For example, if you want to coach a basketball session, is there a full-size court available? If not, can you complete your session in a small hall? Check before planning.
- *Equipment*: Consider whether you have the correct equipment available. For example, are there enough mats available for a gymnastic coaching session? Are all the springs working correctly on a trampoline for a practice session? This should all be checked before the activity planning begins.
- *Health and safety*: Consider the environment and welfare of your participants. Are there any obstacles that a participant could trip over or collide with during the coaching session? All participants should be dressed appropriately. For example, if participants wear jewellery in contact sports, this could pose a potential risk of injury to others. Remember, the participants are in your care, so look after them.

Coaching session components

When delivering a session you should try to follow the basic format of a warm up, main section and cool down.

Warm up

The warm up serves a number of purposes that can help improve a participant's performance in a practical session. Light exercise, such as jogging, causes the pulse to raise, which allows warm blood to circulate around the body. This blood helps to warm the muscles and joints, which in turn helps to make them more flexible and reduces the potential risk of injury. Performing a series of stretching exercises can also help increase the range of movement of the limbs, which reduces the risk of over-stretching and injury. When stretching, try to be logical, for example, stretch from top to bottom starting at the neck, followed by the arms, shoulders, hips, quads and hamstrings, calf muscles and ankles.

More dynamic exercises can also be used in the warm up. These require the participant to move rather than remain stationary, for example, short, fast jogging/striding, or star jumps. The aim of this type of warm up is to raise the participants' heart rate, known as a pulse raiser, which helps to move warm blood around the body, carrying lots of vital oxygen to your working muscles. Warm blood helps to make your muscles more flexible, allowing them to stretch further and reduce the risk of injury.

Link it up

Go to Unit 3 and see the section on planning activity sessions for further information on warm up and cool down activities. This will also be important when it comes to completing the synoptic task in Unit 8.

Group warm up ahead of a main activity session.

Main section

This is where you complete the main aims and objectives of your coaching session. Here you should include the development of simple and complex skills, using the range of techniques you looked at in Unit 3. You should consider this carefully as you need to make the session engaging, enjoyable and developmental. Those involved in the session should show clear progress by the end of the session.

Think about what you are trying to achieve, the drills you could use and the games you could include to develop skills you are wanting to improve. For example, if you are trying to coach the bounce pass in netball, how could you construct an activity that develops this skill? Then consider how you could make it more difficult. This could include making the pass longer, or placing a defender between the two passing players. Developing the skill should be progressive, so make it simple and gradually increase the complexity to make it more difficult over time.

Bounce pass   **Chest pass**

Figure 4.3: Basic drills for coaching a chest pass and bounce pass in netball

Cool down

This is the opposite process to the warm up. The cool down should involve a light aerobic component, for example, a slow jog, followed by some light stretches. The cool down helps to prevent the muscles and joints from tightening. A good cool down will help participants avoid feelings of muscular soreness and decrease the likelihood of injury at the next session – both factors that might reduce the participants' enjoyment of the session.

Coaching plans

Whatever the coaching session you are planning, it is important that you follow a stage-by-stage process to structure your session. An example of a good coaching plan is shown in Figure 4.4.

Date: 13 May	Stage of athlete development:
Duration: 1 hour 20 mins.	Introductory group to long jump.
Venue: Local athletics track.	Age group of athletes: 12–14 years old.
Conditions: Warm and sunny.	Size of group: 18.
Equipment: Cones, pit, rake, measure tapes, result sheets.	
Session goals for the athletes: Will be able to take off from one foot using a short approach.	Personal coaching goals: By the end of the session I will have all participants confidently taking off with one foot and landing with both.

Practical session			
Session	Unit component	Coaching point	Organisation / Safety point
Warm up (15 minutes)	Light jog running forwards, backwards and sideways, changing direction on command. Light stretching of lower back, hamstrings, quads, calves (10-sec hold each stretch). 5 mins of shuttle activity including skipping, running, bounding, hopping, and two-footed jumps. Race time – organised into groups and race against one another.	Head up, chest up, drive up with each jump. Soft landing with knees bent and drive forward with legs and arms.	Use a small grid, 20m apart, running / jumping / bounding to each corner and tag teammate.
Main session unit A (30 minutes)	Standing long jump – all athletes to have three practices after demo. Further five measured attempts into the long jump pit. Short approach long jump – using 5–7 stride approach into a one-footed take off into pit. Measure and mark approach run with a cone.	Hips high in take-off phase. Head up, chest up, using arms to drive the body upwards. Soft landing with knees bent.	Coach demo. Line participants along side of long jump pit for practice, this gives more room and maximises group involvement.
Main session unit B (20 minutes)	Team competition into pit from a short approach. Participants split into groups and each member has two jumps. Distances are added together to determine the team score.	During jump, drive up with eyes and head position focused ahead.	Involve athletes in measuring, recording and adding up their team distance.
Cool down (15 minutes)	Slow jog for 400m followed by arm swinging, hip rotations, stretching of lower back, hamstrings, quads, calves (10-sec hold each stretch).	Position athletes so all can see coach demonstration of the stretches.	Hold stretch for 10 seconds.

Figure 4.4: An example of a coaching plan for a long jump session

Practise

Produce four coaching plans that show the methods you would use to develop a participant's sporting performance. Each of your plans will be separated by three to four days and should be progressive, i.e. improve upon something from the previous session.

Remember, you must lay out your plan clearly, and it should be typed up for potential use.

The plan must contain a warm up, main session and cool down. Each plan must show progression from the previous week's activity, i.e. it must be more challenging.

Delivering an effective coaching session

The delivery of an effective coaching plan can be determined by the range of factors that have been covered within this chapter. It is important that you are able to demonstrate an understanding of the roles, responsibilities and qualities of a coach in order to deliver your coaching plan with success. Remember the coaching techniques you use should identify the participants' strengths and areas for improvement in order for you to apply effective coaching skills.

You should also ensure that your facility (the place where your session takes place) is appropriate for the coaching session you plan to lead. This includes checking that all equipment works. For example, if coaching tennis, do you have enough rackets and balls? Is the court free from obstruction? Is the net working so that it can be wound to the correct height? All these points should be checked prior to the session as they could influence the participants' enjoyment of the activity, and also pose a **HEALTH AND SAFETY HAZARD**. Remember the participants are in your care during the session.

Finally, and very importantly, when you deliver a coaching session, show enthusiasm and encouragement. You should create a positive learning and coaching environment, which will motivate your participants and maximise their enjoyment of the session.

Remember...

☐ Project your voice during any communication, so that everyone can hear you clearly.

☐ Use positive body language by standing tall, facing your participants when not demonstrating.

☐ Give strong eye contact to individuals in the group.

☐ Show confidence, and remember you are leading the session.

What if...?

Sam has been contacted by a local school who have requested some support with their after-school sports club. The aim is to encourage the learners to become more active and raise awareness of health and fitness throughout the school. Sam does not know anything about the participants other than they have mixed sporting interests that range across rugby, netball, gymnastics, football, basketball and judo. To provide activities that cover all these interests in one session is unrealistic, so the sessions will be twice a week, for the next three months, in term time only. Before Sam can plan his activity sessions, he needs to find out some further information, so he decides to contact the school.

1 Sam is concerned that the information he has is very vague. Create a list of information that Sam would need to know prior to commencing his activity session.

2 Write a formal email that Sam could send to the school, covering the key points you have in your previous list. Remember your email must take a formal tone and be clear and concise.

What if...? *(continued)*

3 Sam receives a reply and can now create his first activity plan. Produce an activity plan that can be used within the first session. Remember, it is very important that everyone takes part and no-one is left standing on the side.

4 Sam must try to identify areas that can be modified to support individual needs. How could Sam support the inclusion of mixed age groups within his session? On the plan you produce, provide additional activities that could help to support participation by people of all levels and abilities.

5 The head of the sports department has asked for a copy of Sam's next session. Provide an example that could be used. It should be professional looking, clear and concise.

Skills and knowledge check

☐ Why should a coach demonstrate a skill to a participant?

☐ What planning considerations should a coach have when preparing a coaching session for a group of participants?

☐ What is meant by the term 'modelling' when applied to coaching?

☐ Can you provide a practical example of whole-part-whole practice and provide a practical example of its application?

☐ Can you name three leadership styles and identify their strengths and weaknesses?

☐ Why should a coach use less complex activities when preparing an activity plan for beginners?

☐ Why is a cool down as important as a warm up within an activity session?

⬤ I know how to perform a warm up for an activity session.

⬤ I can prepare an activity plan for a series of coaching sessions.

⬤ I can communicate with groups of participants.

⬤ I can coach to encourage inclusivity.

⬤ I am aware of the legal obligations I have when coaching.

⬤ I know how to coach using whole-part-whole practices.

⬤ I understand the importance of goal setting when planning activities.

⬤ I know how to plan and deliver safe and effective training sessions.

If you have been unable to give positive responses to any of the questions or statements above, please go back and review the section.

B Communicate clearly to others while coaching

B1 Importance of verbal and non-verbal communication

It is easy to take communication for granted, but how effective you are in communicating with participants can have a significant influence on the success of your coaching.

Different types of communication

There are two main categories of communication:

- **VERBAL COMMUNICATION:** this is where you communicate with language, but you change the volume and tone of your voice to meet the needs of the session. It is important to use it appropriately, as constantly shouting may be interpreted as threatening. Similarly, a lower tone may mean the participants cannot hear or understand the activity clearly.
- **NON-VERBAL COMMUNICATION:** this is any communication where language is not used, and is achieved with the use of physical hand gestures, demonstrations and appropriate body language. The coach can communicate with subtle movements and posture, though, again, this needs to be controlled and non-threatening.

Link it up

Communication skills and techniques are also covered in Unit 3.

A football manager providing hand gestures to communicate to his team in an attempt to change tactics and motivate for success.

Practise

In pairs, select a sporting activity and skill you wish to coach to an individual on a one-to-one basis. Take it in turns to coach the skill using an activity of your choice. However, you are not allowed to use your voice and must use only non-verbal communication.

Review this experience. What were the difficulties you found, apart from not being able to use your voice?

Two-way communication

It is important to remember that communication is a two-way process, whether this is direct verbal interaction, or a response to an instruction/coaching point. As you learned earlier, coaches who lead using a democratic leadership style are open to listening to feedback from the participants and therefore rely on two-way verbal interaction. While they will lead the group with confidence, they will listen to feedback in order to make effective changes in the future. It is important that participants feel that communication goes in both directions and the coach is willing to listen to them and Improve their delivery or style in response to feedback.

For example, if you are coaching the smash in volleyball to a group of younger performers, participants may request alterations to the net height so that they are able to practise hitting downwards on the ball yet over the net. The coach could lower the net to help complete the correct technique. Their ability to jump higher will come as the participants mature, and from additional fitness training; at this stage, it is important that they learn the correct technique. By doing this the coach has responded to the feedback and made adjustments to overcome the performance difficulty, yet enhanced the skills practice.

Elements of effective communication

In order for a coach to be successful, they need to be able to confidently interact with their participants. Communication should be effective In order to meet the needs and level of understanding of the participant group. Effective communication can be provided if you use appropriate language and terminology. It is important you remain professional yet build a RAPPORT with your group. You should consider the language you use, keep it clear and concise while using the correct terminology. For example, when coaching the forehand in tennis, rather than just shout 'Whack it!', you could say 'Strike through the ball', as this will encourage greater control of the shot.

Practise

In pairs, select a sports activity and identify a skill you want to coach. Take it in turns to coach the skill. You are allowed to use three sticky notes for all your communication throughout the session. Remember, you should use the correct terminology and this should be professional and technical. All feedback should be clear and concise. You may only use one point on each note.

You are not allowed to communicate verbally, you may only write down the feedback coaching points needed to help them during each attempt.

1 What difficulties did you find?

2 Were there any improvements in your partner's performance?

Avoid over-complicating your coaching feedback or giving too much feedback at once. Do not feel you should keep talking to the participant – sometimes less is more. Try to work on one point at a time. Be courteous, polite and constructive with the feedback you provide. Most importantly, avoid searing criticism or foul language, remember you are a role model and the group looks to you as an example of how to behave.

What if...?

Hannah has managed to secure an exciting new job, coaching netball to a group of primary school children. The team are all highly motivated, keen to learn and thoroughly enjoy their weekly training sessions. Within the team there are five players who are hearing impaired, so Hannah must ensure that all her instructions are fully understood, using non-verbal communication techniques.

In her first session Hannah is to coach two different drills/practices, however they will need to be completed without providing verbal instruction and must show praise and provide constructive feedback. As it is a coaching session it is not appropriate to write everything down, so she must use her skills of non-verbal communication – body language and facial expression – to praise and motivate the participants.

1 Create two activity drills/practices that Hannah can use with her team.

2 Before Hannah can use them, practise them yourself. With a partner, instruct a team player how to perform each activity without using verbal communication. Remember, you are not allowed to write anything down and everything you communicate must be as a result of non-verbal communication.

3 Provide detailed non-verbal feedback to your partner at the end of the activity session.

4 Describe any difficulties Hannah may experience based on your practice.

The England rugby team huddle as one to communicate and motivate each other before a game.

B2 How to motivate and give feedback

MOTIVATION is very important in any coaching session. Consider this: would you want to attend regular coaching sessions that are led by someone who gives the impression that they are not interested or want to be somewhere else? It is unlikely that this would inspire you to achieve greater performances.

There are two different types of motivation (see Figure 4.5):

- **INTRINSIC MOTIVATION**: Having the desire to succeed purely for sheer enjoyment and the satisfaction of achievement. This desire comes from within: a self-interest to be the best you can in order to achieve the results you want, for example, a personal best in the 100m sprint. This type of motivation is most common for those who participate in sport for leisure and recreation.
- **EXTRINSIC MOTIVATION**: Having the desire to succeed due to the reward it may bring, such as money or trophies. This is most common in competitive and professional sporting activities where the desire to gain reward is at its greatest. This could include an Olympic medal, a championship or world cup, prize money or other financial reward.

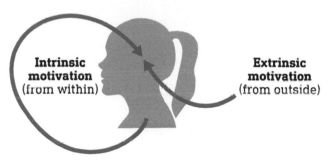

Figure 4.5: Origins of motivation for success

The type of motivation you give will be dependent on the individual you are coaching. For example, many young children may want to be coached in order to be rewarded with a certificate or medal at a sports day event. Others may take part just for fun. While age is not a key determinant of motivation, it can help to increase an individual's competitive nature for future performances. Many performers at amateur level participate in an activity for sheer enjoyment. This can be seen at sports fixtures that are held around the country each weekend. Furthermore, many participants will want to be coached to keep fit, giving them their own personal motivation, regardless of team success.

Whatever the motivation, it is important that all activities have an aim and an objective. A good series of coaching sessions that are effective, clear and concise – and that use a variety of techniques and are well planned to meet individual needs – can help motivate the performer to achieve their future goals.

Skills and knowledge check

☐ Why does a coach use goal setting when preparing coaching plans?

☐ Can you describe the key features of verbal and non-verbal communication?

☐ Why is the difference between voice tone and projection important when coaching?

☐ What is the difference between simple and complex skills?

☐ Name three roles of a coach and justify why they are important to a coach's success.

☐ Why is the use of professional and technical language important when giving feedback?

☐ What are the strengths and weaknesses of the two types of motivation?

☐ Why could it be beneficial to listen to opinions and feedback from participants in your coaching group?

○ I can coach using verbal and non-verbal communication.

○ I can confidently demonstrate a task/activity.

○ I can motivate others.

○ I can provide feedback clearly and concisely.

○ I can be courteous and respectful of my participants.

○ I can use different types of motivation to create interest in activity sessions.

If you have been unable to give positive responses to any of the questions or statements above, please go back and review the section.

Ready for assessment

You have been invited to prepare a coaching session for a group of primary school children, in preparation for their sports day in several weeks' time. The Head of PE has asked you to develop an activity session that will develop their skills for the event.

1. Create a coaching plan in preparation for an activity session of your choice. Remember, the plan should follow a standard format with an introduction, warm up, main activity, and cool down.

2. Select three coaching methods that may be used to help develop the skills of your participants.

3. Coach your participants using the methods you have selected, providing appropriate communication and motivation throughout. Remember, it is important to use the correct technical terminology, build a rapport with your participants, provide encouragement and develop their skills.

4. Review the success of the participants' performance at the end of the activity session, providing them with three coaching tips to practise when they next try the activity.

WORK FOCUS

HANDS ON

There are some important occupational skills and competencies that you will need to practise, which relate to this unit. Developing these and practising them could help you to gain employment as a sport and activity leader.

1 Work as part of a team.

- Select an example from a leisure facility where the importance of teamwork is key to the success of the job role. Provide two examples of how you could contribute to supporting teamwork for this job role.

2 Show you can respect work colleagues, other professionals and adults who come to your leisure facility setting.

- Give two practical ideas for how you could do this.

3 Use appropriate verbal communication methods with adults in the leisure facility setting.

- Give two practical ideas for how you could do this.
- Give two practical ideas for how these may be adapted for different groups of participants, e.g. children, those with disability support needs and active retired people.

Ready for work?

Take this short quiz to find out whether you would be the person chosen for that dream job.

1 I think motivation when coaching is....
- [ ] A important but not essential
- [ ] B very important
- [ ] C something you should consider
- [ ] D something I have to do if told.

2 The responsibility of a coach is to...
- [ ] A act as a role model
- [ ] B lead the group
- [ ] C support the group
- [ ] D treat people differently.

3 A coaching plan....
- [ ] A allows you to provide evidence of planning to cater for all participants
- [ ] B provides you with a guide outlining what you want to achieve
- [ ] C can be difficult to stick to
- [ ] D does not help with my session.

4 Warm up and cool down exercises are important because...
- [ ] A they help you stretch the muscle fibres and create an injury before and after an activity session
- [ ] B they help you stretch the muscle fibres and avoid an injury before and after an activity session
- [ ] C they are exercises you do every time you exercise
- [ ] D it is just the warm up that's really important.

5 When preparing a series of basketball activity plans for young children, the most appropriate practice method is...
- [ ] A variable practice
- [ ] B distributed practice
- [ ] C fixed practice
- [ ] D massed practice.

Your score:

If you scored mostly Ds, you may need to brush up on your interpersonal skills. If you scored mainly Bs then you are ready for employment, if you gained mainly As and Cs you should go back and read through the section again.

5 Developing Skills for Sport and Activity Leadership

Different companies employ sport and activity leaders to lead a variety of sessions with different groups. To be a successful sport or activity leader, there are certain skills and qualities you need to have and show on a regular basis. If you have ever worked with people in a sports team, or led people in sports activities, you may already have some understanding of the skills, attitudes and qualities needed to work in the sport or activity sector.

In this unit you have the chance to discover what it is like to work in the sport and activity industry. You will develop your skills, knowledge and understanding, which will help prepare you for future employment. After exploring employment opportunities, you will work with others and take part in work experience or a voluntary placement. You will learn what the job involves on a day-to-day basis. An excellent opportunity awaits you to get a glowing reference from your employer. It will look great on your CV and will help you to make decisions about your future career.

How will I be assessed?

This unit will be assessed through a series of assignments set by your tutor. You will be expected to research a range of suitable sport and activity leader job opportunities, and document the skills, attitudes, roles and responsibilities involved in carrying them out. You will be expected to lead multiple sport and physical activities, where you will be able to show the relevant skills, attitudes, roles and responsibilities needed to be effective in the role. You will complete a logbook and review your own performance.

Your assessment could be in the form of:

- research documents and a report
- a logbook documenting your leadership activity
- observation records of you leading multiple sessions
- visual evidence of you leading your sessions (video or photographs)
- a written review of your leadership performance with an action plan.

You will record the activities you complete and review your own performance. Your review will give you time to focus on your own skills and you will create your own action plan to help you achieve your future goals and ambitions.

Assessment criteria

Pass	Merit	Distinction
Learning aim A: Find out about the skills needed in sport and activity leader roles and the different opportunities for work		
A.P1 Identify the skills, roles and responsibilities needed in three sport and activity leader roles.	**A.M1** Compare the skills, roles and responsibilities needed in three sport and activity leader roles.	**A.D1** Explain the importance of the skills, roles and responsibilities needed in three sport and activity leader roles and compare and contrast them.
Learning aim B: Demonstrate the skills needed in sport and activity leader roles		
B.P2 Take on responsibilities of a sport and activity leader role and show appropriate skills and attitudes when leading sport and physical activities.	**B.M2** Take on responsibilities of a sport and activity leader role and show effective skills and attitudes when leading sport and physical activities.	**B.D2** Take on responsibilities of a sport and activity leader role and show effective skills and attitudes when leading sport and physical activities, linking them to achieving a desired outcome.
Learning aim C: Review own skills needed in sport and activity leader roles		
C.P3 Identify one strength and one area for improvement and produce a plan providing basic suggestions to improve performance.	**C.M3** Identify own strengths and areas for improvement, outlining why they are significant and produce a plan giving suggestions to improve performance.	**C.D3** Evaluate own strengths and areas for improvement, explaining why they are significant and produce a justified plan with detailed methods to improve performance.

A Find out about the skills needed in sport and activity leader roles and the different opportunities for work

The sports industry is growing rapidly. This means the need for well-qualified and skilful staff is greater than ever. The sports industry is diverse and there are many different career opportunities on offer. Some examples include: sports scientist, sports psychologist, **SPORT AND ACTIVITY LEADER/** coach, sport physiotherapist, nutritionist, sports teacher, activity instructor, sports development officer, sports attendants and lifeguards.

In this unit you will examine the different sport and activity leader job roles available in the sports industry. By investigating these you will gain a detailed insight into the various jobs you might like to do after this course. You will get the opportunity to complete a voluntary placement or work experience where you can work with others already in the industry.

This excellent opportunity means you will learn on the job. You will grow your skills, as well as develop the attitudes and qualities needed for the role – you will have the chance to be a better you. Learning and development is something you will do throughout your career. Even the greatest leaders working in the sports industry today are constantly learning by working with and observing other people.

A1 Different sport and activity leader job roles

There are many different sport and activity leader roles (see Figure 5.1). These can either be paid or voluntary. Most people choose to take part in sport and physical activities in the evening during their leisure time, and many roles in the sports industry require you to work irregular hours, such as evenings and weekends.

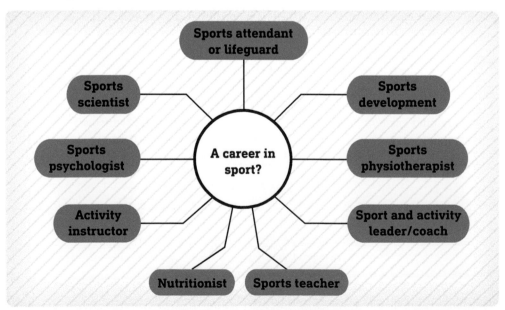

Figure 5.1: Examples of sports-related job roles.

Because of the array of different job roles on offer in the sports industry, there is a wide variety of different employers looking for hardworking, local staff. (An employer is a person or business that pays a salary or wage to an individual in exchange for them completing a job or a task.) A good employer can offer numerous training opportunities, as well as good pay, in return for you performing the job to a high standard.

Key employers in the sports industry include:
- outdoor activity centres
- private health clubs
- local councils or leisure centres
- professional football clubs
- schools
- ice skating rinks
- swimming pools or water sports facilities.

Practise

Make a list of the possible job roles that you could do for each type of employer listed above.

Many people choose to volunteer in the sport and activity sector, and you will find there are numerous local volunteering opportunities that will not require you to travel far. Check at your local sports club, leisure centre, school or activity centre for volunteer opportunities. Your local council is often a good place to start as they often rent out their facilities to local clubs and organisations.

Practise

Research and investigate two employers who you think you would like to work for.

Discuss your findings with a partner, and justify the reasons for your choices.

Examples of sport and activity leader job roles

There are many different opportunities for employment in sport. Some sport and activity leader job roles are summarised in Table 5.1.

Table 5.1: Sport and activity leader job roles

Role	Responsibilities
Activity leader	Organising, planning and delivering a range of activities to groups with different needs, for example, kayaking, rock climbing, arts and crafts or camp building.
Sports coordinator	Organising and running sports programmes. The job is likely to vary from day-to-day and will involve communication with a large number of people. For example, one day it could be running a hockey tournament and the next day organising a triathlon for the over-50s.
Children's activity leader	Organising, planning and delivering a range of activities to groups of children. This could be based at an outdoor activities centre or at a leisure centre.
Multi-sports coach	Planning and delivering a range of sports in the local community. This often involves working with young children to develop their movement and skills. The coach will need to act as a role model and mentor to others.
Community sports coach	Usually specialising in one sport, such as football. The coach will deliver sessions in the local community to a range of ages and experience levels. Professional football teams often work with local schools to encourage learning through sport.
Sports holiday camp activity leader	Organising, planning and delivering sports and activity sessions to children on a holiday camp. Sometimes the leader will stay at the holiday camp accommodation with the participants and take part in night shifts.
Sports technician	Offering support and organisation to the sports centre or department. A sports technician usually manages and maintains all of the sports facilities and sets up equipment.

Table 5.1: *(continued)*

Role	Responsibilities
Play worker	Planning, organising and taking part in leisure activities for young people aged 4–16. A play worker might arrange an arts and crafts session or take children on different outings.
Leader for disability activities	Organising, planning and delivering a range of sport and activity sessions to children and adults with disabilities. The job will involve promoting the sessions to encourage maximum participation from disabled people.

Local councils offer many different employment opportunities. The wide variety of jobs means employees have a greater opportunity for potential involvement in different parts of the industry. For example, many local councils have a gym. This can mean jobs in areas such as personal training or gym instructing are available, as well as maintenance of the equipment and gym management. There will also be opportunities connected to gym operations, such as a sports injury therapist for issues arising during training. There is a variety of qualifications that can lead to any of these jobs. Employers are looking for people who are able to develop their practical skills, as well as have the right level of entry qualifications.

Practise

Identify the four main skills you believe are necessary for a career as a sports injury therapist.

Discuss these with a partner, and rank them in order of importance.

NATIONAL GOVERNING BODIES (NGBs) also offer many different employment opportunities. (National Governing Bodies are organisations that govern and regulate a sport or activity.) Below are some examples.

- *Safeguarding officer*: Works with others to ensure children and vulnerable adults are safe. You will need to organise reports and follow procedures.
- *Stadium store manager*: Runs and manages the store day-to-day, including match days. You will need good social skills to interact with the customers to maximise sales and profit.
- *Social media assistant*: Assists with publishing items on all social media channels. Informs and encourages others to interact with their local sports clubs.
- *Sports development officer*: Responsible for the development of sport in a particular geographical area. Often a specialist in a particular sport. Aims to improve sports participation in the local community.

Link it up

Governing bodies are discussed in more detail in Unit 6.

What if...?

Paul's dream job is to be a stadium store manager at a professional football club. He has worked in a clothes shop for five years and has gained lots of practical experience in the shop. He is always the first to offer if the shop needs any extra help and regularly helps to train other staff on the shop floor. His hobbies include watching football, reading the newspaper and seeing his friends. At the moment Paul has never managed people or a budget.

Complete the tasks below.

1 Research the requirements of the role.

2 Using this information, write Paul an email giving him advice on his next steps. Make sure you include what you believe Paul's strengths to be in applying and what he needs to do in order to be a good candidate.

The role of volunteers

Volunteers provide a lot of support to the sport and activity industry in the UK. A **VOLUNTEER** is someone who gives up their time for no financial gain to complete a job or a task. A volunteer can be of any age, experience level or background. People choose to volunteer for many different reasons. They are often people who enjoy sport and want to give something back. Some volunteers want to make a difference to their community or the people around them. Others choose to volunteer to build up their skills, experience and enhance their CV.

Volunteers play a crucial role in sport and activity provision in the UK today. The London 2012 Olympics relied heavily on help from volunteers. They were known as 'Games Makers', the volunteer army who helped London 2012 run so smoothly. The 'Games Makers' had numerous roles in the Olympics. Some helped with ticketing, others with directions or coordinating transport, while others were at the heart of the sporting action, working with photographers or assisting with drug testing. More than 70,000 people gave up their time to help the huge international event run smoothly. The volunteers were all given a uniform and a travel card to help them navigate their way through London free of charge. The London 2012 Olympic uniform was immediately recognisable, consisting of a purple shirt with beige trousers, and it became an iconic legacy of the games. Afterwards, the volunteers were left with a hugely rewarding emotional experience that they will always be able to refer to in any job interview or to members of their family. Volunteers for London 2012 were vital and their contribution towards that event will be remembered forever.

'Games Makers' volunteers were crucial to the success of the London 2012 Olympics.

Sports volunteer schemes are an excellent way of building your skills and CV.

The largest voluntary organisations worldwide are the Scouts and Girlguiding movements. The Scouts has more than 450,000 members in the UK, and offers many opportunities to get involved in many diverse activities, ranging from leading kayaking sessions to running games for more than 50 scouts at one time.

There is not one type of person that suits any particular volunteer role. People choose to volunteer at different stages of their life. For example, a young person taking a gap year might volunteer in the UK or overseas; someone who is retired might choose to volunteer to give something back to their community. A parent might volunteer with children's groups, or someone might simply have a spare two or three hours a week and want to be more involved in their community.

Volunteering is often an excellent way of meeting new people and gaining new skills. However, a volunteer might already have a set of skills that an organisation really needs. For example, someone with carpentry skills might be able to offer to help maintain the scouting facilities.

Volunteering can be very rewarding and help the community.

Sports charities also rely on, and are usually set up and run by, volunteers. United Through Sport is one example of a UK-based charity that uses sport to help disadvantaged young people. United Through Sport works to improve participation as well as supporting children that have the potential to be elite performers. The charity works both in the UK and abroad. Volunteers are offered the chance to work in countries such as Argentina and Thailand.

Other opportunities that are closer to home include volunteering in local sports or physical activity teams. For example, running a local Sunday league football team is regularly taken on by a parent or a friend of one of the children. However, some people also use volunteering as an opportunity for personal learning and development and this can be hugely advantageous all round: participants and clubs benefit from free coaching, and the volunteer has access to a group of participants with whom they can practise their coaching skills and techniques.

Local youth and activity clubs are also usually set up and run by volunteers. They provide a central and safe location for young people in the community to socialise, play sport and take part in various activities. Volunteers are not just required to lead the activities. Some people might also participate in planning fundraising activities to pay for the equipment and maintain the facilities. Without volunteers, this type of club would not exist in the UK.

Practise

Research a local volunteering opportunity in your area.

Create a poster to help recruit volunteers.

Roles and responsibilities of sport and activity leaders

A sport and activity leader has many important roles and responsibilities. These include organising, planning and delivering a range of sports and different activities to a group of participants. The participants might vary in age, experience, background and culture. Generally the roles and responsibilities are similar for all sport and activity leaders, although there will, of course, be some variety depending on where you are working and who you are working for. The roles and responsibilities of any job will be outlined in the job description, which an applicant would receive before reaching interview stage.

Some of the general roles and responsibilities of a sport and activity leader are given below.

- *Introducing new activities*: Hosting and leading a new activity for a group of participants. This could be introducing a group to a new game or sport. How the session is led depends on the group's experience and ability levels. It might be as simple as introducing a group to trail running, or as complicated as learning to ride a horse. It is important to remember that when people try something new they can be nervous and unsure. As a leader you will need to demonstrate a range of different skills to make them feel at ease.

- *Running suitable activities*: When leading a group through a planned activity, you will need to take charge of the equipment, work out timings, book the **FACILITY** and ensure **HEALTH AND SAFETY** is considered throughout. Examples of activities include five-a-side football, abseiling, hillwalking or a high ropes course.
- *Teaching skills*: Delivering a sport or activity session usually means teaching the group a new skill or set of skills. For example, a badminton coach working with beginners might teach the group how to execute a forehand serve.
- *Organising groups*: When leading sports or activity sessions you will often work with a group. This means managing many participants. Good planning and communication skills are essential.
- *Implementing health and safety*: Health and safety is the main priority in any sports or activity session. As leader you will need to consider this before, during and after the session. It is likely you will need to complete a **RISK ASSESSMENT** to ensure the activity is as safe as possible.
- *Customer care*: Providing a good service to a group of participants by running an effective sport or activity. As leader you will adapt your session to the group's needs to ensure everyone receives a positive learning experience.
- *Dealing with issues and emergencies*: You will need to be prepared for any emergency that you might face. Examples include a fire or a bomb scare. You will need to follow emergency procedures and ensure everyone in the session is safe. You will also need to register participants at the start of every session so you are aware of who is present in case of emergency.
- *Child protection*: Children deserve to enjoy a sport or activity session in safety. As leader you will need to be aware of the different signs of child **ABUSE** and follow the correct procedures if you have any welfare concerns about the child. Companies and organisations give training on this. If you are unsure at any time, ask your manager or supervisor.

Link it up

Refer to Unit 3 and Unit 6 for more details on creating and producing a risk assessment for leading a sport or activity session, and dealing with emergencies.

Unit 1 also looks at health and safety and considers how to ensure participants' needs are catered for.

Practise

Working in small groups, take it in turns to introduce and deliver a new activity of your choice.

Remember to use demonstrations and make sure everyone feels at ease.

As a sport and activity leader, it is important that you always put participants' needs first. Health and safety is the main priority, but it is also important that all sessions are inclusive and fun. An effective sport and activity leader will ensure that everyone in the session learns something new.

Do not feel overwhelmed by this. When a sport and activity leader is offered a job, it is the employer's responsibility to ensure they are given appropriate training and complete any courses they need to, particularly with regard to health and safety and **SAFEGUARDING**. Do not worry if you do not feel that you have mastered everything for your work placement – you will still get the chance to show what you can do, as well as learn something new.

A2 Skills and attitudes required to work in different job roles

In this section you will examine the skills and attitudes required to work in sport and activity leadership. You will be encouraged to reflect on which skills and attitudes you currently possess and those that you think you will need to develop. Remember, in order to be an effective sport and activity leader, you do not have to be outstanding in all areas. Even the greatest sport and activity leaders do not demonstrate excellence in all skill areas. All leaders, whatever their experience, are constantly learning and can always improve. You should always look to develop yourself to be the best you can be.

> **Practise**
>
> Think of a sport or activity leader that you admire.
>
> Make a list of the skills and attitudes that they demonstrate.

Skills required

A wide range of skills is required when leading sport or activity sessions. The skills you need to employ will often depend on the group you are leading and the environment in which your activity is taking place.

Communication

COMMUNICATION is an essential skill for a sport and activity leader. Communication is the exchange of information using verbal or non-verbal methods. Any job that involves working with people relies on good levels of communication. Communication can be split into two different parts: verbal and non-verbal communication.

- **VERBAL COMMUNICATION:** For example, a leader might verbally ask the group to go and collect a bib.
- **NON-VERBAL COMMUNICATION:** For example, they might gesture to a participant to pause what they are doing so they can listen to instructions.

Communication is a two-way relationship between the leader and the participants. Sometimes you will need to use different skills to ensure the participants feel relaxed and at ease. You should always encourage open communication. Without any form of communication a leader will not be able to instruct and direct their group to achieve the **OBJECTIVES** of the session. This means no – or limited – learning will take place.

Teamwork

Most jobs require at least some element of **TEAMWORK** (this is where a group works together cooperatively to achieve a shared goal). It is not surprising that roles within the sport and activity industry often require a large amount of teamwork. Frequently a sport or activity leader will need to work with others to organise and deliver a session. For example, a sports camp activity leader will need to coordinate with other activity leaders to establish groups and assign activities. It is likely they will have to work alongside other leaders, using and sharing the same facility and equipment.

> **Link it up**
>
> For more on communication skills and techniques, go to Unit 3.

However, it is not only other leaders they might need to work alongside. Other staff, such as managers, reception staff, night staff, cleaners and specialist sports coaches might also be on site. Every job is different and, as a sport and activity leader, you will work with many different people. Employers are looking for leaders who can work well with other people and push others to meet high standards.

Practise

Think about the last time you worked in a team. This could be in your group, at home or in a sporting situation. Answer the questions below.

1 What role did you have in the team?

2 What did you do well?

3 What could you improve for next time?

Decision making

When a problem occurs during an activity, it is up to the leader to find, and choose, a solution to solve it. This process requires good DECISION-MAKING skills. A decision can be something really small, such as how many cones to prepare for a sports session. It can also be very large and potentially have dangerous consequences. For example, if an activity leader takes a group of participants hillwalking and suddenly the weather changes, the leader will need to make a decision as to what course of action to take. The health and safety of participants in this scenario is clearly a top priority.

Motivation

All sports and activities require leaders who can influence those around them. Leaders should inspire MOTIVATION in others in many different ways. Sometimes leading by example helps to increase a participant's motivation levels. There are many other techniques a leader can use to increase a participant's or performer's motivation levels. Most importantly, as a leader, to inspire motivation in others, you must be motivated yourself. To be effective, you should be constantly motivated to learn and set yourself regular goals to achieve. By being motivated yourself, you are more likely to inspire motivation in those participating in your activity.

Leadership

LEADERSHIP is defined as the ability to manage a group of people effectively. By demonstrating good leadership qualities, you are more likely to gain the respect of the group. Every leader will have a different style of leadership and, depending on your group and the stage of your career, this can change over time. A leader will need to show they are a good role model to their group and lead by example in their behaviour and conduct.

Problem-solving

The sport and activity environment can be very inconsistent and therefore PROBLEM-SOLVING skills (finding a solution to an issue) are often needed. As leader it is your responsibility to resolve any issues. The participants will expect these to be sorted before the session starts so that the activity can go ahead with minimal disruption. If a problem occurs during the session, it is your job to solve it as quickly as possible to allow the session to continue. Problems can happen in a range of areas. For example, there might be an issue with the facilities, faulty equipment, transport failure, opponents not turning up or participants being unable to attend.

Link it up

The advantages and disadvantages of different leadership styles are looked at in Unit 3 and Unit 4.

What if...?

You are leading a beginners' basketball session in your local sports centre for children aged 10–11. You arrive one hour before your session to set up and are told that the facility has been double booked.

Discuss with a partner how you will handle this situation to ensure your session continues with minimal disruption.

Inclusivity

All sport and activity sessions must be fully inclusive. **INCLUSIVITY** means not excluding anyone based on race, gender, disability, culture or sexual orientation.

The leader should treat everyone in the same way. Working with a range of diverse people is an intrinsic part of the sport and activity leader role. When leading, it is important to understand that different individuals will have different needs and it will be up to you to create a welcoming environment. Working with a range of different people will also help a leader to develop their own skills and attitudes to support every participant.

> **Link it up**
>
> For more on inclusivity, go to Unit 1.

Attitudes required

Good sport and activity leaders are role models. They display an outstanding attitude to their participants at all times (see Figure 5.2). Effective leaders have the ability to inspire, encourage and motivate others to help them to be the best they can. A leader's behaviour, thoughts and feelings all reflect the attitude they have. If a leader shows a negative attitude, this can decrease learning in the session and also have a negative impact on the group. The ability to be positive, enthusiastic and patient is an essential part of the role for all sport or activity leaders.

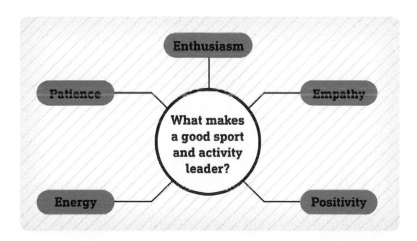

Figure 5.2: Personality traits of a good sport and activity leader

Patience

PATIENCE is an important attribute for a leader to have. Patience is displayed through your own self-control. Sometimes you might feel frustrated with a particular event or situation, for example, if you are a children's activity leader and one of the participants is not demonstrating a good attitude in your sessions. To be a good leader, you will need to consider the needs of the whole group and remember that patience and praise is much better than criticism and shouting.

Empathy

Humans often use **EMPATHY** without realising it. (Empathy is defined as the ability to share and understand someone's feelings.) For example, a participant attending your session may feel worried and anxious about their forthcoming school exams. As an effective leader, you will be able to recall your own experiences in this situation and demonstrate a high level of understanding about how the participant is feeling. Sometimes it is appropriate to share your own experiences of a particular event if you have dealt with it before. Of course, in other circumstances, this would not be acceptable, particularly if it relates to your personal life. You will need to show good judgement in this position.

By showing empathy, it is possible to reassure a participant and help them to get the best out of the session. For example, at a sports camp young people may need to stay overnight. For some it might be the first time they have stayed away from home, and they might feel homesick. As leader you will need to demonstrate that you understand this feeling, but then try and distract the individual and get them to focus on something else. This helps them to take their mind off feeling homesick and enables them to benefit fully from the experience of sports camp.

Positivity

Being positive when leading a group is a fundamental requirement. (**POSITIVITY** is defined as showing a positive attitude.) As leader, you need to display the behaviours and attitudes you expect from your group. By being positive you are likely to inspire others and be a role model. Positivity can encourage participants to work hard and learn from their mistakes. For example, if a multi-skills coach is teaching a new skill and a child is not able to execute it properly first time round, then being positive will encourage them to keep trying and not be afraid of making mistakes. In turn, this means that participants are more likely to have fun in your sessions and keep attending.

An outdoor activities instructor delivering a new skill and activity to their group.

Practise

In pairs, choose a topic to discuss.

1 Choose one person to be consistently negative throughout the discussion. What impact does this negativity have on both your mood and that of your partner? What happens to the quality of the discussion?

2 Discuss the same topic with the other person being consistently positive. What impact does the positivity have on the discussion?

3 Explain how you feel about being involved in a positive discussion compared to a negative one.

Enthusiasm

ENTHUSIASM is a very important aspect of sport and activity leadership. Being enthusiastic engages, excites and helps to motivate participants. It shows a leader is passionate about their sport or activity and shows their desire to be at work. For example, a play worker who is working with children will need to show high levels of enthusiasm towards all the activities they deliver.

Energy

Your energy levels often vary depending on your lifestyle choices. Diet, sleep, stress and alcohol all have an impact on your energy. **ENERGY** is defined as the capacity to be physically or mentally active. When working with any group of people, a sport or activity leader will need to be engaged and show they are physically and mentally active. For example, a sports technician will need to be mentally alert to prepare and organise equipment. It is usually the case that when you enjoy your work you show high levels of energy. This makes it really important to ensure you work hard to get a job that you would like to do, not simply something that just pays the bills. Many people want to work in the sport and activity industry, and competition for jobs is fierce. It is down to you to work hard and improve your skills and attitudes to be the best you can be.

What if...?

Jenni is studying sport at college. She has volunteered at her local leisure centre and has had some experience of teaching children at her old primary school. After studying she would like to become a multi-skills coach. Jenni's lifestyle involves lots of socialising and she often suffers from a lack of sleep. She has a diet high in fat and sugar. Her friends often say she is a really good leader and has a lot of patience. However, she can be negative and low in enthusiasm.

Jenni is not sure what skills and attitudes are most important for her future career. Advise Jenni by answering the questions below.

1 Explain why having high energy levels is important in the role of a multi-skills coach.

2 Outline an example of when Jenni will need to be patient in her future career.

3 Give Jenni advice on how she can change her lifestyle to be the best multi-skills coach she can be.

A3 Suitable employment opportunities and work conditions, and expectations in different roles

Sport and activity in the UK is organised and divided into three sectors. These are the private, public and voluntary sectors.

Opportunities offered by providers in different sectors

Private

The **PRIVATE SECTOR** provides sport and activity services that are owned by an individual or a group. The main aim is to make a profit. These services and facilities can be local, regional or at a national level. They aim to offer a high-quality service and are frequently members-only facilities or clubs. Facilities are normally of a high standard, with members paying a higher price and a joining fee as well as a monthly fee to access the club and facility. Often this means members sign a contract stating they will pay the agreed membership for a set amount of time, such as one year.

Individuals or shareholders usually own private sector companies. The business will pay its own taxes and staff from the money generated. The business aim is to make a profit for the owners and management team. Sometimes the management team may get bonuses if the club or facility is growing and doing particularly well. Private organisations often have investors who initially give the owner(s) more financial help to set up or grow the business. The investors will also be rewarded when the business does well.

There is a wide range of opportunities offered by private sector providers. Each gym, for example, will need personnel such as personal trainers, a gym manager, receptionists, children's club activity leader, sports and activities coaches, sports coordinators, leisure centre managers, activities leaders/instructors, head of operations and a sales team.

The private sector often has excellent facilities and equipment for staff to use.

Practise

Research a local private sports club or activity centre. Investigate the cost of membership compared to a one-off visitor fee.

Public

The **PUBLIC SECTOR** has facilities across the country. These are funded and paid for by the local government out of taxes and sometimes National Lottery money. Usually the local council or authority owns and runs these. They are open to the public and are not usually membership-only. The focus is on increasing mass participation. There is normally an option to pay-as-you-go or join a cheaper membership scheme. They have a policy of making sport and activity accessible for everyone and aim to increase sports and activity participation in the local area. These clubs and facilities are sometimes attached to schools. A school will have access to these facilities in the day as part of their curriculum physical education (PE) lessons. Frequently, these include outdoor pitches and swimming pools.

The public sector will offer similar opportunities to the private sector. What is on offer will depend on the facilities offered at a local leisure centre or activity centre. Examples include lifeguard, receptionist, outdoor activities instructor, sport and activity leader or coach, personal trainer or gym instructor, disabilities instructor, manager, play worker, assistant manager and sports activity holiday camp leader.

This person is an outdoor activities instructor. Do you think you would like to work outside all day?

Voluntary

The **VOLUNTARY SECTOR** is a not-for-profit sector, which is neither private nor public. An individual or a group of volunteers who want to enjoy sport and develop it for their local club and community usually runs the voluntary sector. Voluntary organisations do not normally own facilities but usually rent them from the local authority. One example might be a local walking club. All ages are welcome and by collecting a small payment from each participant every week, costs are covered.

Different organisations and clubs offer volunteering opportunities and sometimes new opportunities can be created. For example, if a local football team only has an under-15 and under-16 team they might propose setting up an under-14 team to compete in the local league. This new team will need volunteer support in a variety of roles.

There are often volunteering opportunities outside of the UK. Sometimes the organisation will fund a volunteer's travel and/or accommodation. The volunteer will then complete the job or task in an agreed amount of time. These opportunities can be excellent additions to your CV and are often looked at favourably by future employers.

Volunteering to coach a local football team can be very rewarding.

Practise

Select two people who you would like to interview regarding their current work. Create a list of five questions to ask them to find out about the sector they work in and why.

Make sure you are sensitive and do not ask them any personal questions, such as how much they get paid.

Link it up

Employment in the different sectors (private, public and voluntary) is also discussed in Unit 2.

Philosophies, advantages and disadvantages

Each sector has a different philosophy and main aim that they are working towards. This means that there are both advantages and disadvantages for working in each, which are summarised in Table 5.2.

Table 5.2: Advantages and disadvantages of working in the private, public and voluntary sectors

	Private sector	Public sector	Voluntary sector
Main aim or philosophy	To make a profit.	To provide accessible sport and physical activity to the community to increase mass participation.	Non-profit organisations or charities, which bring communities together by offering sport and physical activity opportunities.
Advantages	Employees often earn more money and senior staff may get bonuses or performance related pay.	Jobs can often be secure and can be less stressful than the private sector.	Opportunity to 'give something back' and benefit the community and those around you.

Table 5.2: *(continued)*

	Private sector	**Public sector**	**Voluntary sector**
Disadvantages	The owners of the business make the decisions and, if you are not performing well, you might be at risk of losing your job.	For a similar role salaries and pay is generally lower than in the private sector.	The opportunities are not paid. Importantly, sometimes travel expenses can be paid for a volunteer to attend their work.

Local and national opportunities

Searching for a job opportunity can often be daunting. Employers advertise job and work placement opportunities in many different locations. More and more people are choosing to only use the Internet to look for a job. However, this can be a mistake. A job search should involve investigating many different areas to find the very best roles.

Below are four areas you can explore to look for a suitable employment opportunity.

1 *Specific sport and activity leader employment websites*: These websites are regularly updated with new roles in this area (and only these types of roles). Companies often have online applications for candidates to complete from home.

Examples include:

○ www.sportsleaders.org: courses for Sports Leader UK qualifications, and job vacancies for sports leaders

○ www.ukcoaching.org: job vacancies and a range of resources for coaches and people who develop coaches

○ www.uksport.gov.uk: job vacancies, including UK Sport, English Institute of Sport and national governing bodies

○ www.leisurejobs.com: worldwide directory searchable via sector and location

○ www.leisureopportunities.co.uk: searchable directory for UK and Ireland

○ www.leisureweek.com: news and jobs for the UK leisure industry.

2 *Local newspapers and their websites*: If you are looking for a job locally this can often give you a broad idea of the different organisations and providers that are in your area.

3 *Local job advertisement sites*: These can be similar to local newspapers and their websites. You will be able to search specifically for sport and activity roles in your local area, allowing you to gain local knowledge and review the types of roles available.

4 *Local authority sports and activity providers*: Sometimes the best way is to go in to your local sports and activity providers and ask to speak to the manager. Fewer people choose to take this route now, which can often separate you from others. It can be a good idea to hand in a copy of your CV or arrange a meeting with the manager. The manager will also be able to give you advice on your job search so do not be afraid to ask.

What if...?

Dani is currently in year 9 at school. Recently she has started to think about what job she would like to do when she is older. She knows she wants to work in the sport and activity industry.

She plays netball, likes swimming and enjoys keeping fit.

Dani has asked for your help. Complete the tasks below.

1 Use your knowledge to inform Dani about the different job opportunities in the sport and activity industry.

2 Dani has hinted that she is interested in working with people in the community. Explain the differences in working in the public, private and voluntary sector. Make sure you outline the advantages and disadvantages.

Working conditions

Every job has slightly different working conditions. This will vary between sectors but also between different organisations and providers. When a position is advertised the job description will outline the job's roles and responsibilities. This gives the candidate an idea of the type of work they will be required to complete and if they feel that the role is suitable for them.

Normally, the expected rates of pay, working hours and patterns of working, flexible hours, holiday allowance and benefits will be told to you at a job interview. However, sometimes the expected rates of pay and any specific requirements – such as night shifts – will be communicated in the job advert and description. This gives the candidates as much information as possible to see if the role meets their needs. Remember, if the hours and the idea of shift patterns do not appeal to you, make sure you think very carefully before you apply. If the role is full-time you will be completing a large portion of your week at work, therefore it needs to be the right decision.

One way of understanding and gaining more information about the industry and different job roles is to volunteer or complete a work placement.

All job adverts and descriptions vary. Figure 5.3 shows an example of a job description for the role of holiday activity leader.

Job title: Holiday Activity Leader

Reporting to: Activities Manager

Purpose of the role: To organise, plan and deliver a wide range of sporting and non-sporting activities for the summer school.

Location: School premises and off-site for trips.

Rate of pay: Depending on experience.

Working hours: The day will be split into two shifts 7.30 a.m.–4.00 p.m. and 4.00 p.m.–10:30 p.m. The role requires one shift per day, six days a week. The role is for four weeks in total.

Benefits: Use of the on-site gym when you are not on shift.

Figure 5.3: Job description for a Holiday Activity Leader

Roles and responsibilities of the role

- **Session planning and delivering:** Organise and deliver a range of sporting and non-sporting games and activities. All sessions need to be engaging, structured and high in quality.

- **Trips:** To accompany a group of students on a trip, following the schedule and procedures of the school to maximise the enjoyment of the children.

- **Risk assessments/Health and Safety:** To read and understand the risk assessment for every sporting and non-sporting activity. Ensure the children are safe at all times.

- **Welfare:** To be constantly mindful of the children's physical and emotional well-being.

Essential requirements

- Experience with young people aged between 8 and 16. Ideally this will be in a sport or activity-related setting.

- Sports coaching qualifications

- Proven ability of working in a team

- Knowledge of Health and Safety

Key skills and attitudes

- Excellent communication skills

- Ability to motivate a group of young people

- High levels of positivity and enthusiasm

Practise

Select a job role from the following options.

- Leader of disability activities
- Community sports coach
- Activity leader
- Play worker

Research a job advert or job description for a similar role. Answer the questions below.

1 What are the roles and responsibilities of the role?

2 What is the expected rate of pay?

3 What are the working hours and patterns of working?

4 Does the role allow for flexible hours?

5 Are there any holiday allowances or benefits to the role?

Skills and knowledge check

☐ Explain the role of volunteers.

☐ Define the public sector.

☐ Explain one advantage and one disadvantage for working in the voluntary sector.

☐ List five different job opportunities in the sport and activity industry.

☐ Explain a leader's responsibility in dealing with issues and emergencies.

☐ Name the four places you can use to investigate local and national opportunities to work in sport and activity roles.

○ I can list three attitudes required to work as a sport or activity leader.

○ I can explain a leader's responsibility in dealing with an emergency.

○ I can describe two skills that are required to work as a sport and activity leader.

If you have been unable to give positive responses to any the questions or statements above, please go back and review the section.

B Demonstrate the skills needed in sport and activity leader roles

This is your chance to discover what it is like to work in the sports and activity industry. Be ready to develop your skills, knowledge and understanding, and prepare for future employment. You will work with others and take part in work experience, learning what a particular job involves on a daily basis. This is an excellent opportunity that will help prepare you for your future career.

Activities always need to be fun and engaging for your participants.

What if...?

John is confident, hard-working and outgoing. He has been looking forward to his work experience at a leisure centre all year and has just finished his first day. John loved working in the gym at the centre but feels disappointed in himself. He met some of the customers and when they asked him questions, he was so nervous his mind went blank.

Write an email to John with advice on how to approach the rest of his work experience.

B1 Responsibilities involved in being a sport and activity leader

Being a sport and activity leader involves taking on specific responsibilities. As you have seen from Learning aim A (in 'Different sport and activity leader roles'), these responsibilities can vary depending on where you work. A sport or activity leader's main responsibility is always to offer a safe activity and environment to their participants.

Different working roles

When you think of the working day you often think of nine to five, Monday to Friday. While a lot of people do follow this working pattern, there are plenty of other options open to you. Work in the sport and activity industry often involves shift work or irregular hours. Most people choose to exercise in their leisure time, which means many roles, such as sports coordinator, outdoor activities instructor and multi-sports coach, often involve work in the evenings and at weekends.

There is often flexibility in the contracts on offer within the sport and activity industry. For example, some staff might only work in the holidays, while others might work two days a week in term time. Many leisure or activity centres offer holiday work, as this is the time they are most busy, so you might find an opportunity in a role such as sports holiday camp activity leader. Many centres also offer part-time work (where you typically work less than 30 hours per week). For example, a gym might employ a personal trainer to run exercise classes for ten hours per week. This allows the personal trainer flexibility to set up a business or work somewhere else for the rest of the week.

There is, however, a large amount of competition for many jobs in the UK. To stand out you need to offer something different. Work experience and voluntary placements are an excellent way of doing this and allow you to meet new people, build your network and practise your skills. If you do a good job you may also be able to use your workplace supervisor as a REFEREE. (A referee is a person who can provide information (hopefully positive) to a potential employer about your skills, attitudes and personality.)

Responsibilities in the different roles

The responsibilities of a job are first outlined in the job description and will be communicated to you when you first start in your new role. Refer back to Learning aim A ('Different sport and activity leader roles') for detailed information on the responsibilities of being a sport or activity leader.

On your work experience you will have some set responsibilities. This opportunity is exciting and gives you the chance to take control. For example, you might be asked to teach a skill in a session, organise a particular group or work on reception, meeting customers. Make sure you are clear about what has been asked of you and if you are unsure ask your workplace supervisor. As always, health and safety is the priority so make sure you report any issues to your supervisor. Every member of staff needs to follow a set workplace procedure for dealing with emergencies, such as a fire or bomb scare. As you are on work experience it will not be your responsibility to deal with an emergency, however, you may need to assist if a situation arises. Remember to be calm and follow any directions you are given.

B2 Skills required to be an effective sport and activity leader

Leadership takes practice and experience.

How to be an effective leader

Effective leadership is not something anyone is immediately good at. Leadership takes practice and experience. The skills needed to become an effective leader include communication, teamwork, decision making, motivation, leadership, problem solving and inclusivity. Refer back to Learning aim A ('Skills and attitudes required to work in different job roles') for specific details of each of these skills. During your work experience make notes in your diary about when you demonstrated these specific skills.

How to work effectively in a team

Teamwork is a fundamental part of the sport and activity industry. Whether you are working as a steward on match day for a professional football club or leading open-water swimming sessions at a local lake, you are part of a team. You will automatically become part of a team on your work experience and you will work with others to achieve an aim. Working effectively in a team includes listening, following instructions, developing ideas, providing feedback, showing flexibility and being respectful (see Figure 5.4).

Working in a team can be incredibly rewarding but be prepared for it to also be a challenge. Working in a team means you have to be very good at listening to others. By listening you will gain a large amount of information that allows you to learn about the job or industry. You will need to listen a lot on your work experience. You are likely to be given instructions by your supervisor or colleagues. Follow these instructions and always ask if you are not sure or need further guidance. For example, if your supervisor asks you to set up four badminton courts for use at 3.00 p.m., you will need to prepare the equipment, make sure the area is clean and safe, and work quickly to set up four courts. In this example, the number of courts and the time they are required are important pieces of information – you will have needed to listen properly and retain the information in order to perform this task.

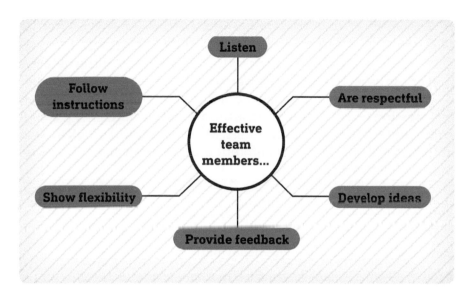

Figure 5.4: How effective team members behave

Working in a team often means helping others. For example, if a person calls in sick, you might need to complete some additional work or change what you have planned. Learning to be flexible is an attractive quality for any future employer. Being flexible can often mean doing a particular job or role that you would not normally do. This can sometimes mean that you develop ideas of how to do the task quicker or better. Do not be afraid to share any ideas you have with your team, especially if it benefits the business or helps others.

You might be asked to a team meeting during your work experience. Managers call team meetings for a variety of reasons. A lot of workplaces have a weekly meeting to share and discuss ideas. Other meetings can be called if a problem has arisen that needs dealing with. If it is appropriate, or you are asked, provide some feedback to your supervisor. This might be as simple as informing them how many participants turned up for a particular session or what canoeing equipment is still in the locker. Be confident in your abilities and be respectful to others at all times.

B3 Learning from working with and observing other people

Being able to work with others is a fundamental aspect of sport and activity leadership. All over the world people learn from others every single day. Professional football coaches often use this as part of their own development. First team coaches in football clubs will regularly observe others to gain new ideas.

On your work experience you will get a chance to work with others who work in the sport and activity industry on a daily basis. Take the opportunity to ask your supervisor and colleagues questions to gain more information on the work conditions, daily life and expectations of different roles. For example, ask about the key skills they need to work well with others and talk about the times when they 'got it wrong' and what the impact of this was.

Practise

During your work experience, you might get the opportunity to ask your workplace supervisor and colleagues some questions.

In pairs, plan a list of questions you might ask about what it is like to work in the sport and activity industry.

It is likely you will be asked to shadow a coach or a sport and activity leader in action. Become a student of their actions. Focus on the little details, such as when does the leader talk and when does he or she listen? Consider how often the leader works with others. Sometimes this might be before and after the session or even during the session. Observe when the leader leads the group and when they follow others. Most importantly, look at how the group behaves and responds to different aspects of the leader's session.

Practise

Observe a coach or leader and complete the following tasks.

1 Make a list of the best-practice behaviours that they show.

2 Explain why these behaviours are important, giving reasons for your answers.

3 Explain what would happen if these behaviours are not shown.

The importance of collaboration

COLLABORATION is defined as the action of two or more people working together to achieve something. On your work experience you will definitely collaborate. This could mean working with someone to satisfy a customer query or working in a team to set up equipment for a group or event.

Practise

In small groups, work together to plan an event that raises money for charity. You will need to collaborate with your team and others in your educational environment to make the event a success.

Be creative in your event choice. You may need to think about:

- who will attend your event
- how you plan to market your event
- where your event will take place
- what jobs you will designate to different people in your group
- what equipment you will need
- what you will need to prepare beforehand
- when your event will be
- how you are going to charge people or raise money for charity.

Working in a team is fundamental to success and often a team will agree a goal to focus on and work towards. For example, a team of multi-skills coaches will work together to deliver a set number of sessions per month. Each person in the team will often bring different skills and qualities, which make the team very effective. Someone in the team might be really good at motivating, not just the participants but also their colleagues. Someone else might be a really good communicator, so is tasked with keeping a record of the number of sessions delivered and communicating this throughout the month to the team. If a team do not collaborate and work well together there can be conflict and goals are likely not to be reached. Building a team that works together is crucial for all employers.

Working well with others is vital to achieve any goal or ambition.

B4 Attitudes required to be an effective sport and activity leader in the workplace

A leader's behaviour, thoughts and feelings all reflect their attitude. Attitudes can be improved and developed over time. They can change and are often influenced by the environment and other people. To work in the sport and activity industry the following attitudes are required: patience, empathy, positivity, enthusiasm and energy.

Appropriate attitudes

The workplace requires staff to have positive attitudes in order to ensure the customers are satisfied. While you are on your work experience make notes in your diary about when you have shown these specific attitudes. Refer back to Learning aim A ('Skills and attitudes required to work in different job roles'), which gives specific details on the attitudes required to work in a range of job roles, including sport and activity leadership.

Skills and knowledge check

☐ Explain the different working roles on offer in the sport and activity industry.

☐ Describe the attitudes required to be an effective sport and activity leader in the workplace.

☐ Describe how to work effectively in a team.

○ I can list the skills required to be an effective sport and activity leader.

○ I know the importance of working with and observing others.

○ I can demonstrate that I am a good listener.

○ I can demonstrate that I am a good communicator.

If you have been unable to give positive responses to any of the questions or statements above, please go back and review the section.

C Review own skills needed in sport and activity leader roles

One of the most difficult aspects of sport and activity leadership is reviewing your own performance. This is the same whether someone is a very experienced leader working with elite players or if they are new to the industry. A sport and activity leader will often spend a significant amount of time planning, organising and delivering their session, but will not put enough time aside to review their own skills and development needs.

Technology today is more advanced than ever before, which often means sport and activity leaders have the opportunity to film sessions they lead (of course with the permission of their participants). They also have access to online session plans and videos. These are resources you should try and make use of – many leaders choose not to use them as much as they could.

A good way to start reviewing your performance is to write some notes immediately after a session and then review them within 24 hours. Asking others for feedback is an essential part of the review process. A good way of doing this is to set up an opportunity to receive feedback. For example, you might ask your workplace manager for ten minutes of their time where you can ask them questions about your performance. When reviewing your performance you will need to take into account other people's opinions. This might come from:

- your manager
- other colleagues
- customers
- your mentor
- a tutor or friend.

Your tutor will have some videos, audio evidence or photographs of you completing your work placement. They will encourage you to review these and they might direct you to other areas for gaining feedback too.

C1 Reviewing performance in sport and activity leader roles

This is your time to reflect on your work experience or voluntary placement. It is really important that you are honest with yourself about your strengths and weaknesses. Even the best sport and activity leaders are constantly learning and reviewing their performance. Learning never stops and there is no such thing as a perfect sport and activity leader.

Remember, if you find it difficult to review your own performance, then try to think about what you would do differently if you did your work experience again.

Mapping personal skills against those required to act effectively as a sport and activity leader

As you are aware, a sport and activity leader needs a range of skills and qualities to be effective. One way of evaluating your own skills and performance is to compare them to the 'perfect model' for the role of sport and activity leader. A 'perfect model' does not exist in reality, but it gives leaders the chance to compare themselves against the highest possible standard, and identify areas that they want to work on to improve.

The skills required to be an effective leader are:
- communication
- **TEAMWORK**
- decision making
- **MOTIVATION**
- leadership
- problem solving
- **INCLUSIVITY**.

Think about what your personal skills are, and use your work experience diary to review and map them. It might be the case that you have not had the opportunity in the sessions you have led to demonstrate or practise all of your skills. Or, you might feel that there are additional skills that you have used with a particular group that should be on the list. Make sure you add these to your personal skills list.

There are many different ways of mapping your personal skills and comparing with the 'perfect model'. One way is illustrated below for you: you are asked to rate yourself out of 10 across a range of skills. A 'perfect model' would receive 10 for each area. But remember, no one is perfect and even the most effective leader will not achieve 10 all the time – the point is to evaluate and review where things are going well, and where you would like to focus your efforts for improvement.

Figure 5.5 shows an example of an activity leader who reviewed their performance after a high ropes session. The review was completed immediately after the session.

Skill to be an effective leader	My rating out of 10
Communication	7
Teamwork	6
Decision making	8
Motivation	7
Leadership	8
Problem solving	6
Inclusivity	9

My main strength was inclusivity. I made sure that everyone was included in the session and I treated everyone equally.

I need to improve my teamwork skills. I did not speak to the other 'Activity Leader' during the session very much. I needed to work with them to confirm the finish time and find out when her group started their first activity. This is something I am going to make sure I do next week.

Overall, I am pleased with the high ropes session and feel it was a success. All of the participants enjoyed the session because it was their first session and they learnt something new.

Figure 5.5: Self review of an activity leader

Mapping attitudes against those required to act effectively as a sport and activity leader

Mapping attitudes is very similar to mapping skills. The attitudes required to be an effective sports or activity leader are:

- patience
- empathy
- positivity
- enthusiasm
- energy.

When reviewing your work experience you will need to consider your attitudes throughout. It is likely that you showed different attitudes at different times or situations throughout your work experience. It is important to be specific in your review. For example, when leading an activity session with children you might have showed a high level of enthusiasm. However, when dealing with a customer on reception you might not have been as enthusiastic and you might have needed to be more patient.

Practise

Using the list below, write down examples of when you showed each attitude during your work experience.

- Patience
- Empathy
- Positivity
- Enthusiasm
- Energy

Choose two of the attitudes and explain the impact each attitude made in your workplace.

Mapping ability to be flexible and deal with a range of situations

All job roles in the sports and activity industry require some degree of flexibility. Being flexible at work and when working with others is a necessary quality. For example, an activity leader might have planned an orienteering session for 12 adults. When the leader arrives they realise that only four adults have turned up. The leader will need to deal with this situation and be flexible to change their original plans to accommodate the new situation. If the leader was planning to separate the group of 12 participants into four teams of three, then the leader might choose to have two pairs instead. They might also need to change the timings or direction of the new groups.

Working in the outdoors means a leader needs to be ready to deal with any situation.

Sport and activity leaders regularly work with a range of different groups. Different groups have different needs. During your work experience you may have had to work with different groups. Examples of different groups include the elderly and active retired people, people with disabilities or teenagers.

It is not just when leading a group that you might have to be flexible and adapt to differing needs. Being flexible in a sport and activity environment can also involve working across the organisation as a whole. For example, you might have to deal with different customers on reception, or you might end up setting up the sports hall at a different time than you had originally planned.

What if...?

Lee has asked for your advice. He has been asked to deliver an introductory tennis session to a group of children and a group of elderly and active retired participants. Lee is delivering the session to the children between 5.00 p.m. and 6.00 p.m. and the session to the elderly and active retired participants between 6.00 p.m. and 7.00 p.m.

He is concerned that he will not have any time between sessions and will need to adapt to the groups' needs very quickly.

Give Lee some advice on how he can deal with this situation.

Reviewing the way you deal with a range of different situations is incredibly valuable. It is also important to speak to others to see how they have dealt with difficult situations. Often you can learn so much from your friends and colleagues. You could also ask your tutor for examples of how they have had to be flexible to deal with groups with different needs.

Link it up

Refer back to Unit 3 for guidance on leaders working with a range of different groups.

Practise

Make a list of the different groups you worked with on your work experience.

Explain how you worked with these groups and give examples of when you showed flexibility.

Identifying personal strengths and areas for improvement

Identifying your own strengths and areas for improvement can be difficult. It requires you to give an honest evaluation of where you are and how you can improve. There is no doubt that by completing your work experience you will have learnt a lot about yourself. You have most likely been pushed outside your comfort zone. Being put into a different situation often provides an opportunity to learn more about yourself, which you might not have expected. It is likely on your work experience there were times when you thought you did something well and other times when you thought, 'Next time I am going to do better'. This is all part of learning.

Refer back to your time on work experience, the feedback you received and study the diary you made. Consider what you did well and what you would like to improve. If you are uncertain of your improvements, think what you would do differently if you did your work experience again. Remember, do not get your strengths confused with the things you enjoy. Your personal strengths are specific to you and are what you can use to your advantage when applying for jobs or working with others.

Make sure you keep the evidence of your identified strengths and areas for improvement. You will be able to look back at this and monitor your progress over the coming weeks, months and years.

Practise

From your work experience, identify three of your personal strengths and three areas that you need to improve. For each area that you need to improve, make a suggestion of how you can improve this moving forward to your future career.

C2 Action planning to develop skills needed for sport and activity leader roles

ACTION PLANNING helps to focus ideas and gives detailed steps of how to achieve specific goals. An action plan will include a timeline for goals to be achieved and the resources that you will require to achieve them.

Good action planning needs to be realistic and achievable. Writing things down can often help you to focus on what it is you want to achieve.

Assessing personal career aspirations against current skills and experience

In order to create an action plan you need to have an idea of which direction you would like to go in. Your work experience will have helped you to understand more about your own current skills and experience. During your work experience there are likely to have been some activities you really enjoyed and others you did not enjoy as much. For example, you might have really enjoyed working in a team or dealing with customers, and maybe you did not enjoy making decisions under pressure.

You may already have it figured out and you might know your dream job. Don't worry if you are not sure at the moment. Think about what job you would like to do after your course has finished and what sector of sport you would like to work in. In order to get there you will need to compare where you are currently with where you would like to be. Assess this against your levels of skills and experience.

Practise

What experience have you got in the sports and activity industry? Think about any volunteering, sports team involvement, your work experience and the activities you do outside school or college.

Once you have reviewed this, create yourself a goal to help increase your experience even further.

An action plan creates clear objectives for both the short and the long term. Planning these actions will help you to address the areas you need to improve. For example, you might assess your current skills and see your leadership as a weak area. One way of improving your leadership skills could be to volunteer at a local school to lead a skill session for the under-7 netball team.

Offering to lead part of a session is an excellent way of improving your leadership skills.

What if...?

After assessing her career aspirations, Fiona decides she would like to work with disabled children. However, she has not had much experience working with this group of people. As a result, she decides to create an action plan. The first thing she decides to do is to volunteer in the sports disability session at her local leisure centre to find out whether this is something she enjoys. Trying it will mean she gains first-hand experience that will help to improve her skills and experience levels.

Next, Fiona will need to evaluate her progress.

1 Explain to Fiona why it is important she evaluates her progress.

2 Advise Fiona on tools she can use to monitor her development. For example, explain to her how performance profiling and setting SMART targets could work for her.

Performance profiling

PERFORMANCE PROFILING is a tool that helps you to identify your strengths and weaknesses by analysing your current performance. It is regularly used in sports coaching to help athletes improve their performance. It can also be used to help focus on strengths and weaknesses in a work situation and motivate individuals to strive towards set goals.

A performance profile assesses your range of skills and qualities – see Figure 5.6 for an example of a completed performance profile. The sections of the performance profile can reflect whichever skills, qualities and attitudes you would like to assess and feel are most important to you and your role. Once you have completed a performance profile you can ask your line manager or mentor to assess your performance. The idea is to compare your thoughts with theirs. This can often be an effective way of gaining feedback and learning more about how others view you. Sometimes you think you are not very good at something and others see it as a strength.

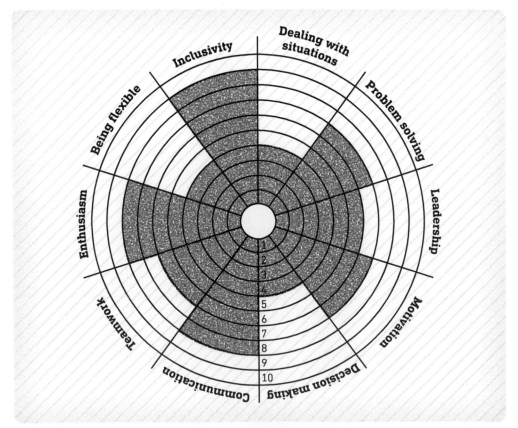

Figure 5.6: An assistant activity instructor's performance profile.

Performance profiling can also help you to monitor your progress over time. When you have completed a performance profile make sure you keep it. In three or six months' time you can then complete another performance profile using the same skills, qualities and attitudes. This allows you to compare the progress you have made. In this way, you will be able to see which leadership aspects you need to focus on.

Practise

Create your own performance profile and assess your performance following your work experience.

SMART targets

After evaluating your performance you will need to set goals to help you improve. The goals will help you to monitor your progress and give you a focus for the future. The goals you set need to be based on SMART targets.

- **S**pecific: they are detailed and relevant to you and your career.
- **M**easurable: this allows for the improvement to be monitored.
- **A**chievable: it is possible and can be completed.
- **R**ealistic: it is challenging but within your reach.
- **T**ime-bound: a deadline needs to be set.

What if...?

Mandy is an aspiring badminton coach. She has played for her county throughout her teenage years and has nearly finished her sports course at college. She did work experience at a local badminton club and really enjoyed it. At the moment she does not have any formal qualifications.

Mandy sets herself a SMART target:

'In one month's time I need to have finished researching the coaching qualifications for badminton and have a course booked.'

Explanation

This is **S**pecific to badminton coaching.

It is **M**easurable as she will either have booked or not booked the coaching course.

It is **A**chievable because one month is plenty of time to research and book a course.

The target is **R**ealistic as she is at the start of her coaching journey. She has a good level of badminton knowledge from playing for her county.

By setting a deadline it ensures the goal is **T**ime-bound.

Mandy completed this target within two weeks. The course she booked on starts in two months.

Set Mandy a SMART target to aim for prior to her course beginning. Explain the SMART target you have chosen.

When a sport and activity leader sets and meets goals they are likely to notice the effect this has on their participants or their work environment. The better a leader is, the more likely they are to have positive influences on everyone around them. It is important to make a note of the outcomes that have improved performance and celebrate them. For example, after Mandy completed her course she became a qualified badminton coach. Not only could she now apply for more jobs and earn more money but she could offer a better service to her participants. She had improved her coaching knowledge of specific techniques and skills, while learning how to deal with different groups of people. This is an excellent outcome for Mandy.

What if...?

Mandy wants to keep improving and progressing but is not sure what to do next.

Set Mandy a new SMART target and remember to explain the target you have created.

Skills and knowledge check

☐ Describe what the word 'SMART' stands for in the term 'SMART targets'.

☐ Create a SMART target for your career.

☐ What is a performance profile?

☐ Explain why it is important to review your own performance.

☐ Identify two areas for improvement detailing the reasons for your answers.

◯ I can explain two of my own strengths.

◯ I can confidently rate my personal skills and give reasons for my answers.

◯ I can link all the attitudes to my work experience and explain when I used them.

If you have been unable to give positive responses to any of the questions or statements above, please go back and review the section.

Ready for assessment

You will need to research and show that you understand the different opportunities for work in three sport and activity leader roles. You will provide comparisons between the skills, roles and responsibilities that they each require.

You have an excellent opportunity to participate in work experience or a voluntary placement. Here, you will be able to demonstrate your skills and attitudes in leading sports and physical activities, as well as take on the responsibilities of a sport and activity leader. During your work experience you will complete a logbook detailing the activities you completed and how you were most effective. Make sure you keep evidence of any written business communications, record the activities you complete and any plans you have created or used. Remember, you are representing yourself and your school or college. You are encouraged to gain feedback from your work experience supervisor, your colleagues, tutor, manager, friends or through the videos and photographs your tutor has collected.

After your work experience you will be ready to produce a report. The report will contain a detailed review and an action plan to develop the skills needed to be a sports and activity leader. Be prepared to be honest with yourself and work hard.

WORK FOCUS

HANDS ON

There are some important occupational skills and experiences that you will need to practise, which relate to this unit and your future career. Developing these now will help you on your path to employment.

You often learn a lot from the people around you without even realising it. You can learn from observing them and working with them. Choose someone you feel you would like to learn from and who is a positive role model for your future career. This might be someone in your school or college, from a local sports team, community centre, gym or leisure centre.

1 **Observe this person for 30 minutes at their workplace or in the community.**

2 **Write down the skills and attitudes they are showing in their work.**

3 **Choose one skill or attitude that you feel they are particularly good at. Explain the impact they are having on their customers or surroundings by demonstrating this skill or attitude.**

Ready for work?

1 The definition of empathy is:
- [ ] A the ability to share and understand someone's feelings
- [ ] B the ability to feel sorry for someone
- [ ] C the ability to plan a risk assessment.

2 The following skills are needed for a sport or activity leader:
- [ ] A teamwork, problem solving and decision making
- [ ] B decision making, inclusivity and dreaming
- [ ] C communication, panicking and leadership.

3 Voluntary work is:
- [ ] A where an individual provides a service for no financial gain
- [ ] B an individual works in the community and receives money for their time
- [ ] C two people work together in partnership with the aim of making money.

4 Which of the following are responsibilities of an outdoor activities instructor?
- [ ] A customer care, dealing with emergencies and introducing and running new activities
- [ ] B organising groups and teaching football skills
- [ ] C introducing and running new activities, advising on diet and watching television.

5 On my work placement I aim to show the following attitudes:
- [ ] A patience, enthusiasm and energy
- [ ] B health and safety, disorganisation and flexibility
- [ ] C sports co-ordinator, energy and asking questions.

6 One way of monitoring performance is to set SMART targets. What does SMART stand for?
- [ ] A Specific, Measurable, Achievable, Realistic, Time-bound
- [ ] B Special, Measurable, Attainable, Realistic, Time-bound
- [ ] C Sports, Must, Action, Real, Teacups.

7 On my work placement I aim to get feedback from the following sources:
- [ ] A workplace manager, tutor, my colleagues and myself
- [ ] B myself only
- [ ] C no one – feedback isn't important.

How did you do?

You should have all As as your answers. It is important to show everything you have learnt from this section to any future employers. If you have not achieved all A answers then please go back to your tutor and review the section.

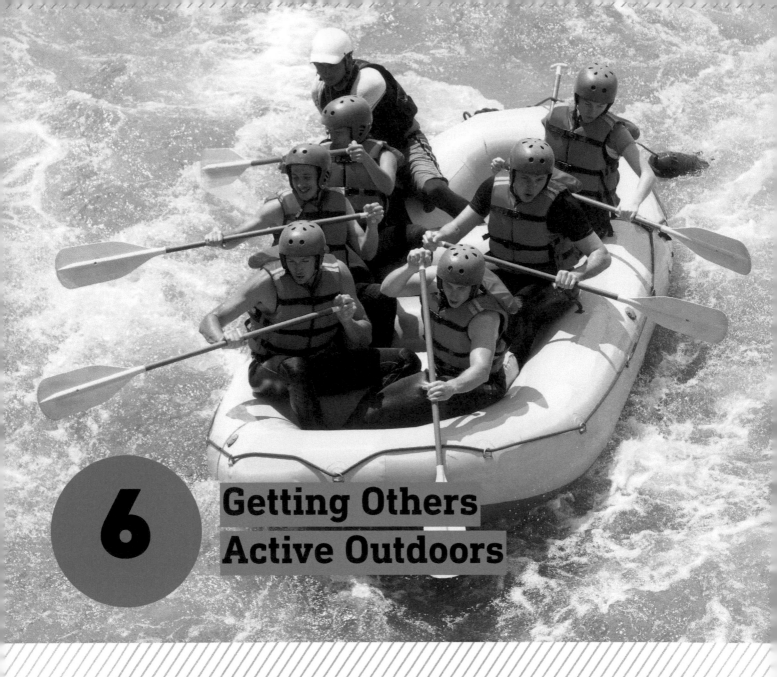

6 Getting Others Active Outdoors

Many people play sport or get involved in some sort of physical activity indoors. However, more and more people are choosing to be active outdoors. Some people enjoy hillwalking in the countryside while others opt for surfing on the coast. Across the United Kingdom, there are numerous opportunities to exercise outdoors, at both a local and national level.

This unit will improve your understanding of why people enjoy outdoor activities and what the benefits are. You will take part in a range of outdoor activities and learn how to lead others safely. As a result, you will develop your leadership skills and qualities, while gaining a deep understanding of a leader's responsibilities.

Get ready to be challenged mentally and physically while increasing your employability. This unit gives you an opportunity to push yourself out of your comfort zone. Take the challenge and be the best you can be.

How will I be assessed?

This unit will be assessed through a series of assignments set by your tutor. You will be expected to investigate a range of rural and urban outdoor activities along with their benefits and barriers for participation. You will be expected to lead an outdoor activity demonstrating both health and safety considerations and your leadership skills.

Your assessment could be in the form of:

- a written report discussing a range of information about three rural and urban outdoor activities, as well as information on the benefits and barriers to participation
- observation of you leading an outdoor activity session, where you demonstrate your practical skills, taking into account appropriate equipment, the needs of your participants and health and safety considerations
- visual evidence of you leading your session (video or photographs).

Assessment criteria

Pass	Merit	Distinction
Learning aim A: Explore the range and benefits of outdoor activities		
A.P1 Identify key features of three rural and urban outdoor activities and provide information on participants and participation trends in the UK.	**A.M1** Describe key features of three rural and urban outdoor activities and summarise information about participants and participation trends in the UK, suggesting possible reasons for them.	**A.D1** Explain key features of three rural and urban outdoor activities and evaluate information about participants and participation trends in the UK, analysing possible reasons for them.
A.P2 Outline benefits of and barriers to participation in outdoor activities.	**A.M2** Describe benefits of and barriers to participation in outdoor activities and offer appropriate solutions to overcome barriers to increase participation.	**A.D2** Explain benefits of and barriers to participation in outdoor activities and offer effective and justified solutions to overcome barriers and increase participation.
Learning aim B: Demonstrate the skills and responsibilities to take part and lead others in outdoor activities		
B.P3 Apply health and safety considerations to one outdoor activity and provide essential information to a participant about the equipment to be used.	**B.M3** Competently apply health and safety considerations to one outdoor activity, suggesting precautions and associated actions, and describing features of the equipment to be used to a participant.	**B.D3** Confidently apply health and safety considerations to one outdoor activity, justifying precautions and associated actions, and explaining features of the equipment to be used to a participant.
B.P4 Demonstrate appropriate techniques and leadership skills and recognise the need to be flexible when leading one outdoor activity (the activity must last for at least 10 minutes).	**B.M4** Demonstrate effective techniques and leadership skills and show a flexible or adaptable approach when leading one outdoor activity (the activity must last for at least 10 minutes).	**B.D4** Demonstrate comprehensive techniques and leadership skills and adopt a flexible and adaptable approach when leading one outdoor activity (the activity must last for at least 10 minutes).

A Explore the range and benefits of outdoor activities

Outdoor activity participation is on the increase. More and more people are discovering the wide variety of outdoor activities the world has to offer. Exercising outdoors can offer a different experience with rushes in adrenaline, unusual challenges and a constantly changing environment (see Figure 6.1).

In Learning aim A, you will not only explore the range and benefits of outdoor activities but also the barriers to participation and what this can mean for individuals.

A1 Different types of outdoor activities

Definition of outdoor activities

OUTDOOR ACTIVITIES are defined as leisure pursuits completed outdoors, often in a natural environment or at a purpose-built facility. These activities can be completed individually or in a team. Many schools and companies are choosing to take their groups to outdoor activity centres as they can offer numerous team-building activities with individuals working together in unusual situations. They give individuals the opportunity to try something new that is completely different to their normal way of life. Activities often involve excitement, physical challenge and RISK. This makes them appeal to a wide variety of people from all cultures and backgrounds. Figure 6.1 outlines some of the advantages of outdoor activities.

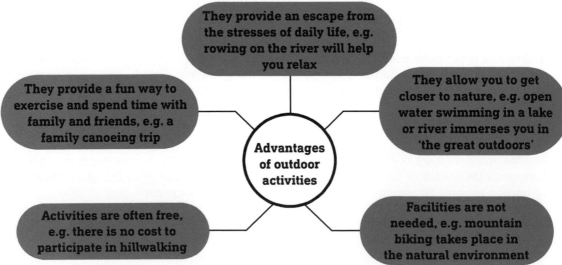

Figure 6.1: Some advantages to outdoor activities

Given the wide variety of choice and the different types of outdoor activities available, it is no surprise more and more people are choosing to participate in outdoor activities, compared to more traditional indoor activities.

Participants and participation trends

Evidence suggests participation is increasing for outdoor activities. For example, Snowsport England reported a 12 per cent increase in participation at domestic slopes for the period February to April and an 11 per cent increase for the period May to August (from 2013 to 2014).

There are many reasons for the increasing popularity of outdoor activities.

1   A larger number of opportunities to participate as an individual or part of a group are available at any time of the day or week. This flexibility around how and when an individual can participate, whether it is on a regular or irregular basis, is becoming increasingly desirable.

2   Social media has raised the profile of outdoor activities. For example, individuals participating in an outdoor fitness boot camp or visiting their local climbing wall share their enjoyment with others through the internet.

3   There are a wide variety of different outdoor activities available at limited or zero cost to the participant.

4   Government campaigns encouraging people to get outside and be active have been popular. There has also been an increased awareness of the health benefits of regular exercise and the consequences of being overweight and inactive.

5   Rising costs mean more and more people are choosing to have a holiday in the United Kingdom. Families and couples are increasingly looking at local facilities for opportunities to relax and get active.

However, not all outdoor activities are accessible for everyone. For example, skiing is traditionally known as a 'middle-class' sport. This is because the equipment is expensive and **PARTICIPANTS** usually need to leave the United Kingdom. There is the added cost of transport and accommodation. In a similar way, horse riding can be very expensive, with participants either choosing to pay for lessons or taking the expensive route of owning their own horse.

Compare this to orienteering, fell running, mountain or road biking and trail running where participation is free or costs a minimal amount. Outdoor activities give everyone options. The choice is yours.

Categories of outdoor activities

There are five categories of outdoor activities, as shown in Table 6.1.

Table 6.1: Categories of outdoor activities

Categories	Outdoor activities	Example
Snow-based	Skiing Snowboarding Ski mountaineering	 Snowboarding in Austria
Mountain-based	Climbing Bouldering Abseiling Caving Fell running	 Caving in Yorkshire, United Kingdom

Table 6.1: *(continued)*

Categories	Outdoor activities	Example
Countryside-based	Orienteering Mountain or road biking Hillwalking High ropes Horse riding Paintballing Triathlon Trail running	Paintballing in Surrey, United Kingdom
Water-based	Open water swimming Canoeing Kayaking Paddle boarding Coasteering Rowing Surfing Sailing Windsurfing	Paddle boarding in East Sussex, United Kingdom
Urban-based	Artificial skiing BMX biking Assault course Parkour Skateboarding In-line skating Indoor climbing walls Boot camp fitness classes	Parkour in London, United Kingdom

Practise

Choose one outdoor activity you are interested in participating in from each category in Table 6.1.

Research where you would need to go in order to take part in this activity, and investigate the equipment and resources you would need.

A2 Different outdoor activity providers

Governing bodies

There are different governing bodies for each category of outdoor activities. Governing bodies have many roles. They can create new rules for their sport or activity and even discipline participants if they break the rules. They help to organise the people participating in their sport or activity and promote where and when someone can take part.

Governing bodies can also be involved at an international level. This is the case if there are international competitions. For example, British Canoeing had athletes that were involved in the Rio 2016 Olympics and it organised and supported the Great Britain team. Table 6.2 gives examples of some UK governing bodies.

Table 6.2: Examples of UK governing bodies

Governing body	Sport/Outdoor activity they represent	
British Triathlon Federation	Represents and promotes triathlon, aquathlon and duathlon in Great Britain.	www.britishtriathlon.org
Royal Yachting Association	The national governing body for certain watersports in the UK, including sailing, windsurfing, motor cruising, powerboating and personal watercraft.	www.rya.org.uk
Surfing England	Promotes surfing in England, and supports surfers, coaches, surf clubs and schools.	www.surfingengland.org
British Gliding Association	Represents and provides services to UK glider pilots.	www.gliding.co.uk
British Orienteering Federation	Develops orienteering throughout the UK from grassroots through to international competition.	www.britishorienteering.org.uk
British Mountaineering Council	Promotes the interests of climbers, hillwalkers and mountaineers and the freedom to enjoy their activities.	www.thebmc.co.uk
British Association of Snowsport Instructors	Creates a reputation for excellence through the provision of the highest quality of training and support services for snowsport instructors.	www.basi.org.uk
British Caving Association	Represents individuals and groups with a genuine interest in caves, karst and associated phenomena, from both sport and science perspectives.	www.british-caving.org.uk
British Cycling	The internationally recognised governing body for cycling in the UK, working across all levels and six disciplines (BMX, mountain bike, cyclo-cross, road, track, and cycle speedway).	www.britishcycling.org.uk
Parkour UK	Governance and regulation of parkour and free running throughout the UK, acting as custodians of the sport/art and protecting the rights and freedoms and interests of practitioners.	www.parkour.uk
Skateboard Scotland	Set up to improve and develop the skateboarding scene across Scotland – run by skaters for skaters.	www.skateboardscotland.com

Centres and providers

Around the UK there are many specialist outdoor activity or recreation centres and residential providers. Some of these are funded by local authority or government funds, while others are private businesses owned by an individual or group of individuals. There are also some centres that are charities.

Specialist outdoor recreation or activity centres often offer a broad range of outdoor activities. Participants are invited to try a mix of activities and attend to develop and learn. Frequently, they offer a residential option where groups of people can stay over and enjoy a break away. These are very popular with schools, businesses and youth groups. They promote their services through the internet, marketing materials and by word of mouth.

Other activity centres might offer a smaller range of activities specialising in just one or two activities. One example might be a centre offering climbing and bouldering. These centres will appeal to a smaller range of participants but are likely to be much more focused. This will attract more experienced participants who are used to the activity and are not just looking at trying something new.

What if...?

Skern Lodge (www.skernlodge.co.uk) is an outdoor activity centre in North Devon. It provides a broad range of outdoor activities. Skern Lodge was established in 1976 and offers a fun learning experience through outdoor adventure.

1 Research the activities that Skern Lodge provides.

2 Which groups of people does Skern Lodge most appeal to?

3 Explain what impact there would be on Skern Lodge if another outdoor activity centre was established locally.

Uniformed youth groups

Uniformed youth groups regularly participate in outdoor activities. Some examples of uniformed youth groups are: Scouts, Guides, Sea Cadets, and Surf Lifesaving clubs. These types of group promote and encourage outdoor participation and often offer badges and awards to their members for completing different challenges.

Uniformed youth groups encourage the learning and development of skills in outdoor environments. They offer unique experiences and regularly help others in their local community. They promote fun and adventure through a range of activities and are regularly advertising for others to be involved. Adult volunteers who are passionate about sharing their experiences with others usually run these groups.

A3 Benefits of participating in outdoor activities

Although participation in outdoor activities is on the rise, there are still many citizens in the UK that choose not to exercise. Often people are not aware of the numerous benefits participation in outdoor activities can offer (see Figure 6.2). It is now your job to inform and encourage others to take part and get involved.

People of all ages, backgrounds and abilities benefit from participating in outdoor activities. The benefits are categorised into four areas: physical, psychological, social and economic.

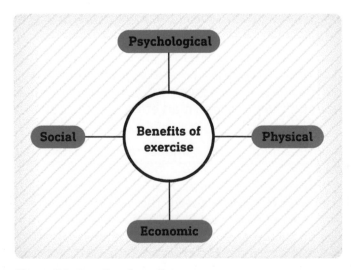

Figure 6.2: Benefits of exercise

Physical

By taking part in outdoor activities you can help to ensure that your body is fit and healthy. The health benefits of physical activity and exercise are hard to ignore. Regular activity helps to prevent or manage a wide range of health problems.

Participation in outdoor activities on a regular basis will increase fitness levels. People engaged in these outdoor pursuits are choosing to lead an active lifestyle. As a result of this they are lowering their risk of chronic illnesses that can result (in part) from a sedentary lifestyle.

A **SEDENTARY LIFESTYLE** is one with limited or no physical activity. A person who lives this lifestyle does not regularly exercise or take part in outdoor or indoor activities. Common examples of sedentary activities include: watching television, playing on the computer, sitting for long periods of time, and using a car/bus for short journeys. It is important that, wherever possible, people try to decrease sedentary activities and increase physical activities.

A sedentary lifestyle can lead to health problems and chronic illnesses, such as coronary heart disease and diabetes.

Coronary heart disease	Type 2 diabetes
This is the most common cause of death in the UK. It is when the blood supply to your heart is blocked or interrupted by the build-up of fat or fatty acids. This can lead to heart attacks and heart failure. Unfortunately this disease cannot be cured. Leading a healthy lifestyle can prevent coronary heart disease.	This is a lifelong health condition. It is often caused by obesity and leading a sedentary lifestyle. Type 2 diabetes is when a person's blood sugar level becomes too high because the body does not produce enough insulin. Type 2 diabetes can cause serious long-term health problems. It is the most common cause of vision loss and blindness. Diabetes can also cause kidney failure and lead to lower limb amputation. People who have diabetes are five times more likely to have a stroke or another complication of cardiovascular disease. As with coronary heart disease, leading a healthy lifestyle can prevent Type 2 diabetes.

Both of these chronic illnesses are related to the build-up of fat in the body and obesity. Exercise and the participation in outdoor activities reduces body fat. Physical activity plays a significant role in helping people to lose weight or maintain their current weight. Taking part in any activity requires energy. You get this energy from the food you consume. Therefore it is important to not just exercise but also to monitor the food you are consuming, making sure you are eating a healthy diet.

Practise

The consequences of leading a sedentary lifestyle are serious.

Produce a poster encouraging people to participate in outdoor activities. Make sure you inform them of the benefits of being active.

Psychological

It is not just your body that benefits from exercise. Choosing to lead a healthy and active lifestyle also has many psychological benefits. Regular physical activity improves mood. This is because, when you take part in exercise, your body releases **ENDORPHINS**. These chemicals reduce any feelings of pain and trigger positive feelings in your body. It is for this reason that physical activity and exercise is often used to treat mild depression.

Making the positive lifestyle choice to take part in outdoor activities can help to build confidence and self-esteem (see Figure 6.3). By positively completing risk-taking activities, you will feel confident in your own abilities. Often this confidence helps in other areas of your life and you can achieve more. For example, if someone is scared and nervous of heights and they complete an abseil, they will experience increased confidence as a result. Next time they feel nervous or worried, they can recall their success in the abseil and their anxiety about the next task will reduce. Their chances of completing it successfully are thus enhanced.

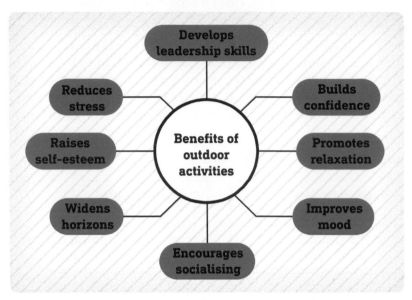

Figure 6.3: Benefits of outdoor activities

Taking part in outdoor activities also reduces feelings of stress and promotes relaxation. Often, when you are exercising, you will notice that you are only focusing on the activity you are completing. Sometimes you realise you have not thought about anything else for ages. Some people call this mindfulness. You escape from your everyday worries and any concerns you may have. Your body becomes much more relaxed, and anything you were worrying about becomes smaller and less important.

Social

Increased participation in outdoor activities also has many social benefits. It is an excellent way of meeting new people and making friends outside normal friendship groups. A wide range of people from different backgrounds and cultures participate and this means you can learn more about the world and people in it.

Outdoor activities provide an excellent alternative to traditional sports such as football, hockey or cricket and can offer the development of skills in risk-taking situations. They are a good way of developing leadership skills. Being outside in the natural environment often means you have to adapt quickly to changes in weather or environment. Individuals have to make quick decisions and help to lead others who might not feel as comfortable. These decisions often bring out different aspects of your personality that you did not even know existed. For this reason outdoor activities are excellent for learning and challenging yourselves.

Being part of a club or activity can often mean you are given the opportunity to volunteer. Volunteering can have a real and valuable impact on your local community. But, while volunteering often helps others, it can also help you too. It can help build confidence, reduce stress, offer fun and enjoyment and potentially advance your future career. There are numerous opportunities to volunteer in outdoor activities. For example, you might choose to volunteer at a triathlon race or rowing competition. You might even choose to volunteer abroad and discover the world.

Practise

Research what options are available to you for volunteering. Choose one of the following locations.

- USA
- Africa
- Australia
- Local to you

As part of your research, answer the following questions.

1 Explain the social benefits of volunteering.

2 Investigate what volunteering roles are available to you in your chosen location.

3 Evaluate the effect volunteering will have on your future career.

Economic

Outdoor activity locations can bring many benefits to the local area. Often people travel to participate in outdoor activities, either in a rural or urban location. This brings more money to the area and promotes jobs and local businesses. For example, a family who choose to go mountain biking in Wales will travel to their chosen location, where they might hire bikes from a local bike shop, eat lunch in a café or stay overnight in a local hotel. All this brings business and word-of-mouth publicity to the location.

Outdoor recreation businesses, both online or on the high street, also benefit. If you are participating for the first time, or trying a new activity, you might need to purchase new clothes, equipment or footwear. Retailers of outdoor recreation clothing and equipment will all benefit, ensuring their continued survival, and the activity as a whole will benefit.

Practise

Design a new range of clothing that is suitable for hillwalking.

Make sure you explain its key features and what sets it apart from the crowd.

A4 Barriers to participating in outdoor activities

There is a range of barriers that can prevent people from participating in outdoor activities. These barriers can be categorised into five groups, as shown in Figure 6.4:

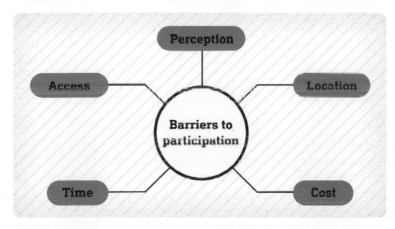

Figure 6.4: Barriers to participation

Perception

PERCEPTION is the way you think about or understand something. Perception is unique to you as it is your own thoughts and feelings. For example, one person might view a triathlon race to be exciting and a challenge; someone else might view it as boring and time-consuming. However, sometimes a perception is based upon limited knowledge and experience. For example, the person that views the triathlon race as boring might never have even taken part in one. How do they know they would find it boring, if they have not tried?

It is important for you as individuals to help others challenge and change their perceptions. It is your role as leader to encourage others to be active and to give something a go. Remember, there are many benefits to taking part in outdoor activities.

Sometimes people use a previous negative experience or stereotype as an excuse to prevent them from participating. For example, a stereotype could be 'only slim and fit people go hillwalking'. This, of course, is not the case. A wide range of people from all backgrounds, experiences, fitness levels and abilities participate in hillwalking. While it might be true that some people complete a 30-mile hillwalk, others might choose to opt for a three-mile hillwalk. You can adapt outdoor recreation for everyone. It is **ACCESSIBLE TO ALL**.

Time

People often say lack of time is the reason they cannot take part in physical and outdoor activities. Modern life can be very busy and often when people have families, work and other commitments they struggle to find time to exercise. However, this can be a matter of priorities. Some people say they have no free time for activity, but will watch several hours of television on a daily basis. These people need to be encouraged to see this as time that might be much better spent taking part in physical activities.

Link it up

See Unit 1 for more on how to meet the needs of diverse groups of participants.

Access

Access is not just about the physical requirements that allow people to take part in outdoor activities, but also the types of facilities and activities that are provided. Different groups of people may have different access requirements and if these are not met it can prevent participation.

Practise

Choose someone who you know does very little physical activity. Create a set of questions to ask this person.

Interview this person. Find out whether they have any barriers to participating in outdoor activities. Remember to use effective communication skills to handle the interview professionally and sensitively.

Location

Location can often prevent an individual from participating in outdoor activities. For example, someone that lives in Birmingham (central England) might find sailing difficult, as they are not located near the sea. In this way, your location might not prevent you from participating altogether but might dictate which outdoor activities you do take part in.

Cost

Cost can be a barrier for participation in outdoor activities. Outdoor activities that require travel or a lot of equipment can sometimes be very expensive. An example of this is skiing.

However, due to many outdoor activities being accessible in the local natural environment, cost is often less of a barrier than it is for traditional sports. An example of this is hillwalking.

Skills and knowledge check

- ☐ Give a definition of the term 'outdoor activities'.
- ☐ Explain why skiing is traditionally known as a 'middle-class' sport.
- ☐ Identify one barrier that prevents people from participating in outdoor activities.
- ☐ Identify the five categories of outdoor activities. Give an example from each category.
- ☐ Explain the role of a governing body, using an example.
- ☐ Evidence suggests that participation in outdoor activities is increasing. Give one reason for this change.

- ○ I can confidently discuss the benefits of outdoor activities.
- ○ I can provide an example of a uniformed youth group.
- ○ I can define the term 'sedentary lifestyle'.

If you have been unable to give positive responses to any of the questions or statements above, please go back and review the section.

B Demonstrate the skills and responsibilities to take part and lead others in outdoor activities

B1 Equipment and facilities used in outdoor recreation activities

Outdoor recreation activities take place across a wide variety of outdoor terrains and facilities. Participants might find themselves in the mountains, in the countryside, on the water or in the man-made environments of a city or town. Equipment needs will vary depending on the activity, but thought needs to be given to finding suitable equipment to match the requirements of the environment or facility.

Unlike many traditional sports, some of the facilities are free or part of the natural environment. This means that the participant needs to be even more aware of health and safety considerations. For example, mountain biking tracks cover large areas and are part of the natural environment. Because of this, it is unlikely that they will be regularly safety checked. It is important that participants either go with an experienced cyclist or they tell someone where they are going, especially if they are new to mountain biking.

Types of equipment common to outdoor activities

The activity market is swamped with many different types of equipment and clothing for outdoor recreation users to wear. A particular activity might require a certain type of clothing to keep participants warm, dry or safe. For example, when skiing, low temperatures on the slopes mean that skiers will need to be dressed to keep their body temperature at an adequate level, but also take into account that body temperature rises during exercise. Specially designed ski wear will allow for warmth but will also be breathable to release increased body heat and sweat. To be properly equipped on the slopes, a skier will need a ski jacket, ski trousers (sometimes called salopettes), ski goggles, base layers, ski gloves, hats and a mask. When catering for a family group, this can be very expensive. However, some equipment will be suitable for more than one type of activity – for example, ski gear can be transferred to other snow pursuits, such as snowboarding and ski mountaineering.

Practise

In pairs, choose an outdoor activity. Create a video or audio clip informing others about the types of equipment needed.

As part of your video/audio clip, give health and safety tips on how to use the equipment. Use demonstrations where necessary.

Activity-specific equipment

A huge range of different equipment and facilities is needed for all the different outdoor recreation activities on offer, reflecting the varied environments in which they take place – snow, mountains, countryside, water or man-made environments. Equipment needs can range from almost nothing to some very specialised equipment. For example, compare a hillwalker to a horse rider. The horse rider needs an extensive range of specialised equipment.

- For a start, the horse rider needs a horse.
- The minimum requirement for a beginner or novice is a helmet. Riding stables often have these to borrow but it is recommended you get your own.
- Riding gloves, trousers and comfortable boots are also advised. Riding trousers are called jodhpurs. These are tight-fitting but comfortable trousers that help a rider to feel comfortable and stay safe.
- Boots are also important; these need to have a heel, which helps to grip on the stirrup.
- Many riders like to wear a pair of riding gloves. Not only do they keep your hands warm but they help to grip the reins of the horse.
- For more serious riders, other equipment is likely to be required, such as a crop or a whip. These are for advanced participants who need to give feedback to the horse.

This equipment is all specific to horse riding. The helmet, jodhpurs, heeled boots and riding gloves will not be applicable or be appropriate for any other types of outdoor activities.

Compare this specific equipment to that of a hillwalker.

- A hillwalker needs some suitable footwear, loose but warm clothing and preferably a map and compass.

The hillwalker will spend much less money on equipment than the horse rider. The equipment they need is not very complex and is widely available. It can also be worn for other activities. Horse riding equipment is more specific and complex. As you will see later in the section, this sort of equipment requires maintenance, as well as supervision and comprehensive checking when in use.

The equipment needed for outdoor activities is often unique to the activity. As leader you will need to ensure that you are fully aware of the health and safety aspects associated with each piece of equipment. You will need to complete training in using the equipment and pay special attention to detail. Always prepare for the activity by practising putting the equipment together safely and effectively beforehand.

Practise

Produce a presentation to outline the activity-specific equipment needed for the following outdoor activities:

- snowboarding
- abseiling
- high ropes
- windsurfing
- skateboarding.

Importance of using appropriate equipment

Assessing the equipment needs for a particular activity is usually straightforward. For example, to take part in a kayaking activity, a participant will need a kayak, but they will also need a lifejacket, a paddle and a helmet. This basic equipment will meet the requirements of the activity, as well as keep the participant safe and dry.

Kayaking requires appropriate equipment.

Sometimes equipment needs to be adapted to suit the particular needs of a participant. For example, horse riding is often adapted for disabled participants. The Riding for the Disabled Association (RDA) is a UK-based charity run by volunteers that offers horse riding therapy to disabled adults and children. Trained, experienced and gentle horses are used. Horses can be trained to stand while a hoist is fitted to support a disabled participant. This example shows that appropriate equipment (in this case a specialised horse) is incredibly important for the safe delivery of an activity.

However, for other outdoor activities, basic equipment is often appropriate for all participants whatever their particular needs. For example, British Canoeing guidance states that there is not always a need for specialised equipment for disabled paddlers and that equipment can be modified for use if needed. They emphasise working with the needs of the individual to identify what works best for them.

Volunteers help and support disabled riders on specially trained horses.

Choice of equipment really depends on the needs of the individual and it is the leader's responsibility to ensure these are met. A good leader will present these options to their participants and recommend the equipment that best suits each person.

Outdoor activity centres need to invest a considerable amount of money in buying and maintaining appropriate equipment, as it is often too expensive for an individual to purchase their own. Offering the full range of equipment will bring more business to activity centres or providers, but they must always follow HEALTH AND SAFETY LEGISLATION set by the government. This will give current and future participants the peace of mind that all of the equipment has been checked, assessed and maintained correctly. Someone purchasing their own equipment would need to either be highly experienced themselves and know what they were looking for or check with experts that the equipment was appropriate.

Link it up

Go to Unit 3 to understand more about health and safety considerations regarding equipment.

Benefits to performance and safety from selecting appropriate equipment

You have seen how using appropriate equipment for an activity keeps participants safe. This can be ensuring clothes are suitable to keep participants warm and dry or by providing extra support to reduce the chance of injury.

Specific equipment is also important for performance. While, of course, this does not necessarily apply to a beginner, the more experienced a participant becomes, the more likely specialised equipment will have an impact on performance. For example, in road biking a specialised bike is likely to help increase performance levels, and an experienced participant will look at power, aerodynamics and comfort when choosing a road bike. Each individual is different and different bikes will suit different people. British Cycling encourages participants to be fitted properly at bike shops. Among other things, the saddle position and height of the handlebars are important. Some bikes are more aerodynamic, making them suitable for time trial rides while other bikes are more about comfort, for riders who will be in the saddle for long periods of time. It is clear this helps performance but it is also important from a safety point of view. Depending upon the event, cyclists can spend long periods of time in the saddle and an incorrectly positioned saddle or wrongly adjusted handlebars creates a much higher risk of injury. Selecting the appropriate equipment at the outset will bring both performance and safety benefits to the participant.

Specialised road bikes were made for the London 2012 Great Britain Olympic team.

Suitable clothing and footwear

Suitable clothing and footwear are important for many outdoor activities. They help to minimise the risk of any dangerous accidents or injuries taking place. There are numerous different types of suitable clothing and footwear and the market for these in the UK continues to grow.

As an activity leader, you will complete a detailed check of participants before the activity starts. It is important to check that everyone is wearing the correct clothing. Sports and loose-fitting clothing should be worn for most activities. Incorrect clothing can cause injury, and jeans should generally be avoided. For example, a climber wearing jeans will find the material not only limits their ability to perform at their best but may restrict movement so much it could cause injury.

Clothing also needs to be suitable for varying weather conditions. Waterproof clothing – both a jacket and trousers – is essential for many outdoor activities. If people are outside for a long period of time in the rain, then they are likely to get cold very quickly. This can be very dangerous. Although waterproofs might seem like a basic piece of equipment, they are there to keep a participant safe and dry.

One of the most important items of equipment for most outdoor activities is footwear. Some activities might require laced-up trainers while others require specialised shoes or boots. Apart form helping complete the activity, it is always safer to wear the correct footwear. Road runners need special footwear as pounding on the tarmac over a period of time can cause injuries and long-term impact on knees, feet and hip joints. If someone is completing the activity frequently, it is worth investing in some good quality running shoes. These can be expensive as a lot of research goes into making them suitable for the activity. They are important for providing comfort and support. Surfing can also require specialised surf boots. It is likely the leader and the activity centre will provide you with these. Surf boots are not just useful in the winter but can also give extra protection to your feet when in shallow waters.

Practise

Research a range of road running shoes and choose your ideal shoe.

Create an advertising poster to promote this shoe. Focus on the benefits that it can offer to a road runner to run safely and increase their performance.

B2 Realistic management of risk and health and safety in outdoor activities

Selecting activities that are appropriate for users

In order to ensure risk is managed and all participants are kept safe, an outdoor activity leader must ensure they select activities that are appropriate for their users. For example, if a child has expressed an interest in climbing, then the activity centre will need to make sure the level of climbing is appropriate for the child and their experience level. It would be ridiculous to allow a young child to climb a challenging course over difficult outdoor terrain. Not only would this be unsafe for the child, but is also likely to make them feel worried and will affect their self-confidence and self-esteem. It is likely that the child would not enjoy such an activity, as they would not have the skills to effectively complete the climb. A more suitable alternative would be a smaller indoor climbing wall. Climbing centres have different walls for different abilities. A beginner can start on an easier route with larger holds. Once they are competent on this, they can progress to more challenging walls, and eventually climb in the natural environment.

Health and safety guidelines

A key responsibility of an activity leader at an outdoor centre is managing the health and safety of everyone who is involved. Health and safety will need to be considered before, during and after all sessions. If you have taken part in many activities or played sport you are likely to be aware that injuries can and do happen. However, this is not usually because of the activity centre or leader. It is normally due to the sport or activity itself.

Most sports or activities have a **NATIONAL GOVERNING BODY** (NGB). A list of UK governing bodies can be seen in Table 6.2 on page 173. NGBs often issue health and safety guidelines to support clubs and centres deliver their sport or activity effectively.

Adventure Activities Licensing Authority (AALA) is an organisation created in 1996. It ensures that all activity providers follow good safety management procedures and practices. The main aim of this is to allow young people to enjoy stimulating outdoor activities without being exposed to risks that can be avoided. The AALA was created after a tragic canoeing accident in which four teenagers lost their lives at Lyme Bay, Dorset. Unfortunately this was due to a series of errors by the activity centre. The creation of this legislative body now means that all activity providers and centres are inspected and have to apply for a licence.

Link it up

For more on health and safety, go back to Unit 3.

What if...?

You are working as an assistant activity instructor at your local climbing centre.

You have just taken a booking for a group of disabled adult beginner climbers in one week's time.

1   Work in a small team to select appropriate activities that will be appropriate for this group.

2   Give reasons for your choices.

As you are already aware, many outdoor activities have a certain level of risk associated with them. This means accidents and injuries can happen. An activity centre has a **HEALTH AND SAFETY OBLIGATION** to ensure the level of risk is minimised as far as possible. This level of care begins with the completion of a **RISK ASSESSMENT**.

Types of risks and hazards

When completing a risk assessment, a sport and activity leader or activity centre needs to identify the **RISKS** and different types of hazards that are associated with the activity they are delivering. **HAZARDS** are categorised into three areas (see Table 6.3):

1   human hazards
2   environmental hazards
3   mechanical hazards.

Table 6.3: Different types of hazards

Human hazards	An inexperienced participant would fall into the **human hazards** category. A beginner is at a higher risk than a more experienced participant. A beginner will have less knowledge about an activity. Their skill level is likely to be at novice level and, as a consequence, might cause more harm to themselves or others. For example, someone that has never skied before will be less able to stop if they are going too fast and are likely not to know how to fall correctly. Compare this to a more experienced skier who will be more aware of their limitations.
Environmental hazards	Outdoor activities frequently rely on the environment for facilities for participation, and **environmental hazards** will need to be assessed. An example of this is sailing. The sea can be unpredictable (as is all of nature) and, therefore, this level of risk needs to be accounted for. Other hazards, such as bad weather conditions, will need to be taken into account when completing a risk assessment. Another example is abseiling, which needs calm weather conditions. Heavy rain, wind or snow increases risk of harm in this activity.
Mechanical hazards	Different outdoor activities require different equipment, and these mechanical hazards need to be assessed and managed. **Mechanical hazards** involve anything to do with equipment or facilities. For example, a bike centre that hires out bikes will need to check all of the parts on each bike to make sure it is safe to use. An example of a mechanical hazard is faulty bike parts. This is because it has the potential to cause harm to someone taking part.

Practise

Visit your local sports hall or activity centre. Take some sticky notes, on which you have written the following labels: human, environmental and mechanical.

Work with a partner to place the notes on any hazards you can find. Take a photograph of your work before you collect them in.

Risk assessment

Every activity facility has to have a risk assessment by law. The aim is to safeguard the staff and participants to ensure their health and safety is the priority. The purpose of a risk assessment is to:

- identify hazards: for example, poor weather conditions
- give a risk rating: multiply the likelihood by the severity
- state the measures to minimise risk: for example, review the weather forecast before the activity, cancel the activity if the weather is unsuitable.

Application of the risk assessment process

In order to complete the risk assessment process an individual needs to follow a step-by-step approach. As you have learned, this begins with the identification of risks and hazards. Remember, these are categorised into three sections. See Figure 6.5 for an example of a risk assessment.

Link it up

Look back to Unit 3 for more information and guidance on completing risk assessments.

Risk Assessor's Name: Jenni Joyce				Date: 20.5.16		
Name of Activity: Horse Riding				Location: Stable Nowhere		
Hazard	Who is at risk?	Likelihood (0-3)	Severity (0-3)	Risk Rating	Risk Level (H/M/L)	Measure to minimise risk
Injury during activity (HUMAN)	Learners, tutors/helpers	2	2	4	M	Ensure the route is suitable for the least able rider. Communicate emergency procedures to the group at the start of the activity. Check ability of riders beforehand. Ensure all participants are wearing a helmet and appropriate clothing.

Figure 6.5: An example of a risk assessment

Any risk assessment created needs to be specific to that site and area. The risk assessment Is dynamic, which means that it often changes. This means that it is very important to update the risk assessment on a regular basis.

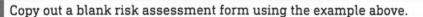

Practise

Copy out a blank risk assessment form using the example above.

Visit your local sports hall or activity centre. Complete your risk assessment form for an activity of your choice.

Aim to identify and rate a minimum of four hazards.

Physical Activity Readiness Questionnaires

All activity centres or providers have a **DUTY OF CARE** (a legal responsibility to safeguard people who are in their care or taking part in their activities) to new and current participants to keep them safe. When someone is new to a centre or provider they need to complete some paperwork. This is to keep that person safe and check that the activities are appropriate. It is also to protect the centre against any lawsuits or accusations of negligence or malpractice made by participants. Activity centres issue a **PHYSICAL ACTIVITY READINESS QUESTIONNAIRE (PAR-Q)** (a form that assesses an individual's medical history and needs to see if they are ready to take part in physical activity or exercise).

A PAR-Q includes a series of 'yes' and 'no' questions based around an individual's medical conditions and symptoms. For example, 'Do you feel pain in your chest when you do physical activity?' If an individual answers 'yes' to any of the questions, they will need to seek medical advice before being able to take part. Gathering this important information means you and the participant know they cannot take part in any activity that may cause them risk, injury or harm.

Practise

Work in pairs. Research two different Physical Activity Readiness Questionnaires issued by activity centres.

Using your findings, create your own Physical Activity Readiness Questionnaire for your partner to complete.

An activity centre will also ask participants to complete and sign a **LIABILITY WAIVER**. This is a legal document that acknowledges that the participant is aware of the risks involved in any activities they undertake. This means that the participant cannot then bring legal action to the activity company for any injuries incurred.

B3 Personal skills needed to participate in outdoor activities

Development of skills

Outdoor activities are often challenging and demanding. They require individuals to push themselves to their limits, which in turn means they learn a lot about themselves and their personal skills.

Practise

Take part in two different outdoor activities.

For each activity, work in pairs and discuss the personal skills you needed to participate in your chosen activities. Make notes of your findings.

What skills do these participants need in fell running?

Self-sufficiency, responsibility and perseverance are three skills that are regularly necessary and should be developed when taking part in outdoor activities.

Self-sufficiency

SELF-SUFFICIENCY is defined as being able to rely on yourself without the need of external assistance. It allows a person to be independent and to support their own goals and desires. The outdoors provides opportunities to develop self-sufficiency. Participants are placed in challenging situations where they need to adapt and think quickly. Being self-sufficient is a valuable skill to acquire; it allows an individual to grow in confidence and be comfortable in their own skin. For example, someone taking part in an orienteering competition will rely on their own map-reading skills, and will be required to find checkpoints and adapt to any environment changes, such as a change in weather or terrain. They will need to have full trust in their own skills and ability to complete the task and thrive against the competition.

Responsibility

Being placed in an unusual and challenging environment can make someone more responsible. RESPONSIBILITY is defined as having a duty or control to deal with someone or something. An individual may be given a job or task to complete and it is their responsibility to ensure it is finished to a high standard. Individuals need to learn a range of skills to allow them to be more responsible. The outdoor environment can change very quickly and to be prepared and ready for varying weather, the leader has to plan ahead and be well equipped. In the outdoors, the responsibility levels can be high; a person may have someone's life in their hands. For example, in team abseiling a participant will have the huge responsibility of selecting and tying the correct knot for their teammate to abseil down a cliff face. Outdoor activities demand someone to take charge and lead others. This requires a large amount of mutual trust and, of course, practice and training.

Perseverance

When overcoming fears and taking on new challenges, you develop perseverance. PERSEVERANCE is defined as being continually determined to do something, despite it being challenging or difficult to achieve. Outdoor activities frequently require a lot of determination. For example, if someone is kayaking and they are paddling against strong wind, perseverance will keep them going to the end destination. A triathlon regularly needs a high amount of perseverance. A triathlon consists of three disciplines: swim, cycle and run, which makes it very demanding. Completing three different activities in the same race often requires mental strength too. Participants will most likely favour one of the activities less and getting through that challenge alone requires high levels of perseverance.

Practise

In small groups play the game 'Ball Juggle'. The object of the game is to juggle as many balls as possible.

The rules are simple: all players form a circle and one ball is introduced to the group. The group can throw the ball to anyone in the group except the person next to them. Once the group has got used to one ball, gradually introduce more balls.

The group will then aim to find ways to process handling the additional balls and move the balls quicker.

After the game, discuss the importance of taking responsibility and how this evolved in 'Ball Juggle'.

The open water swim is the first discipline in this triathlon taking place in Anglesey, North Wales. It is an activity that requires determination and perseverance from participants.

Practical techniques and skills

Not only are personal and mental skills developed through participation in outdoor activities, but also practical skills and techniques are learned and mastered. Practical skills and techniques in outdoor activities are fundamental to completing the activity safely. For example, the skill of landing and vaulting in parkour is learned through practice. If this skill is not learned, and a participant cannot land safely, they are likely to injure themselves.

Outdoor activities such as sailing require a high level of skill and the mastery of various techniques. For example, sail trimming is a skill that is developed over time. This is when the sail is pulled until it fills with wind. The individual needs to get this to an exact point, and it takes practice and skill. The sea can be a dangerous place so, even if an individual has the skills of self-sufficiency, responsibility and perseverance, they will not be able to sail by themselves without the development of these practical skills.

B4 Personal skills needed to safely lead and motivate others in outdoor activities

The skills needed to safely lead and motivate others are different to those skills needed to participate in outdoor activities. Being a leader requires someone to be a role model. LEADERSHIP is defined as guiding a group of people or an organisation. There are many examples of people leading others in our society, including: the prime minister leading the country, a restaurant manager leading his or her team to serve customers, or the hockey captain leading her team to achieving a gold medal in the Rio 2016 Olympics.

Anyone can be a leader. A leader can be any age, from any background and have varying levels of experience. It is likely you have been a leader on numerous occasions without realising it. For example, if you have ever been involved in a sports team or club it is likely at some stage you will have led the group. Leadership is important for achieving goals, increasing an individual's confidence and encouraging others. The chance to lead is often created when someone is challenged in an unusual situation. For example, if a group of beginners are orienteering then someone will often take responsibility for the map and directions, despite it being the first time they have been in this situation. Outdoor activities can teach individuals about themselves in many ways in extraordinary settings.

Practise

Think of the last time you were a leader. This could be in your group, at home or with your friends. Explain the skills you needed to successfully lead the group.

Leadership skills

In order to lead and motivate others you need to show you have leadership skills. Teamwork, communication and decision making are three skills that are regularly needed and developed when leading and motivating others in outdoor activities.

Teamwork

As a leader, you need to be able to work with a variety of different people to achieve a target. In a sports example, this might be a football captain working with their team to win the game or the league. In a restaurant this could be a manager leading a team to successfully serve 150 people for dinner in one evening.

Organisation

Leading any team requires good organisation. In outdoor activities this often means being able to support individuals in situations that are physically and mentally demanding. Being a leader in a team requires you to be a role model to others. This can often be very difficult but is developed with experience. For example, a leader in hillwalking would need to encourage their team to reach their final destination despite facing varying weathers and terrains. The leader would have overall responsibility to get their group safely and efficiently to their destination. Working in a team often means using everyone's strengths. In this example, if the leader felt someone in the team was really strong at map reading, they might delegate this responsibility to them. Importantly, the leader is not expected to be the best at everything or to complete all of the tasks. A good leader will work with the team and combine all their efforts to achieve the goal.

Communication

In order to be able to share out the tasks in this way you must be able to communicate effectively. We all communicate every day. This morning you might have communicated with your parents, guardians, brothers or sisters about the forthcoming day or recent events. You have probably already greeted your friends or your tutor before looking at this book. Communication is everywhere and, to be a leader, it is crucial to develop this skill to get the best out of a team or situation. If you fail to communicate effectively, your team may be left feeling confused or demotivated. Communication can motivate others. For example, if you are completing a trail run with a team of four other runners, verbal encouragement to someone who is struggling can give them the confidence and reassurance that they can carry on and complete the task. It is common that a leader in outdoor activities will often be required to communicate towards those lacking in confidence.

What if...?

You are leading a paintballing team. One of your team members has never been paintballing before and is feeling worried and nervous. They are not sure what to expect and are concerned they are going to let the team down.

Describe how you would use your communication skills to settle their nerves.

Link it up

Look back to Unit 3 where a leader's verbal and non-verbal communication is explained. This will also be examined later in this section.

Communication is really important in many other outdoor activities to achieve a goal. For example, in canoeing, a team will need to communicate effectively to ensure their strokes and movements are in line with each other. If they do not communicate, they are likely to not be in time and therefore the canoe will move more slowly through the water. Another example is a group of people completing an assault course – the team members need to be able to give clear instructions to each other to ensure they complete the obstacles as quickly and efficiently as possible.

Communication is important when trying to achieve a goal.

Decision-making

Leaders need to make decisions, which may be big or small. Some decisions can be the difference between a competitor winning or losing. Others could be the difference between life or death. Imagine a leader taking a group of beginners surfing. If the leader makes the wrong decision to surf in the incorrect place this may mean the individuals are at risk from strong currents. Or consider a leader in ski mountaineering, an activity that involves climbing mountains and then skiing back down. This activity involves a huge number of decisions starting from the planning stage. The ski leader needs to use their experience and knowledge to ensure that the participants are safely led to the top of the mountain and return safely to the bottom of the mountain.

Decision making in outdoor activities is not always quite so critical but it is important. A simple decision might be which way the team should climb on an indoor climbing wall. This might be decided solely by the leader, or it might involve other members of the team. A leader in a boot camp fitness class might ask participants which type of exercise they would like to complete or which challenge they would like to do first. The most important thing to remember is to always ask for help if you are unsure about making a decision in an outdoor activity environment.

What if...?

You decide to try mountain biking for the first time with a friend. There are a range of tracks available. Your friend says he wants to try the most difficult track first because he 'is not afraid of falling off'.

Using your decision-making and communication skills, answer the following.

1 Which mountain biking trail do you decide to go on? Give reasons for your decision.

2 How do you communicate this to your friend?

Leadership qualities

As well as developing a range of skills, you will need certain qualities to be an effective leader. Outdoor activities regularly require you to positively influence others and motivate a group or team. Whether you are a natural leader or have been chosen to lead a particular group of people, developing the right leadership qualities takes hard work. Self-confidence, professionalism, patience and enthusiasm are all qualities needed to safely lead and motivate others in outdoor activities.

Self-confidence

SELF-CONFIDENCE is having the confidence and trust in your own abilities and judgements. Having high levels of self-confidence encourages you to be a leader not just in outdoor activities but in your own lives too. Self-confidence does not just come from winning or losing. Many outdoor activities do not include a competitive element to them. Self-confidence often comes from completing a task and overcoming a fear.

What if...?

There are two very different teams competing against each other in a game of paintball. Your team has a leader with high levels of self-confidence. The other team has a leader with very low levels of self-confidence.

1 Compare the behaviour of each leader.

2 What characteristics does each leader show?

3 Which team would you rather be in? Why?

4 Explain how each team is most likely to react to their leader.

5 Which team do you think has a better chance of winning? Give a reason for your answer.

Professionalism

Frequently, participants that take part in outdoor activities are nervous and anxious. Imagine you are going open water swimming for the first time. You are a strong swimmer but have only ever been swimming in a pool. You are hoping that the person in charge is self-confident and professional. You feel you are placing trust in them and want to safely enjoy the activity. A person showing they are professional would appropriately welcome you, go through all of the safety procedures and what you are going to do in the session, give you demonstrations where necessary and be focused on the job at all times.

There are many ways of showing PROFESSIONALISM. Being professional means demonstrating the skills and behaviour expected of a person who is trained to do a particular job. A professional is usually a role model and someone that is well respected, is good at their job and does everything right, even when they think no one is watching. Take a professional footballer, for example: they get paid to perform well on the pitch. However, when they are at the training ground and at home they have to do all the right things. This includes going to the gym regularly, eating the correct diet, not drinking alcohol and working to prevent injury.

Patience

Another key quality needed by a leader of outdoor activities is PATIENCE. Imagine that you are leading a group on an assault course. One of your participants is showing they are really worried about completing one of the activities. How would you handle this situation? You would need to wait and encourage them to complete the activity. It is important never to get annoyed if a participant does not want to do an activity. It is often very worrying when you first try something new. Show a level of self-confidence and professionalism to reassure this person. Imagine how happy they will be if they complete it – this can be very rewarding for them and you.

Enthusiasm

Continuing with the assault course example, while you are showing levels of confidence, professionalism and being patient, it is important also to be enthusiastic. Consider the nervous participant on the assault course again. Would you say things like: 'Well, the activity is okay – do it if you want', or 'I have completed it many times – it is boring now'? No, you would not. As a good leader, you would show excitement about the activity, and motivate the reluctant participant to achieve their goal. By doing this you would be motivating others to achieve the same goal. This kind of strategy is especially important if a participant is completing the activity for the first time. It will be helpful to try to recall a time when you were in this position and how you felt. Showing enthusiasm for everything you do creates positive feelings all round, and is very contagious.

Practise

Reflect on your favourite leader or tutor.

What qualities do they have that have helped you to succeed?

Leadership responsibilities

A **LEADER** is someone who provides direction, instruction and guidance to a group. A leader in outdoor activities is responsible for guiding a group of people to safely complete an activity. A leader has responsibilities to participants in their activity, but also to:

- the parents and guardians of the participants (if they are under 18)
- the team, school or club that the participants are representing
- the activity centre or provider they are working for.

Instructing

A leader has a responsibility to instruct the participants to complete the task safely. A leader must give clear instructions that are suitable for the individuals in the group. Being an outdoor activity leader is often a varied role. On a Monday you might be instructing a group of ten-year-old children, and on Tuesday you might be instructing a group of accountants who have been sent by their company for team bonding. Therefore you need to be able to adapt your instructions according to the group you are leading.

Link it up

Refer back to 'Planning with different groups' in Unit 3 for more information.

For example, when working with children, you will need to be aware that children often get excitable and will not be as aware of their limitations as a group of adults. You may also need to remind them to keep hydrated. You will need to deliver instructions in smaller chunks. Compare this to working with adults who are more aware of their own health and safety, as well as their own limitations. This can mean that an adult is more likely to be worried or anxious about completing a higher risk activity. Your instructions will need to be specific but also encouraging and supportive. Depending on the ability level of the group of adults, they are more likely to be able to process more information, at a faster rate.

What if...?

You are working as an assistant activity instructor at your local outdoor activity centre. You regularly assist with the canoeing activities for the under-16s at the weekend. One of the parents regularly uses bad language and speech, which is inappropriate. The activity instructor you are working with is trying to ignore it but you know you need to do something about it.

What do you do?

Activity leaders will often have to attend training courses. This is so they can develop specialist knowledge in specific areas. They can then deliver a high-quality service to the group. An activity leader will need to know the specific instructions and explanations that they are delivering. Many outdoor activities that you have looked at are very specialised. For example, a climbing instructor will not only need to provide instructions on how to climb safely. They will also need to give instructions on tying knots, belaying and working with harnesses. This requires a significant amount of knowledge that needs to be communicated appropriately and accurately.

A climbing instructor will need specialised knowledge to ensure the activity session is safe for all participants.

Control risk

Most physical activities of any kind have an element of risk to them. Of course, it is natural that some outdoor activities have a higher risk associated with them than others. However, it is the activity leader's responsibility to control and minimise this risk.

The assessment of risks should be carried out on a regular basis with the results recorded. The risk assessment will be signed and dated by the person who carried it out. A note of the date and time it was completed will also need to be recorded.

The activity leader will also need to continually assess and control the risk throughout the session. For example, if a group were paddle boarding in the sea and the weather changed, a leader would need to assess if the activity was safe to continue or not.

For more information on risk assessment, refer back to 'B2 Realistic management of risk and health and safety in outdoor activities' in this unit.

Check equipment and facilities

Activity centres and providers all have a responsibility to maintain the equipment and facilities they offer to their participants. Activity leaders need to do a thorough safety check before an activity takes place. They should allow themselves sufficient time before a session begins to make the necessary checks of the area, equipment and facilities.

The equipment must be safe, secure and in good condition before allowing participants to take part. The specific checks an activity leader undertakes will vary considerably depending on the activity and the location. For example, an activity leader facilitating a high ropes session will check that the ropes and structures are in good useable condition. They will also monitor the previous weather and the weather forecast for the day. Due to the nature of the activity, the activity centre will follow strict guidelines on maintaining and checking this equipment on a regular basis. Any damage will need to be reported immediately and an appropriately qualified person will carry out the repair according to the manufacturer's guidelines. If it is not possible to do this, then the equipment must be removed and not used until it has been repaired and thoroughly checked.

Check:

- ☐ equipment is safe, secure and in good condition
- ☐ conditions due to previous weather
- ☐ weather forecast for the day
- ☐ damaged equipment is removed and repaired.

Compare this to an activity leader facilitating an orienteering session in a small area. The leader needs to ensure all the checkpoints are visible and in good condition. They may also need to check compasses and maps where appropriate and be aware of the weather forecast. Depending on the size of the area, the activity leader might ask the participants to make contact at a particular point to check everyone is okay. Alternatively, the leader might be with the whole group, all of the session. It is clear to see that the high ropes session has a much higher risk than the orienteering session in this example. The high ropes equipment has a higher potential to cause more harm if it is not checked and maintained appropriately.

Practise

For an outdoor activity of your choice, complete an equipment and facilities check. You will need to plan what you do, complete your check and follow up with a review of how it went.

Checking and maintaining the high ropes equipment is a key responsibility for an activity leader.

Promote a safe activity environment

An activity environment should be safe for all participants. You have seen it is a leader's responsibility to instruct appropriately, control risk and check the equipment and facilities. These all contribute to promoting a safe activity environment. The following is a checklist of the steps you should take in order to achieve this.

PROMOTE A SAFE ACTIVITY ENVIRONMENT

STEP 1

☐ Promotion of a safe environment starts before the session. Make a health and safety check of the facilities and equipment and complete a risk assessment.

STEP 2

☐ Once the participants arrive, make sure they have all of the appropriate paperwork completed.

STEP 3

☐ Complete a visual check to ensure the group are wearing appropriate clothing and footwear. If equipment is being lent, then you will need to make the relevant safety checks of this. For example, if a participant is being fitted with a harness, it will be the leader's overall responsibility to check it is worn correctly and will protect the participant adequately.

STEP 4

☐ Give a welcome briefing, highlighting what the participants can expect, including all safety features.

STEP 5

☐ During the session be aware that it is your job to continually promote a safe activity environment. Be alert at all times and aware of all of the participants. Provide regular safety reminders and repeat the welcome briefing if necessary. Constant communication ensures that the group feels safe and reassured.

STEP 6

☐ After the session, discuss with the participants their enjoyment and experiences. Recap on any safety procedures the participants were involved in. This will help to prepare them for upcoming sessions or activities. It is important to encourage communication at this point to ensure no one has been injured or harmed during the activity.

STEP 7

☐ After the participants have left, review the session, including the health and safety features.

Practise

You have enrolled on a training course to help develop your leadership skills and understand your responsibilities as leader.

Design a poster to give information on the range of leadership responsibilities required in outdoor activities.

Verbal and non-verbal communication skills

Communication is a vital skill needed by all leaders. Leaders need to effectively communicate with participants in order to safely lead and motivate others. Communication can be either verbal or non-verbal. A leader might give direct instructions through speaking to their group or participants. For example, a direct instruction from a caving instructor will help the group to understand the direction they need to go in.

Verbal communication can also be used to support and motivate others. Outdoor activities are frequently demanding, both physically and mentally. Sometimes leaders will need to motivate and help others to achieve their goals. Individuals might be anxious or worried at the prospect of doing something out of their comfort zone. The challenging aspect of these activities can mean leaders have to develop skills that enable them to reassure participants while encouraging them to push themselves.

Good communication is vital when delivering instructions. A leader taking a group abseiling needs to give accurate guidelines and directions to make sure the participants complete the activity safely. If the participants do not receive or understand this information they are likely to panic and this could potentially mean they lose confidence in participating. The participant and the leader need to communicate well to achieve the overall goal: communication is often a two-way process.

It is important to use appropriate language when leading outdoor activities. Firstly, this includes being professional and speaking to the participants in the correct manner. You should never use slang, be biased or make insulting comments. Secondly, the language must be appropriate to the group you are leading. For example, you will use different language when working with children compared to when you are working with adults. A leader that is leading a similar age group to themselves will need to make sure they use different language to distinguish this activity from a social situation. In this situation, the leader will need to be professional and well practised. Sometimes it helps to think that this is now a 'work situation'. It is important to be able to adapt from being sociable with friends to then leading these same people on a potentially high-risk outdoor activity. The group is placing trust in their leader to keep them safe and motivate them where needed.

Do	Do not
✓ be professional	✗ use slang
✓ use age-appropriate language	✗ be too familiar
✓ be supportive and motivate	✗ be insulting
✓ actively listen.	✗ talk over participants' concerns.

You often use **NON-VERBAL COMMUNICATION** without even realising it. Non-verbal communication includes active listening (see Figure 6.6). **ACTIVE LISTENING** is where the listener concentrates on what is being said and responds to the speaker to show they understand.

Link it up

Refer back to Unit 3 where verbal and non-verbal communication for sport and activity leaders is discussed.

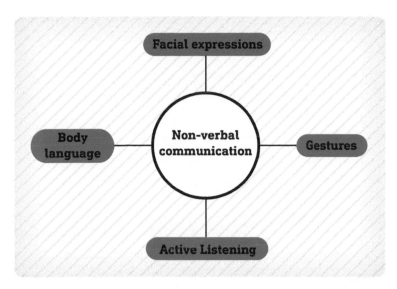

Figure 6.6: Non-verbal communication

Active listening is a skill that can be learnt and is developed with practice. It helps to build **RAPPORT**, understanding and trust. You can show you are active listening by making eye contact, nodding, smiling or saying words such as 'yes' or 'hmm'. By doing this, the speaker feels more at ease and therefore can communicate openly and honestly. For example, if a participant is feeling worried about trying skiing for the first time they might not want to open up and share their feelings. By speaking to them and showing you are actively listening to their responses they are more likely to share their fears. This can help you to encourage them to take part and give them reassuring messages.

Providing a positive outdoor activity experience for others

A positive outdoor activity experience and environment does not just happen, it is created. There are many things that contribute to this experience. The activity centre facilities and equipment need to be of a good standard and well maintained. All of the equipment needs to be appropriate for the group and set up and checked. In order for this to happen, the leader needs to be trained well and have the ability to engage and manage a group of participants. Having the necessary practical skills and the knowledge to plan and lead an activity is essential. As leader you will need to be able to adapt to situations or events that are unplanned, and respond in a calm and confident manner. As with any sports session, you must ensure you plan sessions so that participants enjoy and learn.

Forming a positive learning experience will allow all participants to feel comfortable, safe and engaged. If someone is given the opportunity to feel all of these things they are more likely to learn more and want to participate again. By giving people positive experiences you are enhancing their physical and mental well-being. They will feel more self-confident and, one day, they could be the leader of an outdoor activity experience themselves. In this way, providing positive experiences inspires people to be the best they can be.

Skills and knowledge check

☐ Give a definition of the term 'patience'.

☐ Explain two leadership skills that are needed to lead outdoor activity sessions.

☐ Name the three categories of types of hazards.

☐ Explain the importance of using activity-specific equipment.

☐ Give examples of the different types of clothing and footwear used for an activity of your choice.

○ I can confidently complete a risk assessment for a chosen outdoor activity.

○ I can define the term 'non-verbal communication' and give an example.

○ I know what a liability waiver is and why it is used.

○ I know I have the skills and knowledge to prepare me to lead an outdoor activity session.

If you have been unable to give positive responses to any of the questions or statements above, please go back and review the section.

Ready for assessment

For this unit you will need to show that you understand the scope of outdoor activities and can demonstrate the appropriate skills to take part and lead others safely and effectively.

You will produce a report that discusses a total of three urban and rural outdoor activities. You will include information about the activities, such as the number of people that participate in them in a specific area of the UK. You will report on the different types of people, their barriers to participation and the benefits to choosing to get involved. Be sure to investigate how barriers can be overcome to encourage even higher participation levels.

Following the completion of your report, you will take part and lead an outdoor activity of your choice. You should show that you can be flexible and adaptable while leading the activity and, most importantly, ensure the safety of yourself and your participants at all times.

Relish the opportunity to showcase your skills and qualities that you have developed throughout the unit. This will help to ensure your participants have a positive outdoor activity experience. Remember, be the best you can be.

WORK FOCUS

HANDS ON

Julie has played sport all of her life. She has a good level of fitness and enjoys being competitive. She currently works as a personal trainer and is looking at volunteering opportunities. Recently, her friends have been telling her about their experiences in outdoor activities and she is keen to get involved.

Julie has asked for your help and has requested more information about the variety of outdoor activities on offer to her. Julie lives near the sea and some mountains. She mentions to you that she thinks water activities would be enjoyable.

You work at a local activity centre and you recommend that Julie visits you. You want to give Julie a 'hands on' experience of one activity to see if she enjoys it.

1 **Select an activity that you feel is appropriate.**

2 **Create a step-by-step plan of everything you will need to think about to give Julie a safe and enjoyable experience. Consider the following.**
   • Equipment and facilities.
   • Management of risk and health and safety.
   • Your personal skills, qualities and responsibilities.

Ready for work?

Complete the quiz below to see if you are ready for work.

1 When working as an outdoor activity instructor, you will need to complete a variety of risk assessments for each activity you lead. Do you:

☐ A sign and date each one on the day you complete it

☐ B sign and date the forms for a year in advance

☐ C never sign and date the forms?

2 It is important to understand why people choose not to participate in outdoor activities. There are five categories. Which of the following is correct?

☐ A Perception, time, access, location and cost

☐ B Time, cost, access, location and laziness

☐ C High motivation, self-confidence, patience, professionalism and enthusiasm

3 Working at an activity centre will mean you often have to meet new customers and give them an introduction to the site. Part of this introduction will include some paperwork.

A liability waiver is:

☐ A a legal document signed by an individual who acknowledges that there are risks involved in the activities they are going to complete

☐ B a questionnaire that assesses the medical conditions of a participant

☐ C a document where a participant reviews their experience of an outdoor activities session.

4 A customer asks you what equipment they need to buy to go on the high ropes course. You explain that the centre provides the equipment for free and you are there to guide them. By selecting the appropriate equipment for the customer to wear:

☐ A their safety levels are increased and their performance is enhanced

☐ B their safety levels are decreased and their performance is diminished

☐ C there are no consequences to the customer.

You should have all As as your answers. It is important to show everything you have learnt from this section to any future employers. If you have not achieved all A answers then please go back to your tutor and review the section.

7 Leading Different Groups

Encouraging mass participation within sport and physical activity is very important. You know that taking part in sport and physical activity keeps you healthy and is great fun, but it is often forgotten that it helps you make friends, and increases your self-confidence. Participation should be about inclusivity, meaning that you should provide opportunities for everyone to take part regardless of their age, gender, ethnicity or employment status.

There are many reasons why some are keener than others to take part in sport and physical activity. It is important that you take time to consider how to encourage participation and meet the needs of all those taking part.

In this unit you will learn how to support the needs of different groups and lead sport and activity sessions that are designed to encourage inclusive participation.

How will I be assessed?

This unit will develop your skills to deliver a range of activities that meet the needs of different groups. You will gain the essential knowledge that can be used to help support inclusivity and provide enjoyment for all.

Your assessments will be designed by your tutors to cover the essential grading criteria while reflecting the requirements of your working career. Assessments may include developing scenario-based practical activities, providing research reports on participation barriers and reviewing their outcomes, developing activity plans to increase activity participation, demonstrating communication and appropriate interaction methods with different groups, and practical observations. As part of the documentation, tutors may record evidence using observation records, filmed footage, and/ or annotated photographic evidence of your assessment.

Assessment criteria

Pass	Merit	Distinction
Learning aim A: Find out about factors that influence participation in sport and physical activity for different groups		
A.P1 Identify the influences on and benefits of participation in sport and physical activity for three different groups.	**A.M1** Describe the influences on and benefits of participation in sport and physical activity for three different groups and outline how barriers could be reduced.	**A.D1** Analyse the influences on and benefits of participation in sport and physical activity for three different groups and explain how any barriers to participation can be overcome, offering effective solutions.
Learning aim B: Show how sport and physical activity can meet the needs of different groups		
B.P2 Select a suitable sport or physical activity for a specified group and produce an appropriate plan to encourage them to take part.	**B.M2** Select a relevant sport or physical activity for a specified group and produce an effective plan to encourage them to take part.	**B.D2** Select a relevant and justified sport or physical activity for a specified group and produce an effective and detailed plan to encourage them to take part.

A Find out about factors that influence participation in sport and physical activity for different groups

A1 Influences on participation for different groups

There is no doubt that we all have our individual reasons to participate in sport and physical activity. For the majority, these reasons tend to be for our own enjoyment and the help it can give us in keeping fit. If you reflect on your sport and activity experiences, you may be able to think of all the social experiences you have gained too. Sport and activity allow us to make new friends and develop relationships with like-minded people. Moreover, taking part in physical challenges as part of a team can be a deeply enriching experience.

Children and teenagers

Many of us are introduced to sport and activity when we are children. This might not be as part of organised activities, such as netball, tennis, rugby, etc., but may form part of natural play, such as catching a ball, timing a run in the garden or kicking a ball into a small goal. While our early experiences may not be in structured games with formal rules, they often encourage our interest in taking part.

School is often the place where children first experience a structured sport or game. A school's provision of facilities, and the access to coaching it can provide, often determines the activities a child takes part in and potentially influences their interest in competition. Many schools are able to excel in sport due to the **FACILITIES** and/or coaching staff they are able to offer their pupils, whereas others with limited resources can struggle.

What if...?

Well-resourced schools, such as Millfield School in Somerset, can provide not only the sports you would normally recognise in most schools, such as rugby, football, netball, basketball, etc., but also additional facilities to encourage wider participation. For example, Millfield School is able to develop the talents of its pupils in a wide range of activities including equestrian, fencing, golf, rowing, karate, ski racing and many more. Many of these sporting activities take place on site, owing to a large investment to support up-and-coming sporting talent.

1 If a parent were to ask for your views on the benefits of attending this and other schools that are able to offer exceptional sporting facilities, what would be your response and why?

2 How could the experience the pupils receive in this instance influence their overall schooling?

The exceptional facilities available at Millfield School have led to many pupils completing their education and going on to perform at national and international level. While the facilities were a big help towards their success, many former pupils acknowledge the support and inspiration they were given by a teacher. Regardless of what facilities are available, the influence of a good motivator can encourage success and bring about the determination needed to achieve.

A child's attitude to sport is often influenced by the experience they gain at an early age. Positive praise can help to build self-confidence (a belief in your own ability to succeed) and encourages a child to participate more frequently. When a child receives regular negative comments, they are more likely to give up. For this reason, it is important you are always positive when coaching children as this will nurture their interest and talents, and increase the chances of them continuing to participate in the future.

The influence of our parents is an important factor in our attitude to sport and physical activity. Many children take part in activities that their parents enjoy too. Their parents may have competed/played in the activity prior to having a family, and it is natural that their interests will influence their children. Other influences are siblings' interests – a brother or sister's participation in a sport can often inspire a child to take part, either for enjoyment or out of a sense of rivalry.

England international rugby player and former Millfield pupil Chris Robshaw developed his talents through the facilities provided at the school.

Young people may also be inspired by a friend they look up to, or a ROLE MODEL, such as a famous athlete. A role model is an individual whose behaviour, attitude, actions and success are emulated by others. This is very common in children and teenagers, and role models provide opportunities to promote fair play and future success. Negative role models can often display unacceptable behaviour that is often not in keeping with the spirit of the game, for example, cheating, violence and inappropriate aggression towards others.

Many young athletes look up to performers such as Usain Bolt (100m/200m) and Mo Farah (5000m/10,000m) and aspire to reach similar achievements in the future. While such athletes have exceptional talent, many children can use the achievements of their heroes and heroines to motivate themselves to develop the dedication needed to become top national and international performers.

a) Usain Bolt, the world record holder, Olympic gold medallist and World Champion, for both the 100m and 200m, b) Sir Mo Farah, Olympic gold medallist and World Champion for both the 5000m and 10,000m.

a)

b)

As children get older, they develop both physically and mentally. The stage of physical development can often contribute to the level of success they experience. It is this success that can be a key determinant to sustaining interest and participation. Older performers will naturally be stronger and potentially fitter so it is unfair to create competition between participants who are, for example, 18 and 11 years old. For this reason, many sports use an age-range divide between leagues or performers. For example, sports may operate an under-11s (U11s), U15s and/or U18s age range for each level of performers. Others may categorise the performers as juniors, intermediates and seniors.

Whatever the system, it creates an identity for the performer, and separates their abilities based on their physical development.

Practise

Think about the sports facilities that are open for young people in your area, including your school or college.

1 Make a list of all the sports you could take part in within a short journey of approximately 20 minutes from where you live.

2 For each activity, provide a brief outline of the facilities and coaches/trainers available that would enable you to participate.

3 Which of the facilities and coaches/trainers do you think you could use most. What has influenced your choice?

Women

Female participation has come a long way since the early 1900s. Female competitors were first allowed to take part in the Paris Olympic Games in 1900 with just 22 participants competing in two events. Male participants made up the remaining 975 competitors and had a greater range of sport and activities to compete in. Since then, female competitors have regularly provided more than 40 per cent of the total number of participants, competing across a range of 28 events, in subsequent Olympic Games. As a result of success in the Olympics and many other high-profile events worldwide, female participation in sport and physical activity has continued to rise. While this has been a positive response, many females of all ages still experience BARRIERS TO PARTICIPATION.

The availability of activities can make participation difficult for many women. For example, women's rugby and football has continued to develop and bring significant success over recent years, however, the number of teams offering playing opportunities is limited. Without the availability of activities, many female PARTICIPANTS continue to miss out on taking part in a range of sport and activities. If you consider the availability of teams, consider how many teams there are for football or rugby in your area. It is very likely that there are more teams available for male performers than females.

The relationship status of many women can have an impact on how much leisure time they have available to take part throughout the day. Female participants with few commitments will naturally have more time and are more likely to take part in some form of activity. With fewer responsibilities, female participants are often able to commit time to play sports, join a gym and do other activities. When it comes to raising a family, the additional commitment to childcare and family responsibilities can make it difficult to dedicate free time to sport and activity. While many families spread and share the responsibilities, it is recognised that women frequently take on a much larger role in raising children, which may provide them with less leisure time than men.

Practise

Consider the sport and activity facilities available in your area, e.g. a gym facility. Research the activities that are dedicated to female participants.

1 Make a list of the classes available for female participants.

2 How frequent are the classes throughout the week?

3 At what time of day do the majority of classes take place? Give possible reasons for this.

4 Which do you feel is the most popular class, based on your list?

5 What factors could influence the choice of activity by a female participant?

Many sport and leisure providers recognise the difficulties that may be experienced by female participants and so provide kids clubs, crèche facilities and mixed child–parent activity clubs. Gyms and leisure centres may also provide women-only activity classes, e.g. aqua aerobics, swim classes, aerobics, etc., to encourage participation. To support this further, many activity classes are organised and timetabled to avoid clashing with home life commitments, such as school drop off and/or pick up and evening mealtimes. Check out your local leisure centre or gym provider's fitness timetable. If they offer female-only classes, what time do they start and finish? You may find that this is consistent with a particular time of the day.

Despite ongoing positive developments, attitudes towards female participation can vary among different sports and activities. Participation within some sports may often be discouraged, and others encouraged. For example, many women may choose to swim, run or play netball, as these are traditional female physical activities. However, there is an emerging trend towards increased female participation in **IMPACT AND COMBAT SPORTS**, such as rugby and boxing, which are traditionally played by men. (Impact and combat sports are sports/activities where there is a significant forceful contact with the body, for example, striking of the body in boxing, or a rugby tackle.) Historically, very few women have been encouraged to take up such sports, though successful international performances have continued to inspire new entrants to the sport. These role models are helping to change attitudes and encourage female athletes to take part with confidence. Nicola Adams MBE is one such example. When women's boxing was introduced at the 2012 London Olympics, she became the first woman to win an Olympic boxing title.

What if...?

Nicola Adams MBE became an instant national role model for many up-and-coming female boxers after her outstanding performance in the 2012 London Olympic Games. Having become the first woman to win an Olympic boxing title, she proved to many that the sport is not something that should be dominated by male performers. While there are significantly fewer female boxers, she has contributed to developing the sport further and encouraged wider participation.

1 Why is it important that we increase female participation within impact and combat sports?

2 What could be the key to encouraging and developing greater opportunities for all to participate?

Nicola Adams (blue), on her way to winning gold in the London 2012 Olympic Games.

Such combat sports, or other sports that are traditionally viewed as more masculine or 'manly', can often deter female participation. Many women avoid physical impact sports as they may feel self-conscious and worry about how they will be seen by others. It is important to realise that, while combat sports are currently male dominated, they should never be considered as male-only activities.

BODY IMAGE can have a significant influence on female participation. (Body image is how you perceive your body – either positive or negative, consciously and subconsciously. A negative body image can reduce self-confidence.) We live in a culture where the body is regularly judged and compared, and this may lead many women to avoid participation in certain sports. For example, some women will avoid activities that might seem overly masculine, or that will give them a muscular physique (e.g. weightlifting). They might avoid sports that could attract unwanted sexual attention. For example, in sports such as swimming, some women may feel self-conscious in a swimming costume, and in other sports or in gyms they may feel vulnerable if they are required to wear tight-fitting clothing (e.g. leggings or tops). They may feel inadequate when seeing their own body compared to other participants. All these factors can lead to women choosing not to take part. It is important to recognise these barriers and help female participants to overcome them.

Disabled groups

DISABILITY SPORT has continued to make significant progress throughout recent years. (Disability sport is any activity played by individuals with any partial or total mental or physical inability to perform daily life activities.) With greater access to facilities and an increase in the number of specialist coaches nationwide, the number of sports participants continues to rise, and it has become more popular as a spectator sport.

Participants eligible to compete in disability sport vary, based on the type of disability or level of impairment. For competitive purposes, the

International Paralympic Committee (IPC) categorises each disabled participant to encourage fairness among participants (see Table 7.1).

Table 7.1: International Paralympic Committee standard of impairments (adapted from IPC Handbook: International Standard for Eligible Impairments, 2016)

Category of condition	Typical impairment
Reduced muscle power	The body's ability to generate muscle force is reduced in one limb or lower section of the body. Example of these impairments include sufferers of polio, spina bifida conditions and spinal cord injuries.
Restricted passive range of movement	The range of movement or flexibility in the body's joints is significantly reduced permanently. Sufferers typically show signs of one or more limbs being in a permanent extended/flexed state, making it difficult to move in the opposite direction. The condition is known as arthrogryposis.
Limb deficiency	Joints or bones of a limb are either partially or totally absent from the body. This may be as a result of an injury (e.g. accident), illness (e.g. bone cancer) or as a result of a birth deficiency.
Leg length difference	A limb has been shortened due to loss (e.g. amputee) or as a result of a birth deficiency.
Short stature	The body has a reduced standing height due to abnormal dimensions. Typically as a result of a growth hormone deficiency.
Hypertonia	The body suffers an abnormal increase in muscle tension, which makes it very difficult to stretch muscles fully. This is usually due to a related brain condition and can include sufferers of conditions such as cerebral palsy and multiple sclerosis. Brain injury can also be a cause of hypertonia.
Ataxia	The body has a severe lack of muscle coordination. Like hypertonia, this is usually due to a related brain condition and can include sufferers of cerebral palsy and multiple sclerosis, or as a result of a brain injury.
Athetosis	The body has difficulty in maintaining balance and produces a range of involuntary movements. The body has difficulty in maintaining a symmetrical posture, e.g. level shoulders, and can result from a number of conditions, including cerebral palsy and multiple sclerosis, and as a consequence of suffering brain injury.
Visual impairment	Eyesight has been totally lost or the participant is partially sighted.
Intellectual impairment	The participant may have a significant learning disorder that affects their everyday life, from both a social and practical point of view, and they may have difficulty composing accurate thoughts.

Paralympian Dame Sarah Storey, multiple gold medal winner, competes without a fully functioning left arm.

Disability sport is very diverse, with a wide range of participant needs being supported to encourage **INCLUSIVITY**.

WHEELCHAIR SPORT (any sport where a participant is confined to a wheelchair that can be adapted to suit the requirements of the sport, e.g. long-distance performance, impact performance, increased manoeuvrability, and many more) continues to increase in popularity, with a wide range of clubs and facilities available nationwide. Sports for wheelchair users include basketball, rugby, tennis, fencing, athletics, and many more. As with all disability sports, rules are adapted to support individual needs. Regardless of whether the performers are **AMPUTEES** (partial or total absence of limb or limbs from the body), **VISUALLY IMPAIRED** (partial or total loss of sight) or **HEARING IMPAIRED** (partial or total loss of hearing), activities can be adapted to suit their needs.

Practise

Disability sport is often overlooked within the community, or its availability is poorly publicised.

1 Research how many disability sport or activity clubs are available in your local area.

2 List the types of disability sport they offer, where they take place and how often they occur.

3 For one of the sports, identify the disability they support for participation.

4 Design a publicity poster that could be used to inform the public about a disability club in your area. Remember, it must be informative, with details of when it takes place. Try to create interest – your aim is to encourage a disabled participant to take part.

Examples may include athletics for amputees, whereby the runners wear blades to enable them to run around a running track. Visually impaired football players may play using a rattle/bell within the ball to guide them to the ball, where to pass and when to tackle. Hearing impaired players are not recognised by the International Paralympic Committee as this disability is not seen to affect performance enough to warrant extra support. Within many sporting activities, hearing impairment is not viewed as restrictive to competitive performance. There are many successful hearing impaired performers worldwide who compete regularly in a range of sports, including athletics, golf, volleyball and ice hockey.

There are a range of disability sport organisations nationwide.

- WheelPower (www.wheelpower.org.uk) provides opportunities for people with a physical disability to be introduced to wheelchair sport.
- British Wheelchair Athletics Association (BWAA) (www.bwaa.co.uk) supports wheelchair sports performers who have suffered spinal cord injuries to compete in athletic throws events.
- British Wheelchair Racing Association (www.bwra.co.uk) supports road and track wheelchair racing opportunities.
- LimbPower (www.limbpower.com) promotes sporting participation for amputees and those with limb impairment.

- British Blind Sport (www.britishblindsport.org.uk) promotes opportunities for the visually impaired to take part in sport and recreation.
- UK Deaf Sport (www.ukdeafsport.org.uk) provides opportunities and information for the hearing impaired to participate in sporting activities.
- Dwarf Sports Association UK (DSAuk) (www.dsauk.org) promotes the development of competitive sport for those athletes who have restricted growth.
- Cerebral Palsy Sport (CP Sport) (www.cpsport.org) supports sporting opportunities for athletes with cerebral palsy.
- Mencap Sport (England) (www.mencap.org.uk/sport) supports sporting opportunities for individuals with learning disabilities.
- UK Sports Association for People with Learning Disability (UKSA) (www.uksportsassociation.org) supports the development of talented athletes with learning difficulties.
- Special Olympics Great Britain (www.specialolympicsgb.org.uk) provides training and competitive opportunities for individuals with intellectual disabilities.

Paralympian Ellie Simmonds OBE developed with a short stature and has produced multiple gold medal performances since the age of 13.

The level of difficulty and surrounding support network will ultimately influence participation in a disability sport. Without adequate support of specialist coaches, adequate training and activity facilities, and even transport links to the venue, disabled participation can prove difficult. For some, such as wheelchair users, additional costs such as specialist wheelchairs can also make participation difficult. The nature of disability can provide a barrier for participation and these barriers should be carefully considered when trying to encourage inclusivity for all.

BME (Black and minority ethnic) and BAME (Black, Asian and minority ethnic)

Members of **BME** (Black and minority ethnic), and **BAME** (Black, Asian and minority ethnic) groups have continued to make great advances in participation and success throughout the past few decades. Following a period of restricted participation, sportsmen and sportswomen have achieved much success throughout the last century of sport.

These successes have produced many iconic athletes and performers that span the decades across a range of sports. For example, participants such as British athletics stars Mo Farah and Katarina Johnson-Thompson have achieved many successes throughout their careers and continue to inspire participants nationwide. Positive role models can help to influence sports participation and change attitudes to sport. These role models can encourage participation, motivate mass participation and develop stars of the future.

Katarina Johnson-Thompson is a multiple gold medal-winning performer and provides a positive role model for up-and-coming performers.

Regardless of ethnic group, role models are able to influence the choice of sports that young performers take part in. It is not unusual for widespread participation in a particular sport to result from extensive media coverage on television, the Internet and magazines. Positive role models are essential for young performers as they enable them to aspire to be like their heroes or heroines, and inspire them to improve their own performances.

While you should encourage participation, for some minority groups taking part may be restricted due to faith and religion. For example, participants may be unable to take part on a Sunday or another day of religious significance; some may be unable to wear appropriate sports clothing due to the need to keep their body covered up; and others may need to wear headwear that potentially restricts their use of protective equipment. No matter what religion or faith an individual follows, it should never lead to their exclusion from participation. You should always try to support participation in all activities and use alternative methods to fully encourage inclusivity. Remember, leading different groups should encourage full participation and promote respect for people's faith and religion.

Muslim athletes dressing in accordance with their beliefs while competing at the London 2012 Olympic Games.

Negative experiences such as **RACISM** (the unequal treatment of an individual based on their race or ethnic group) have no place within sport and society. Sport is about passion and participation. It should be remembered that, whether it is an activity session or a competition, you are competing against a fellow competitor, regardless of their **ETHNICITY** (the state of belonging to a social group that shares a common and distinctive culture, religion or language). Racism in sport breeds racism, whether it is experienced during participation or through spectators/supporters. It can only promote negative experiences for sports participants. Sport should be a pleasurable experience, and unacceptable behaviour, such as racism, can influence peoples' participation. Racism in sport often causes performers to give up and never return. Unacceptable behaviour during a match or activity can create widespread feelings of hostility. Should you ever witness or experience racism, it is important that you report it. It should never be tolerated. All information should be detailed and ideally written down as a witness observation of what happened. This should then be passed to a senior manager, sporting governing body and/or the police.

Practise

Racism has no place within society or a sporting culture. Whether you are competing to win, or simply taking part, race is never an issue.

1 Reflect on any negative experiences you have had or witnessed throughout your sporting career and consider how that made you feel.

2 Identify any campaigns that sporting governing bodies have run to enhance BME/BAME participation.

3 Consider the sports available in your community. Are these promoted sufficiently to the BME/BAME community? What could be done to make them even better?

4 If you were in charge of a campaign to encourage BME/BAME participation, what would you do?

Elderly and active retired

Physical activity is very important for maintaining long-lasting health, and this is no different for the elderly and active retired. Keeping fit and active can help prevent or even overcome health conditions that affect day-to-day living.

When encouraging any elderly or active retired person to take part in physical activity, it is important you check for any possible **ACTIVITY-LIMITING HEALTH CONDITIONS OR PHYSICAL LIMITATIONS** (anything that prevents an individual from performing everyday activities), as you could potentially make any condition worse if you fail to take medical guidance. For example, your participant may suffer a respiratory condition or have a heart-related condition that could be made worse by over-exertion during a sport or activity. It is up to you to find suitable alternatives, for example, you could use different activities or sports that allow them to take part but that limit the risk of damaging their health further, e.g. walking football or swimming. Remember, when leading any physical activity, it is your responsibility to look after your participants at all times.

If a participant suffers from physical limitations, such as back and knee joint problems due to injury or wear and tear, arthritis or swollen joints, try to plan activities around this. For example, activities that require a limited but controlled amount of bending or agility running can help to alleviate joint soreness and/or avoid further long-term injury damage, e.g. weightlifting at the gym or an active game of cricket.

Creating fun activities and providing a welcoming **ACTIVITY ENVIRONMENT** (where the activity takes place) is very important to encourage participation. A welcoming environment can help to develop self-confidence and a desire to succeed. Medical professionals often prescribe activity as a means of improving health. However, it is not unusual for the elderly and active retired to deliberately avoid some exercise environments. For example, if you are a regular gym user, look around the exercise space and try to identify how many people are elderly or at retirement age. It is fair to assume that you will count very few in terms of a percentage of total users.

Many elderly and retired individuals can feel intimidated or 'out of touch' with exercise. They may have exercised regularly when at school or later in life, however, going back to it can be difficult. Many report feeling embarrassed that they are not as proficient as others, or feel the exercises are uncomfortable. This can knock their self-confidence. As a result, when planning an activity session, design exercise environments that encourage participation.

All-female Pilates class for active retired participants.

Link it up

You can use a PAR-Q to check a participant's health and fitness – see Unit 6.

To overcome these difficulties, some gyms offer special sessions where participants can feel more at ease. Working out with a group of similarly aged people is likely to encourage people to participate and return in the future. Not only will the participants feel more motivated, they will meet new friends of a similar age group, with whom they have much in common. Activity sessions may take part in over-60s exercise clubs and include Pilates, aerobics, swim clubs, water-aerobics and dance classes. Exercising alongside people of a similar age and ability can often relax participants and encourage them to take part more frequently. It is not unusual for the elderly to assume they are too 'out of shape' or sick, or just too old to exercise. As an activity leader, it is important you try to get past this PERCEPTION, and raise awareness of inclusivity.

It is important as an activity leader that you try to encourage and motivate the elderly to participate in exercise regularly. Not only does it improve physical health, it also enables SOCIALISATION (the activity of mixing socially with others) and can stimulate the mind. Remember, activities can vary from structured exercise or games to regular walking or rambling. When leading an activity, it is important to think of varied exercise in order to encourage participation.

Practise

Consider the sport and activity facilities available in your area, e.g. a gym facility. Research the activities that are dedicated to elderly and active retired people only.

1 Make a list of the classes available for elderly and active retired participants.

2 Which three do you feel are the most popular? Why do you think this is?

3 At what time of day do the majority of classes take place? Why do you think this is?

4 What could you do to encourage greater participation among elderly and active retired people?

5 Prepare promotional resources that could inform the elderly and active retired about classes and activities available in their area. You may want to produce leaflets, posters and/or presentations.

Unemployed

Financial constraints and the possible psychological impact of long-term unemployment can mean that people who are out of work are often unable to take regular exercise. This puts them at greater risk of suffering a range of health conditions. These include higher levels of cholesterol, cardiovascular disease and even some cancers. Therefore, it is important you try to encourage their participation in regular activity.

The unemployed may be financially disadvantaged when it comes to taking part in activity. Joining a gym or belonging to a club can be expensive. In addition, there is often an associated expense of buying appropriate clothing, such as trainers, or equipment, such as a bike. Therefore when encouraging participation and planning appropriate activities, it is important to keep costs as low as possible to allow those from low incomes to take part.

Not all activities have to be expensive and, with careful planning, many activities can be developed to accommodate low incomes. These may include:

- running
- stair climbing
- free exercise workout download apps for mobile phones
- DIY bootcamps, e.g. press-ups, star jumps, squats, shuttle runs, etc.
- home exercises, e.g. sit-ups, press-ups, squats
- skipping.

It is important for you to remember the many health benefits of exercise. These aren't just physical, but can be psychological too. Exercise can improve SELF-ESTEEM, raise confidence and boost self-worth. (Self-esteem is how you feel about yourself as an individual – positive self-esteem means you feel good about yourself and gives you that 'go get' attitude.) This, in turn, develops positivity, which will help an individual seeking employment, who may be facing many pressures. There is truth to the old expression 'Healthy body, healthy mind'. Regular physical activity can help to contribute towards a positive mindset and a sense of purpose, giving you greater strength to tackle difficulties you may be facing in your daily lives. It is important that you always try to encourage participation in order to promote both physical and mental well-being.

It is not unusual for people to take part in physical activity with friends and/or relatives. Joining forces in this way can be very beneficial, as the influence of other people can help to encourage and sustain participation. Sometimes people form partnerships, which might mean attending fitness classes together, or could be a regular sports partner (e.g. for tennis or squash), a training gym partner or a team buddy. Participating with others in familiar surroundings can be an enjoyable and enriching experience.

A2 Barriers to participation in sport and physical activity

Health-related

As previously mentioned, some health-related conditions can cause difficulty for those who wish to take part in exercise. Health conditions can be a result of many factors including age, gender, family history and lifestyle.

MEDICAL CONDITIONS can have a number of effects on the body that might prevent an individual from taking part in physical activity. (A medical condition is a disease or disorder of the body.) They can vary in severity but, as a sport and activity leader, you should aim to overcome them in order to promote participation. However, it is very important to seek medical advice before leading any activity with an individual who has a pre-existing medical condition.

Table 7.2 summarises some common medical conditions you might come across.

Table 7.2: *Medical conditions that may be a barrier to activity participation

Medical condition	What is it?	How could it affect participation?
Asthma	Lung condition that causes breathing difficulties, e.g. breathlessness, wheezing, coughing	Participants may become breathless when taking part in running activities. They may become quickly worn out as they can find it hard to get enough oxygen through the lungs to the working muscles. Always check they have their inhaler with them as this can help overcome potential breathlessness or asthma attacks.
Diabetes	Condition where body fails to absorb sugar properly, therefore has potential difficulty maintaining blood sugar levels	Exercise is important for a diabetic, as it can help them control their blood sugar levels. It is important for diabetics taking part in any activity to monitor their blood sugar levels because if they become too low, it could cause them to faint. Always keep a fruit drink or sugary snack nearby that can be used to help them recover.

*It is very important that a participant seeks advice from a doctor before taking part in any physical activity.

Table 7.2: *(continued)*

Medical condition	What is it?	How could it affect participation?
Epilepsy	Brain condition that can cause loss of awareness or seizures	A misconception with epilepsy is that it is always caused by flashing lights. While this can be a trigger for some, a seizure may occur due to poor sleep, stress, excess fatigue or as a result of a head injury. You should never panic on witnessing an attack. If a participant collapses, keep calm, call for help, and simply hold and protect the head from injury until the seizure is over. For them to recover, simply roll the participant onto their side, or into the recovery position, supporting their head with a jumper/towel – and monitor their recovery. As a sport and activity leader, it is important that you are aware of anyone suffering from epilepsy in the group. For example, during a swimming session, you (or another coach or lifeguard) should be on standby in case they have a seizure in the pool. During contact activities, such as rugby, always provide head protection to avoid a significant impact that could trigger a seizure.
Obesity	Condition when someone is very overweight	Some obese participants can find it difficult to take part in activity because they are physically limited by their size. They may find it difficult to take part in exercise for long periods of time, or movements such as running or jumping might be too strenuous. As leader, it is important that you promote inclusivity and make all activities enjoyable for all participants. Activities where there may be excessive running, such as football, basketball or cross country, may not be enjoyable to these participants due to difficulties with their size. While exercise is important to your health, you should always remember that it is a slow development process and it can take time to reduce the effects of this condition on the body. Remember, you always want people to enjoy an activity session, so supporting their needs is essential.
Arthritis	Condition that causes pain and swollen joints	Participants suffering arthritis may find it difficult to take part in activity that requires bending or that impacts on their joints. As leader, it is important that you avoid activities that involve frequent jumping or movements that require quick changes in direction, as this can put a strain on the joints. Activities such as swimming or cycling are ideal, while football, rugby and basketball are less so.
High blood pressure	Condition where the heart requires a high pressure to force the blood around the body, which can be dangerous to both the heart and brain.	The causes of high blood pressure are poor diet, a sedentary lifestyle or genetics. It is important for participants suffering from high blood pressure to avoid over-exertion as this will raise blood pressure further. They should also avoid heavy lifting or any strength-based activities using weights as this can put extra strain on the heart.

*It is very important that a participant seeks advice from a doctor before taking part in any physical activity.

PHYSICAL INJURIES can also limit an individual's participation in an activity, although the impact they have will be dependent on the severity of the injury. Some physical injuries are minor, such as a sprained ankle or a pulled muscle. Others can be more severe, such as a broken limb or a joint injury. Whatever the injury, always try to adapt activities to support the individual's needs. For example, if a participant is recovering from a recently pulled hamstring muscle, it is important to use activities that avoid the muscle becoming overly stretched, e.g. avoiding excessive running.

What if...?

As an appointed sport and activity leader for your local leisure facility, your employer has enabled you to attend a training event to gain further knowledge on how to support those with health needs. This has been a valuable opportunity and you have learnt much from the event. The course has made you aware how important physical activity is, and how you can adapt it to meet the needs of different participants. The course has also raised your awareness of keeping all your participants safe from harm throughout any activities you prepare. The course has taught you that it is important to remember that anyone who takes part in physical activity must be fit to do so.

1 Select three different medical conditions and give an outline of what they are and how they can affect an individual's participation.

2 Design activities that you could use to encourage their participation and that are suitable for someone with their medical condition.

3 Explain what measures you should take before leading the activities you have chosen.

Just as with any medical conditions, injuries should be checked thoroughly prior to taking part in physical activity. You should always try to protect the participant from any further injury. If an injury requires full rest, e.g. a broken limb or severely damaged joint, then this is a priority in order to avoid any further damage. While there may be a desire to keep exercising, it is important that the body is allowed to recover through rest.

During a period of rest and recovery, fitness levels can drop, so make sure that anyone returning to exercise takes it slowly to avoid a repeat of injury. A drop in fitness levels can also cause a participant to tire more quickly, so develop activity sessions that are more gentle to start with, and build up the level so it gets progressively harder over the following weeks/months.

Environmental

As mentioned in 'Influences on participation for different groups', the availability of facilities can significantly affect sport and activity participation. A lack of **SPECIFIC OR ADAPTED FACILITIES** can create a barrier to participation for disabled users. (Specific or adapted facilities are those that are designed primarily for a target population, such as the disabled.) For example, any sports hall facility should have ramp or lift access for a disabled wheelchair user. Sporting activities may include wheelchair basketball, wheelchair rugby, indoor tennis, etc., and all require an appropriate indoor facility. As a result, the facility has been specifically adapted to support the needs of the user. The Equality Act 2010 protects the rights of the disabled, making it unlawful to discriminate against people in respect of their disability. It is important that facilities are adapted to allow the disabled full access, alongside able-bodied participants.

What if...?

You have been asked to lead a sport and activity session at your local leisure facility. However, you are aware that the facilities could make it difficult for your participants to gain access. You decide to view the facilities in advance to check for access issues in order to perform an activity class of your choice.

1   Visit a leisure facility and identify the barriers that could restrict disabled participants from taking part.

2   Identify methods to overcome these barriers, by making recommendations for specific and adapted facilities.

3   Why is it important that you provide access for all, regardless of physical and psychological abilities?

The availability of facilities within the local area can determine the activities on offer, and may be a barrier to participation. For example, the number of swimming pool facilities available in local communities is currently in decline. These are expensive to run and represent an ongoing maintenance cost. Although it is generally known that swimming is an excellent form of exercise for fitness, and learning to swim is a vital life skill, lack of money is forcing many sport and leisure centres to close their pools, denying the local community the opportunity to participate in this fun activity.

Another example is the use of 4G pitches (multi-purpose all-weather activity surfaces). Some leisure providers are investing large sums of money in order to provide these facilities; however, with an area the same size as a football pitch and costing as much as £800,000, they are not cheap. While expensive, they do have many benefits over traditional grass pitches, and are often used to play a range of activities that would otherwise be limited by poor weather conditions.

Allianz Park is the home of Saracens rugby team and has a unique 4G surface.

Many sport and leisure providers create INITIATIVES (also known as campaigns) to encourage people to take part in sport within the community. The aim is to provide opportunities for people to keep fit, develop their talents, create new hobbies and interests and to socialise and to enjoy free leisure time.

While these initiatives can be successful, a lack of adequate transport can prevent many from taking part. Leisure and activity facilities are often built near good transport links, with some bus companies offering a service to and from the leisure centre. By providing good transport links, it is more likely to encourage people to attend and participate in sport and activity.

Psychological

As you learned earlier, it is not unusual for some participants to lack self-confidence when taking part in physical activity. For those who have not participated in much physical activity in the past, it is understandable that they might feel self-conscious in front of others, whatever their age or background. This anxiety could be owing to a fear of injury or a perceived lack of skill, or to simply being worried or anxious that something will go wrong. Other reasons include:

- lack of motivation
- a belief that they are 'not the sporty type'
- they have never enjoyed sport before
- they feel self-conscious in front of others
- they are anxious about the changing facilities.

Psychological barriers are particularly problematic in activities such as cycling, skating and skiing. For example, cycling is a very good form of exercise for general fitness, and over 1.5 million people cycle regularly in the UK. For some, taking up cycling as a new sport can be intimidating. They might fear potential injury from falling off, or be anxious about being hit by a car while cycling on the road. Some may feel that they cannot ride a bike as it has been so long since they tried. Encouragement is key, and with some practice they can soon build skills and self-confidence.

A3 Benefits of sport and physical activity

As a sport and activity leader, you will be required to educate your participants on the benefits of exercise. You may have been told on many occasions that it is important to keep yourself fit and healthy. But why is it important? Knowing that it is important is one thing, knowing the reasons why is another.

Practise

What do you already know about the benefits of sport and activity for the body? Think about the following questions.

1 What do you think are the physical benefits of exercise?

2 Using a PowerPoint presentation, provide five different adaptations you could expect to take place in your body as a result of regular physical activity.

3 Summarise your presentation with an outline of the improvements those adaptations may have on your overall health.

Physical

It is widely recognised that physical activity has many benefits for the body. Regular exercise can help reduce many life-threatening illnesses and medical conditions, such as heart disease, diabetes and even cancer. Exercise is not a cure for these conditions, however, it can reduce the risk of them developing. Exercise and physical activity give you the greatest opportunity to live a long and healthy life.

Medical research has shown that as little as 150 minutes of regular exercise throughout the week can significantly reduce your risk of illness or a health-related condition developing. Table 7.3 summarises some of these.

Table 7.3: Benefits of regular exercise on reducing the risk of illness, (adapted from www.NHS.uk/Livewell)

Medical condition	Reduction in risk
Heart Disease and Stroke	up to 35%
Type 2 Diabetes	up to 50%
Breast Cancer	up to 20%
Colon Cancer	up to 50%
Depression	up to 30%
Dementia	up to 30%
Osteoarthritis	up to 83%
Early death	up to 30%

Many of the conditions named in Table 7.3 can lead to early death. The earlier you start exercising in life, the greater the long-term benefits you will feel.

Many people think that exercise means going to a gym, and the thought of doing this is just too much effort. However, exercise does not have to take place in an indoor gym. Nor does it have to be excessive to be of benefit. The only rule is that it should be active, and simple changes to a daily routine can make a big difference. For example, instead of driving to the local shops, walk to them. Instead of driving to the station, walk there. While it appears minimal, over a long period of time, small changes such as these can make all the difference to your health.

The long-term improvements to health and fitness from regular exercise can include:

- a fitter, stronger heart
- an increase in the efficiency of lungs and improved breathing
- improved blood circulation to carry oxygen around the body
- a reduction in blood pressure
- stronger muscles, bones and joints
- a reduction in early symptoms of arthritis
- a decrease in symptoms of osteoporosis (a weakening of the bone structure).

Regular exercise is also important for weight control over a long period of time. While a healthy diet is always important, the amount of exercise you perform is key to weight control. It is a question of balance: the amount you eat must be used by your body in equal measure. For example, chocolate bars can contain as much as 200 calories, which equates to the amount of calories burnt during an hour of fast walking. So next time you eat something sweet, consider how many calories it contains and the amount of exercise you will need to complete to remove it.

By taking part in some form of exercise regularly, you can manage existing medical conditions, such as high blood pressure, cardiovascular disease, osteoporosis, obesity, diabetes and back pain. Epilepsy has also been shown to be improved as a result of light aerobic activity, reducing the stress that may trigger seizures throughout day-to-day living. Remember, exercise does not have to involve a strenuous gym work out or a high-impact aerobics class. It can consist of regular walking, cycling or jogging. When leading different groups of participants, consider how you can motivate them to be active and the benefits it could bring to their health by sharing this knowledge.

Psychological/emotional

Exercise and activity is very important for psychological and emotional well-being (see Figure 7.1). Exercise helps to release hormones that make you feel good about yourself. You may have experienced this soon after finishing an exercise session, as you usually feel so much better for it. This is due to the release of endorphins, often referred to as pleasure hormones, which can create a psychological 'high' following exercise.

As exercise releases large quantities of endorphins it can help to improve your psychological well-being by reducing depression, stress and anxiety. This, in turn, will enhance your self-esteem and positive mood. Endorphins can also block feelings of pain and discomfort, which is why feelings of soreness and tiredness will be minimal during an exercise period, and why an injury during a game does not feel as painful as it will a couple of hours later.

Why is exercise good for the brain?

- Boosts memory
- Increases neurochemicals that promote brain cell repair
- Lengthens attention span
- Prompts growth of new nerve cells and blood vessels
- Improves decision-making skills
- Enhances multitasking and planning

Figure 7.1: Examples of the psychological benefits of exercise.

The post-exercise feeling of relaxation makes you feel at ease with yourself, and this boosts your ability to handle daily stresses and strains. Often when contemplating exercise, you really do not feel like it and look for excuses not to go – perhaps you feel too tired, or decide to go tomorrow instead. Remembering the pleasure feeling that you get after an exercise session is a huge motivator – physical activity nearly always ends with that 'feel-good' factor.

Social

Exercise is a good way of socialising with like-minded people. If you attend a gym, play a team sport or engage in regular walking with a group of ramblers, there are plenty of opportunities to make new friends and socialise. For example, when playing a team sport, such as rugby, socialising is an important part of team bonding, and teammates soon become friends. Similarly, attendance at a gym-based class gives you the opportunity to make friends, and walking with a group allows you to develop friendships while participating in a very enjoyable activity.

Feelings of isolation are often accompanied by negativity and depression. When you foster a connection with your community by getting involved in a group physical activity this sense of separation and loneliness will be reduced. Everyone thrives on making new friends and communicating with them. Exercise provides the opportunity to socialise and develop a support network of friendships, many of which may be lifelong.

Skills and knowledge check

- ☐ What are the main medical and health barriers to sport and physical activity?
- ☐ Name the barriers that can influence the participation of women in sport.
- ☐ Name the barriers that can influence participation in disability sport.
- ☐ Provide examples of why role models are important to the success of sports participation.
- ☐ Why is the sport and activity leader important in overcoming barriers to participating in exercise?

- ◯ I can explain what the social benefits of physical activity are.
- ◯ I can help support someone to overcome the psychological barriers to exercise.
- ◯ I can explain what the health benefits of physical activity are.

If you have been unable to give positive responses to any of the questions or statements above, please go back and review the section.

Ready for assessment (part 1)

You work with the local sports development officer and have been tasked to try and encourage people into sport and activity. You are aware that many people in your community could be more active, though they are unaware of the benefits and opportunities available to them.

Your manager informs you that this needs to change so you decide to look into the benefits of participation, and how you can encourage your community. Using a PowerPoint presentation, you must present your findings to your boss during the next team meeting.

1 Analyse the influences on and benefits of participation in sport and physical activity for three different groups.

2 Explain how any barriers to participation can be overcome, offering effective solutions.

3 Provide a printed handout of the presentation for them to take away to discuss with senior executives. It is important you take time to ensure all your details are clear and well presented.

B Show how sport and physical activity can meet the needs of different groups

B1 Provision of sport and physical activity for different groups

Using adapted equipment or activities for different groups

As you know, it is very important that you try to provide opportunities for everyone within sport and activities. To achieve this you can adapt equipment and activities to accommodate different groups to allow participation. The changes you make can still keep the sport theme, but you can make the activities more suitable for the specific group you are working with.

For example, in children's rugby, there is often a concern, particularly among parents, that tackling may hurt, or that there is a risk of serious injury when tackling. To overcome this, the session can be adapted to touch rugby, where touch is used to represent a tackle. Many of the other rules remain similar to the traditional game. This adaptation enables children to develop ball skills for passing and catching, along with gaining an awareness of the rules of the game, and fostering the respect and self-discipline that are needed in rugby.

Walking football is another sport that has been adapted to promote inclusivity. Many elderly or active retired individuals may not be able to run great distances or have sufficient agility to enjoy football on a full-sized or five-a-side pitch. Due to the pace of the game, they may not be able to keep up making it less enjoyable to play. Walking football uses a five-a-side pitch and enables the elderly and active retired to play football but with the adaptation of allowing only walking on the pitch. The game remains as exciting, rules remain similar to the standard game, however, the game pace is much slower, which enables those less mobile to take part.

Walking football provides a smaller, slower paced version of the full sized regular game.

Goalball is an exciting ball game played by visually impaired sports participants. The game uses a ball that has a bell inside in order to allow the players to determine its location on a court. The playing area is approximately the same size as an indoor volleyball court. The aim of the game is to roll or bounce the ball down to the opponent's end to score a goal past their defence. The defence will attempt to block the ball and gain control. The adaptation of equipment enables the visually impaired participants to rely on their sense of hearing, making for an exciting and challenging game.

A competitive game of goalball. The ball contains a bell and the visually impaired participants must defend the goal based on the whereabouts of the sound of the ball.

What if...?

You have been asked by a disability rehabilitation centre to help provide some adapted games for their patients. They have a group of 12 partially sighted learners, 10 wheelchair participants, and 10 limb amputee participants. As the group is diverse you need to ensure you are able to prepare two games for each group of disabled participants.

Provide two different games for each of the disabled participants, e.g. two games for partially sighted, two for wheelchair participants, and two for amputee participants. The games must be exciting and enjoyable for all. You must include a scoring system and an end point to the game, i.e. there will be a winner and runner-up.

For some, participating in sport and activity at a gym or leisure centre can be expensive. This does not always have to be the case. Some local leisure providers are able to offer **SUBSIDISED ACTIVITIES** (e.g. reduced prices for those on low income or income support), such as swim access, and games such as football and basketball. This is a supportive method that helps to overcome the financial burden of some sporting activities, enabling people to keep fit while seeking employment.

Although some sporting activities can be expensive, there are plenty of activities that can be enjoyed at a very low cost. For example, running, stair climbing, trim trails and DIY bootcamps. Changes in lifestyle can also enhance fitness, for example, cycling to work instead of taking the car, and fast walking instead of your normal pace. All these require a minimal financial outlay, and all are good methods of keeping fit and healthy.

Acknowledging different needs and exploring how to meet them

As you have seen, the benefits of exercise extend far beyond just the taking part. Exercise can help you make new friends and build your self-confidence. **COOPERATIVE GAMES** (such as rugby, football, netball, and basketball) are great games for working as part of a team, developing communication skills and working towards group achievement. The feeling of being part of a team can be exhilarating, helping to produce positive body language and good communication skills and raise self-esteem while reducing stress and pressures of the day. Sport and activity have an important function within the lives of participants, and can spread enjoyment across a wide-ranging population.

B2 Initiatives to promote increased participation

Children and teenagers

Understanding the positive benefits of exercise for your health and the enjoyment it brings is important when you try to encourage others to take part. There are many initiatives today that promote physical activity for children and teenagers. These include:

- *Get On Track* – Led by Olympic athlete Dame Kelly Holmes, this initiative encourages more than 3000 vulnerable young adults between the ages of 16 and 25 to take part in sport and activity. It aims to encourage participants to keep playing sport and become sports mentors within the community.
- *Sporting Champions* – An initiative that supports the Sainsbury's School Games Festivals. Retired athletes and sports performers provide their expertise and knowledge to help inspire young people into sport.
- *StreetGames* – A charity that helps more than 600 community organisations to take part in sport. The aim is to change the lives of disadvantaged young people through the delivery of sport within the community. It supports a range of sporting activities through funding from the National Lottery.

> **Practise**
>
> There are many initiatives that aim to improve and develop talent both within sport and within a wider context, as citizens.
>
> 1 What could be the benefit of children and teenagers participating in sport within the community and not just within school?
>
> 2 How does the National Lottery support sports participation within the community?
>
> 3 How would you, as a sport and activity leader, benefit from the activities you are able to offer? *(Provide a real-life example from a community you are aware of.)*

Women

Like the promotion of sport for children and teenagers, there are many initiatives and organisations that aim to encourage female participation in sport. These include:

- *Active Women* – An organisation that promotes the development of a healthy lifestyle in the Southend-on-Sea area. It provides free exercise sessions for women in activities such as Zumba, boot camp, Pilates, yoga and aerobics.
- *This Girl Can* – Developed by Sport England, this national campaign promotes female participation in sport and activity, along with celebrating their successes. The campaign aims to overcome the fears women have of judgement when taking part in activity.
- *Go Where Women Are* – A campaign that aims to engage women who are coming to terms with physical or emotional difficulties. It provides opportunities for women to remove the barriers and emotional triggers in their life to become more physically active and, in turn, to help overcome any emotional issues they may have.
- *I Will If You Will* – A programme that markets sports and activity sessions for women to encourage participation. It aims to overcome the barriers that typically prevent women from taking part in regular activity. It promotes sports participation while helping them overcome emotional and self-confidence concerns.

People with disabilities

As you have previously covered, disability sport has become very popular in recent years. This has been spurred on by the successes Great Britain achieved within the 2012 London Paralympic Games. Many initiatives continue to develop its popularity, encouraging participation and providing specialist facilities for those who compete.

- *Get Equipped* – A disability fund that aims to promote sports participation across 145 local sports clubs. It provides support by purchasing equipment to encourage inclusivity regarding the disabled population.
- *Inclusive Sport* – A sports programme that aims to increase disability sport with the community. It is overseen by Sport England and provides support for participants of 14+ years of age.

What if...?

You have been asked to develop ideas for a promotional campaign for participants with disabilities. The aim is to increase mass participation, therefore you must ensure you meet the needs of your local community. Before you begin your campaign you need to research what other opportunities are out there. There are many programmes already in existence, so it is essential that your analysis reveals what is already on offer.

1 Select four of these initiatives and provide examples within clubs, gyms and associations where these are used. These must be actual examples, which are currently being used by appropriate organisations.

2 Provide a summary of their use and what they are achieving.

BME/BAME

The promotion of sport and activity for BME/BAME groups continues to be a very important component of encouraging inclusivity. Initiatives such as Sporting Equals, and campaigns such as 'Let's Kick Racism Out of Football', aim to promote equality and remove racist attitudes from sport. It is very important that you always promote tolerance and respect.

Many campaigns aim to promote sporting activities across a range of cultures and ethnic backgrounds. Within sports such as basketball and cricket, approximately two-thirds of the participants are from a BAME background, however, in sports such as cycling and golf, BAME participation is minimal. Campaigns and increasing awareness of successful role models are helping to break down the barriers of participation, and balance the participation of groups across sports.

Promotional campaigns try to not only encourage participant numbers, but also develop a greater number of coaches from ethnic minority groups. In 2015, of the 230 clubs that make up the top seven divisions of English football, just 14 of the managers were black. This is not uncommon in many sports, and campaigns are often used to promote coaching and team managing for all BAME groups.

Unemployed

The unemployed may be supported by a range of local initiatives within the community to encourage their interest in keeping fit. One such initiative could be reducing participation costs for community sport such as swimming, football and basketball.

Charity programmes such as Street League aim to promote education through the use of physical activity. Free sport is coupled with employment courses for individuals aged 16–24. These courses aim to develop work and job-seeking skills, such as interviews and CVs for future career applications. By combining activity with education for the unemployed, it supported over 1200 young people into employment, education and training in 2015–16 and continues to encourage individuals back into the workplace.

The combination of jobs and sport can prove a successful one, and it is important to remember that activity can be used as a positive tool to help support the unemployed.

Skills and knowledge check

☐ What is meant by the term inclusivity?

☐ Name the environmental barriers to participation in sport and physical activity.

☐ Name and explain four barriers to exercise participation for the elderly and active retired.

☐ Provide six physical, psychological and social benefits to exercise.

☐ Why is it important we use initiatives to encourage participation in sport and activity?

◯ I can develop games and activities to promote inclusivity among disabled participants.

◯ I know how to respond to racism in sport and activity.

◯ I am aware of a range of initiatives that encourage mass sport and activity participation.

If you have been unable to give positive responses to any of the questions or statements above, please go back and review the section.

Ready for assessment (part 2)

The work you produced for your manager went down well with senior executives and they have asked for your help again. The presentation you produced on the benefits of exercise and the barriers that are limiting mass participation was very interesting.

As a result of your good work, they have asked you to produce an effective, detailed plan to encourage people to take part in sport. They have asked you to select two groups from a list they have produced and develop a further PowerPoint presentation to be delivered within the executives' meeting.

They want you to base your plan on two of the following:

a) Children and teenage participants

b) Female participants

c) Disabled participants

d) BAME participants

e) Unemployed participants

1 Select two different groups on which to present a plan.

2 Produce a plan that could encourage your chosen groups to take part.

3 Provide a printed handout of the presentation for the executives to take away to discuss with senior management. It is important you take time to ensure all your details are clear and well presented.

WORK FOCUS

HANDS ON

There are some important occupational skills and competencies that you will need to practise, which relate to this unit. Developing these and practising them could help you to gain employment as a sport and activity leader who supports different groups.

1 Work as part of a team.

- Take part in a practical activity that involves a coordinated task, e.g. create a raft or move people using restrictive equipment.

- In an activity, provide ideas and contributions, and avoid non-participation.

2 Show you can respect work colleagues, other professionals and adults who come to the setting.

- Greet a friend/colleague/customer with an appropriate smile, tone of voice and welcoming positive approach.

- Always use appropriate and positive body language. Avoid crossing arms, wild arm gestures or a threatening tone.

3 Use appropriate verbal communication with adults in the setting.

- Use appropriate spoken language to describe and explain the points your friend/colleague/customer may need to understand.

- Never swear and avoid signs of anger and frustration.

Ready for work?

Take this short quiz to find out whether you would be the person chosen for that dream job.

1 On your first day at work you should...

- [ ] A dress to impress
- [ ] B turn up late
- [ ] C use your phone for personal texts and calls
- [ ] D avoid asking questions.

2 When working with elderly participants you should...

- [ ] A create activity plans to support their needs
- [ ] B work them hard, regardless of their ability
- [ ] C speak quietly
- [ ] D ignore them.

3 When struggling to complete a task you should...

- [ ] A try your best to complete it
- [ ] B ask for help
- [ ] C give up and tell someone
- [ ] D do something else.

4 When working with a young participant you should...

- [ ] A show encouragement to help them succeed
- [ ] B watch and say nothing
- [ ] C shout at bad performances
- [ ] D get angry.

5 When leading a group of disabled participants you should...

- [ ] A check they are okay regularly
- [ ] B create interesting activities to support their needs
- [ ] C show little interest in supporting the participants
- [ ] D show little interest in adapting the activities.

Your score:

If you scored mostly Ds, you may need to brush up on your interpersonal skills. If you scored mainly As then you are ready for employment; if you gained mainly Bs and Cs you should go back and read through the section again.

8 Delivering a Sports Activity Event

The role of a sport and activity leader can be varied, from leading activities and coaching different groups, to getting people active and encouraging them to develop new skills, or developing appropriate sports events. When creating your own sports event, it is important that you are able to take charge confidently, or to support the delivery of activities, in order for the event to run smoothly. To be successful, it is important that you are able to work with others, communicate effectively and do lots of 'behind the scenes' planning.

In this unit, you will develop an understanding of how to organise and deliver a one-off sports activity event that may extend across a full day. You will explore the important roles needed to contribute to its success, as well as appreciate and understand the various roles necessary for the day to go well. You should be able to identify the resources you may need, as well as how they will be used throughout your event. You will become familiar with how to promote an event, draw up an event plan, develop a schedule of play and ensure it is delivered clearly to all of the participants. After the event, you will review your own performance, to reflect on your successes and identify areas where you could improve in the future.

How will I be assessed?

This unit will develop your skills to deliver a range of activities to prepare you for work within a sport and activity leadership environment. Your assessment will be practically based and designed by your tutors so as to reflect your future working career. This unit will be a synoptic assessment, requiring you to plan, carry out and evaluate a sports activity event that you have led or contributed to its completion.

The assessment evidence may be in the form of an event plan, a logbook of documents including plans, observation records and/or annotated filmed footage or photographs of the event. The assessment will be spread across much of the duration of your course, allowing you the opportunity to draw upon the knowledge and skills gained throughout the qualification.

Assessment criteria

Pass	Merit	Distinction
Learning aim A: Plan a sports activity event		
A.P1 Produce a suitable plan for a sports activity event, identifying the factors to be considered for delivery and the roles and responsibilities of those involved.	**A.M1** Produce a detailed plan for a sports activity event, describing the factors to be considered for delivery and explaining the roles and responsibilities of those involved.	**A.D1** Produce a detailed plan for a sports activity event, justifying the factors to be considered for delivery and analysing the importance of roles and responsibilities of those involved.
Learning aim B: Demonstrate teamwork skills to achieve an agreed goal		
B.P2 Show appropriate teamwork skills to achieve an agreed goal when contributing to organising and delivering an event.	**B.M2** Show effective teamwork skills to achieve an agreed goal when contributing to organising and delivering an event.	**B.D2** Show effective and consistent teamwork skills and initiative to achieve an agreed goal when contributing to organising and delivering an event.
Learning aim C: Evaluate your own contribution to event and make recommendations for improvement		
C.P3 Identify individual contribution to organising and delivering an event and set targets to improve future performance.	**C.M3** Describe individual contribution to organising and delivering an event and explain set targets to improve future performance, identifying strategies to achieve them.	**C.D3** Evaluate individual contribution to organising and delivering an event and justify set targets to improve future performance, describing strategies to achieve them.

A Plan a sports activity event

Link it up

Go back to Unit 7 and look again at inclusivity and ways of ensuring opportunities for everyone to get involved.

A1 Types of suitable sports events

As a sport and activity leader, it is important that you are able to prepare and plan suitable events to meet the needs of selected **PARTICIPANTS**. The participants may be of different ability and skill levels and have different individual support needs. As a sport and activity leader responsible for organising the event, it is important you choose the most appropriate activity to ensure everyone is involved. The key term is **INCLUSIVITY** – you are trying to get all participants involved and ensure they enjoy the activities provided.

Small-scale sports events and competitions

To support introductory events, it is useful to include small-scale sports events and competitions. These are activities that require fewer participants, or less competitive space, yet include basic skills of the game. For example, you could create a half-court 3v3 netball competition, or a five-a-side football match. Competitions such as these **SMALL-SIDED GAMES** involve a competitive application on a smaller scale, and this will encourage the development of player skills, eventually leading to a full-size game. Games such as badminton and tennis can also be used for small-scale participation by reducing the space, e.g. short tennis or half-court badminton.

The main focus of these small-scale events is to promote enjoyment and encourage participation. You may have come across similar activities at school, as they are popular as lunchtime or after-school sports clubs, and are often good fun as they provide the opportunity to turn up and try games and activities, which you would not have otherwise participated in. Small-scale competitions are also popular with school sports day events as they can encourage learners to take part in a competitive event in a less formal activity, either through individual participation or inter-form team events, e.g. five-a-side football or netball.

Competition formats

There are many different **COMPETITION FORMATS** you can use to encourage participation. The aim of a competition is to allow participant(s) to play against each other. Two forms of competition you can use are:

- round-robin tournaments
- knockout tournaments.

Round-robin tournaments provide the opportunity for all players/teams to play one another, regardless of whether they lost or won their previous game. Unlike a knockout tournament, a round-robin enables the player/team to play all games and not leave the tournament after one game should they lose. A table may be set for each of the teams to play one another a maximum of two times, allowing for points to be collected for a win, loss or draw. In this format, a player/team could win a tournament despite losing games throughout the competition. Figure 8.1 shows an example of a score sheet template for a round-robin tournament.

Player/Team name	1	2	3	4	5	6	7	8	Total points	Final position
1:										
2:										
3:										
4:										
5:										
6:										
7:										
8:										

Win = 3 points
Draw = 1 point
Lose = 0 points

Figure 8.1: Template for a round-robin tournament/competition

What if...?

You have been asked to prepare a round-robin sports activity in the sports hall for an indoor racket sport, e.g. badminton and/or table tennis. There are six participants who all need to play each other and you have been asked to design a tournament that will allow this.

1 Prepare a round-robin schedule for each of your six players so that they play one another within the competition.

2 Complete the tournament using the round-robin structure, recording the results from each game.

3 Accurately determine the final position and winner.

A knockout tournament differs from a round-robin tournament in that a player/team can be 'knocked out' of a tournament after they compete in their first game, if they lose. The tournament relies on a simple win or lose format, with the winner progressing to the next round and onto the final, where they compete for first place. A knockout competition is often used within the final stages of a competition, such as the final 16 of a tournament. Players/teams will play another team, who they have been drawn against and then progress through the competition to the final. Figure 8.2 shows how a knockout tournament is structured.

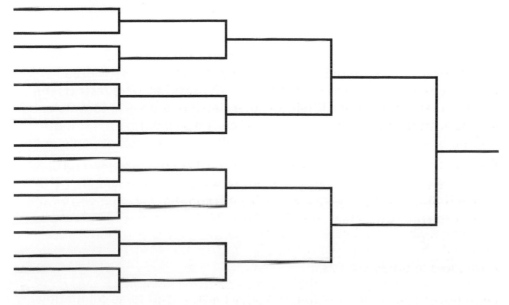

Figure 8.2: Template for a knockout competition

Indoor and outdoor events

When creating a tournament, try to think about the wide range of locations available. Activities and events can take place in a range of locations, including sports days in a park or fun runs on closed roads. The venue you select – whether for a five-a-side football tournament, a basketball tournament, a short-tennis tournament or a table tennis tournament – will have both benefits and potential problems. It is important to consider these in advance.

For example, while not all events/activities/tournaments are suitable to take place outside (e.g. table tennis, badminton), others can benefit from such a venue (e.g. athletics, tag rugby). Outdoor facilities can provide plenty of space to take part, as well as rest and spectator areas. However, there are always possible problems with outdoor locations – even in the middle of summer it is impossible to predict the weather. If the weather is wet then this may cause problems, such as muddy conditions and slip hazards. It is made more problematic if the event is held on grass. The weather can also influence participants' enjoyment of the event, as not many people enjoy getting wet. You should always be mindful of issues such as this when planning an outdoor event.

A successful sports day will have ample space for supporting friends and family to cheer on the participants.

While indoor activities may avoid weather problems, they may present other issues, such as limited space. For example, a five-a-side football tournament will take up most, if not all, of a sports hall. This restricts the space available to non-participants (e.g. a viewing audience) to watch and engage with the activities. A restricted area can also hinder the smooth running of the event, which again could influence participants' enjoyment.

With all this in mind, remember to always consider the location and venue for your event carefully. While you want to encourage enjoyment, try to remain realistic and choose a location that is suitable for what you would like to achieve, both safely and effectively.

Sponsored charity events

It is important to remember that not all activities need to be competitive. Many people enjoy the 'taking part' rather than winning. There are many opportunities for encouraging participation in an activity, such as **SPONSORED CHARITY EVENTS**. These events can include walks, bike rides and fun runs. Opportunities for sponsored participation are plentiful and aim to provide a fun experience rather than a competitive one. Sponsored events target participants of all ages, abilities and support needs. Examples include:

- the London Marathon and other marathon events
- the Great Run events
- Race for Life
- London to Paris cycle ride
- local area charity fun run, walk and cycle activity events.

Participants raising money for one of many worthy charities nationwide.

A2 Factors to consider when planning a suitable sports event

When preparing an event, you will need to plan it carefully, and most importantly write your planning down (see Figure 8.3). There are many factors that you need to consider in order for your event to be a success.

Suitable formats for event planning

When planning a sports event, it is important to take time to develop its structure (thinking about what you would like to achieve and what the content of your event will be). You should consider the format of the event and how you could present the event plan for others to follow. For example, you could consider:

- *duration*: How long will the event last? Will it be an afternoon, a full day or an evening event? Remember, if it is too long, participants may become bored or tired and lose interest
- *resources*: What do you need? How much do you need and where will it come from? Inadequate numbers or broken equipment can affect the delivery of the activity, e.g. you will need sufficient badminton rackets for a knockout tournament
- *participant/organiser numbers*: How many people will be involved? How many people do you need to help support you on the day? Too

many participants with too few organisers can be chaos. Make sure you are able to keep the event under control and ensure everyone is informed about what they should be doing and when

- *venue:* As mentioned above, this is an important component to the success of an event. Ensure it is safe, appropriate and suitable for both the participant numbers and the event you are going to deliver.

These are all important factors to consider when planning a sports event, so make sure you take your time to think about all of these issues and prepare your event plan carefully.

Aims and objectives of the event

Your event plan should show the **AIMS** and **OBJECTIVES** of the event. Think about what you are trying to get out of the session.

- Are you trying to improve participants' fitness? If so, you will need to include lots of activities that will develop this, e.g. running in a ball game to improve aerobic endurance.
- Are you trying to develop skills? If so, consider the skill you want to develop and what activities could be used to support this, e.g. a gymnast doing a handstand could start off supported and progress through to becoming independent.
- Are you trying to make it a fun day to introduce new sports? If so, you could create fun activities to encourage participants throughout the day, e.g. an introduction to the sport of handball could develop basic throwing and passing skills that progress to a full game event.

An introduction to new sports such as handball can increase participation and competition.

Nature of the event

In order to run a successful event, you need to plan carefully and focus on what you aim to gain from the day. What is the nature of the event you want to lead? In your plan, you should include the activity type, the number of participants and where it is to be held. As you have already covered when looking at indoor and outdoor events, the size and location of the event can be critical to its success. For example, for a large charity fun run to improve people's fitness, it would be more suitable to hold it on a field or on a closed road rather than in a sports hall. Similarly, if you are organising a skills development event for football for a small group of players, using a full-size pitch may not be suitable as it could be too big to perform skills-related play. An alternative location might be a smaller five-a-side pitch, where the smaller group can listen better and you, as coach, can be close enough to all the participants to give meaningful feedback.

Figure 8.3 shows an example of an event plan template on which you could base your own plan.

Link it up

For more on adapting activities and facilities to suit the needs of participants, go to Unit 7.

EVENT PLAN			
Event:		**Date:**	
		Duration:	
Venue:		**Age group of participants:**	
		Size of group:	
Preparation check:			

Preparation check:

    Correct staffing (separate sheet with list of names)

    Advertising information

    Venue prepared

    Welcoming team

    Equipment checked (list on a separate sheet)

    Refreshments available (inc. toilets)

    Access to all facilities

    Safety check (inc. risk assessment and first aid)

    Lost property area

Emergency contact:

Facilities contact:

Event aims and objectives:

Event plan

Task (inc. time)	Component	Delivery plan	Organiser / facilitator
Welcome / introduction	\<Brief outline of content\>	\<Full content of task\>	\<Person responsible\>
Warm up			
Main activity			
Cool down			
Close			

Figure 8.3: A typical event plan template

Link it up

For more information on medical support needs for active participants, and for adapting activities to meet the needs of different participants, go back to Unit 1 and Unit 7.

Participants

Once you understand the aims and objects of your event, you should consider the type of participants you are trying to involve. Your target participants may vary and you should consider their:

- *age*: this could range from primary and secondary school groups, to college students
- *ability level*: your group might comprise accomplished performers or beginners and novices
- *medical support needs*: your participants may have health conditions (e.g. asthma, epilepsy) that require adapted activities.

It is important that the activities you choose are relevant to your participants. They should be exciting and engaging for your target group throughout. Adapting games to meet the needs of participants can also be beneficial to the success of an activity.

When planning for primary level children and younger, it is beneficial to create activities that are not too complex, and that develop simple skills. For this young age group, it is important to keep activities fun as this will encourage participation. The ability of younger children to complete complex activities is significantly less than for older children, so your planning should consider this carefully. If a group of children keep complaining that they 'can't do it' or 'it's too difficult', then they are more likely to give up. Similarly, if the activity is too easy for an older age group, children may become bored and lose interest without even completing the activity.

Event timing considerations

The length of time you spend on each of the activities should be appropriate – you do not want participants to become bored, but neither do you want them to feel rushed. Pacing is key to ensure you have enough time to meet your aims and objectives, but avoid participants becoming tired or disengaged.

There is inevitably a certain amount of introductory information to communicate at the start of the event, but avoid speaking at too much length at this stage as participants will be keen to make a start. Make your introduction welcoming, and explain clearly and concisely what you will be doing throughout the day. Be positive and enthusiastic, as this can create an upbeat start to the event. You will need to explain what activities will take place during the day, along with what the aims of the day are. Point out where the refreshments are, the first aid facilities, fire exits and safety procedures, should you be in an enclosed space such as a sports hall. Keep all details informative, clear and concise.

After an introduction, you can start to warm up your participants. A warm up is important as it helps prepare the participants for the activities ahead. Its main purpose is to act as a pulse raiser that causes the blood to carry warmth, oxygen, waste carbon dioxide gas and valuable nutrients to and from the working muscles. When the muscles are warmer, they are less likely to over-stretch and cause an injury, so it is important to have a thorough warm up at the start.

Your main activity will be dependent upon the nature of the event you are running. If the aim of your event is to develop a skill, then games and activities will need to be centred around this element. If you are preparing an activity for young children, you could prepare skill drills and games to encourage accuracy of a skill, or those that build upon basic skills. You can then structure your activities to make them progressively difficult.

For example, if you are preparing an activity session for basketball that aims to develop the skills of young children, you could use different drills and games to achieve this. Once you have completed a warm up, you could use a basic ball bouncing drill, using alternate hands while standing still. This could then be extended to alternate hands while walking and running. This could be further developed by getting the group to dribble around cones and then move on to dribbling racing games around cones to develop competition and encourage ball control. This could be one small **COMPONENT** of an activity event, and you should think carefully about how you can extend basic skills for fun.

Link it up

For more on the different types of sessions and their structure, go back to Unit 3.

Link it up

For more on types of drills and practices, go back to Unit 4.

Using some simple activities can help to develop a skilled basketball player.

The time you spend on each development or activity can vary, depending on the complexity of what you are trying to achieve. Remember, the time you allocate to an activity or event should be realistic. Try not to rush as participants may feel that they have not developed their skill sufficiently. Similarly, try to avoid excessive periods of time for a basic skill as it is easy for participants to become bored.

As part of the main event it is useful to include a game or competitive element at the end. This is often a good way of summarising what skills the participants have developed. To continue with the basketball example, you could have a small basketball game, or a miniature round-robin tournament with small teams (e.g. 3v3). A competitive game can be useful to end an event on a high, so consider this when completing any planning.

Following the main event, it is important you complete a full cool down for your participants. This will help with the recovery process and can prevent sore muscles and excessive fatigue soon after. Remember, when completing an event the participants are in your care so try to look after them and send them away with a positive feeling. Figure 8.4 shows an example of a step-by-step event day plan.

A fun mass warm-up for participants taking part in a charity fun run.

When closing the event, always remain positive and congratulate any good performances. Enthusiasm throughout an event is very important and ending on a high can leave the participants with an enjoyable recollection of the day.

EVENT DAY				
WELCOME	**WARM UP**	**MAIN ACTIVITIES**	**COOL DOWN**	**CLOSE**
Welcome your participants and explain the event. Give instructions and provide clear information on the facilities available.	Complete a 5 minute jog followed by warm up stretches. Use an aerobic component, stretches and games.	Deliver the main event with appropriate equipment. Include games and activities. Record results for closing comments.	Complete a slow jog followed by gentle stretches.	Provide event closing comments. Congratulations / prizes / special mentions. Give thanks to participants and organisers. Provide handouts for completion before participants leave.
Checklist				
Meet and greet participants Provide event instructions Inform participants of event facilities, e.g. toilets, refreshments, first aid, fire evacuation	Aerobic activity e.g. jog, game Warm up stretches Activity warm up game	Activity instructions Activity equipment, e.g. balls, bibs, cones, rackets, bats, posts, net, etc. Clipboard, pen and paper Game activity	Aerobic activity, e.g. jog, game Cool down stretches	Closing instructions Prizes / awards / feedback Questionnaires

Figure 8.4: An example of a step-by-step event day plan

Resources needed

You need to plan the resources you will need for your event. This will include additional facilities and access to additional equipment to overcome any difficulties that occur on the day. A good check prior to the event will ensure you are fully prepared. If, on the day, any resources are unavailable or there are not enough of any particular equipment (e.g. balls, rackets, cones, etc.), you will need a **CONTINGENCY PLAN** to deal with this. The plan will help you overcome difficulties such as unexpected weather conditions (e.g. rain), equipment restrictions (e.g. lost or insufficient numbers) or incidents during the activity (e.g. a flat ball) and many more. Having a good awareness of the available equipment can help you to prepare for the worst-case scenario and help your event run smoothly.

You might also want to think about how you can help participants remain comfortable throughout the event. The provision of refreshments can support this. You do not have to provide an extensive supply of different types of refreshments – a simple drinks station, water fountain and/or vending machine is sufficient. If free refreshments are available, then this can be a bonus for participants, however, providing them for free is not a necessity.

Link it up

There is more on contingency planning in Unit 1 and Unit 3.

Equipment awareness can help you to prepare your contingency plan.

A race drinks station at the Royal Parks Foundation Half Marathon provides extra comfort for participants.

Health and safety considerations

For the safety of participants it is important that there is a **FIRST AID RESOURCE** nearby. This might be in the form of a basic kit or a dedicated facility. It is important that a nominated, trained first-aider is available at the event in order to deal with any minor incidents. There should also be good access to a telephone/mobile phone in order to alert emergency services should an incident be more severe. It is important that a trained first-aider assesses any injury in order to ensure that the participant is safe at all times.

Participants' safety is paramount: to help you achieve this you should carry out a **RISK ASSESSMENT** (see Figure 8.5) prior to the event that identifies any potential areas of danger or **HAZARD** that may cause harm to your participants. Hazards may include things that cause slips, trips and falls, and danger from broken or faulty equipment, e.g. sharp edges, etc.

Link it up

For more on risk assessment go back to Unit 3.

EVENT RISK ASSESSMENT

Event organiser:		Event date	Time
Event:			
Location:			
Assessment carried out by:	(Print)	(Date)	(Sign)

Hazard	Who is at risk	Risk rating	Existing control measure	Preventative measures	Responsibility

Risk Rating = High / Medium / Low

Figure 8.5: A typical example of a risk assessment that may be used for an event (the number of hazards may be extended)

Practise

Make a copy of the event risk assessment form (Figure 8.5) that you can write/type on. For a sporting activity or event of your choice, complete a full risk assessment prior to it taking place.

1 Use the form to record any potential hazards that may be found within the activity space. Remember to show detail and think about it carefully. Consider slips, trips, falls, uneven surfaces, head height, sharp edges, equipment use, equipment storage, fire exits, etc. Remember, the number of rows can be expanded, so do not just limit your hazards to the five rows provided.

2 Identify who you feel is most at risk from the hazard, the participant group or other individuals (identify them).

3 Rate the risk that may be found with each of the hazards you have identified using 'High', 'Medium', 'Low'.

4 Identify the current existing control measures that are in place for each of your hazards. For example, tape, area storage, temporary fix, cleaning equipment (e.g. brush/mop).

5 Identify the methods that could be applied to prevent a hazard from occurring. For example, to avoid slippages, you could permit consumption of drinks only away from the playing surface.

6 Identify an individual, or group of individuals, who are responsible for maintaining the area.

7 With a partner, compare your form and responses. Justify each of your responses and complete a paired risk assessment to summarise both assessments.

Ready for assessment (part 1)

You have been tasked to prepare an event for a group of 20 children aged 6–8 years old. They will need to be warmed up using fun activities, have an enjoyable main event and a fun, active cool down. The children are all excitable youngsters who enjoy being very active, therefore this should be considered within your planning. Before you start to plan your session, you need to prepare a risk assessment for your event.

1 Make a copy of the event risk assessment form (Figure 8.5) that you can write/type on. Complete a risk assessment of the area that you aim to use for your event.

2 Prepare an event plan for your event. Decide on what type of event you want to deliver. Remember the children will not want to be static for long so make it active and as fun as possible.

3 Develop a series of fun warm up activities for the children.

4 Develop a main event that is interactive and enjoyable for the children to take part in. Remember this needs to be linked to your aims and objectives of your session.

5 Develop a fun and active cool down activity that can be used at the end of the session.

6 Provide two examples of how you could reward the children's efforts and explain the reasons why they may be suitable.

A3 Roles and responsibilities involved in planning and leading an event

When planning an event, it is important to remember that you cannot be everywhere at the same time. It is impossible for you to keep time, keep the score, serve refreshments and meet and greet new participants at the same time. Therefore, you should plan to delegate roles and responsibilities to fellow supporting organisers of an event.

Selecting individual roles and responsibilities

When establishing individual roles and responsibilities in a group, always play to your strengths. Select individuals for roles and responsibilities that allow your team of organisers to achieve the greatest success. The use of human resources can determine the success of an event, so it is always important to give it careful thought rather than just randomly choosing people. Some fellow organisers may have characteristics and qualities that suit a particular role. For example, a member of the support team may be very creative and therefore could be very good at creating advertising and communication literature. Another individual may be very outgoing and confident at approaching new guests with positive ENTHUSIASM, which may make them more suitable for meeting and greeting new participants.

Roles and responsibilities

There are a number of roles and responsibilities that need to be fulfilled in order to make an event run smoothly. These include:

- event advertising and communication
- equipment supervision, including preparation of facilities

- equipment setting up and taking down
- health and safety checking prior to and during an event
- a trained first-aider or access to facilities nearby
- meeting, greeting and directing participants to relevant areas
- event timekeeper (if appropriate)
- game scorer (if appropriate).

Take time to consider who will take on these varied roles – and remember, always build your team to their strengths.

What if....?

Your manager is organising an event that will be held in two weeks' time, and you have been asked to prepare some information to advertise it. The event is a fun day at your local leisure centre, and will include five activities for participants to try out for the first time. The advertising must be eye-catching and grab the attention of a passing audience to encourage them to take part.

1 Prepare a poster that advertises the event. Remember, it must be eye-catching, clear and concise. Use plenty of colour if possible and include a date and time. Pictures are useful and can help catch the attention of the passing audience. Remember to include a list of the five activities.

2 Produce a small programme for the event. It should include an eye-catching front cover, brief introduction to the day and a programme of event timings.

3 Ask someone to explain the event from your advertising. Are they able to give all the information accurately, based on what is shown?

4 Reflect on what the strengths and weaknesses are of using paper-based or online advertising.

Figure 8.6: Event advertising for a college sports event.

As an organiser, you have a range of responsibilities that you must fulfil throughout an event. These can be divided into two categories:

- **CORE RESPONSIBILITIES** – ensuring you follow appropriate professional conduct, maintaining event health and safety and providing **INCLUSIVITY** and **EQUALITY**
- wider responsibilities – maintaining child protection policies and procedures, following **LEGAL OBLIGATIONS**, conducting activities in an ethically correct manner and ensuring that appropriate rules and regulations are followed.

Core responsibilities

As an organiser, you have a range of important core responsibilities. These influence the way you behave in front of the participants and surrounding audiences. Your **PROFESSIONAL CONDUCT** must be just that, professional. For example, the tone of your voice and the language you use should be appropriate, polite and respectful. You should never use malicious verbal content nor should you behave in a way that makes your participants feel uncomfortable. Remember, your participants are there for a fun event because they *want* to be there, not because they *have* to be.

As mentioned above, maintaining health and safety is key to avoiding incidents and hazards that could cause harm to your participants. When a participant is involved in activities that you have prepared, they are in your care, so look after them. You should always pay attention to their needs and support their safe inclusion within the activities. Individual participants may have particular needs, for example, wheelchair users will require wheelchair access to a sports hall. You should also consider whether the area is safe for them to enter. As part of your core responsibilities, you should consider carefully whether all participants have an equal opportunity to take part in the activity or event.

Link it up

Go back to Unit 1 to find more information on equal opportunities and health and safety.

Wider responsibilities

As part of your wider responsibilities, you must ensure that you follow **CHILD PROTECTION POLICIES** and **SAFEGUARDING LEGISLATION**. These are legal obligations that are outlined within the Children Act 2004, which must be followed in order to protect the safety and welfare of participants under the age of 18. It is extremely important that the welfare of participants in this age group is a priority, and you should understand the expectation of appropriate behaviour. Any activity should be ethically sound, meaning that you should conduct yourself responsibly and with integrity. You should make every effort to minimise the risk of harm to those in your care and treat all with respect and dignity. For example, you should avoid unnecessary physical contact and ensure participants are appropriately clothed throughout. Following appropriate sporting rules and regulations will support this process and every governing body will have its own requirements based on the nature of the activity .

Link it up

For more on the national governing bodies for different sports and activities, go back to Unit 6.

Skills and knowledge checklist

☐ Why is it important to introduce an event properly?

☐ Do you know how to create an appropriate event plan?

☐ Explain what knockout and round-robin tournaments are.

☐ Describe the core and wider responsibilities of an event leader's role.

☐ Can you identify appropriate facilities for different types of activity events?

☐ Do you understand the importance of an event leader's roles and responsibilities?

○ I am able to prepare activities that use suitable event times.

○ I can organise a round-robin tournament.

○ I can carry out a warm up for a group of participants.

○ I can prepare and carry out a cool down with my participants.

○ I can carry out a risk assessment.

○ I can show professional conduct to my participants at an event.

If you have been unable to give positive responses to any of the questions or statements above, please go back and review the section.

B Demonstrate teamwork skills to achieve an agreed goal

Link it up

Go back to Unit 4 to find more information about the attributes and qualities of an effective sport and activity leader.

As you explored in Unit 4 (Coaching sport), there are many skills and qualities that are needed to be an effective leader. These components can also be useful when guiding a team to complete an aim or objective.

B1 Attributes and qualities of effective sport and activity leaders

A self-assessment can be a useful method of reflecting on your own personal skills, attributes and qualities. While you will have your own opinion of where your strengths and weaknesses lie, the reality of their application at an event can be different to what you first thought. A self-assessment allows you to grade your abilities against a number of skills and qualities. Using such a system enables you to decide where your strengths and weaknesses are. When delivering an organised activity, you should consider your:

- skills, such as communication, preparation and organisation of equipment and knowledge of the activity
- qualities, such as professional appearance, enthusiasm and the confidence with which you demonstrate to participants
- additional qualities, such as your leadership style, motivation, personality and use of humour to relax or support participants.

Self-assessment can also be used to reflect on your performance as leader after the event. As mentioned above, you may find your attributes and qualities are different to what you first thought when they are applied to a practical situation. The assessment of your own abilities should be honest and realistic to gain the most from the results.

The use of a self-assessment wheel (see Figure 8.7) can be a valuable tool for recognising your strengths and areas for development, and help you decide where your skills may be best applied for future activities. For example, if you have very good leadership skills, you may be best suited to taking control of the event or managing a group of organisers to achieve success. Assessing attributes and qualities can be essential when considering individual roles within a team.

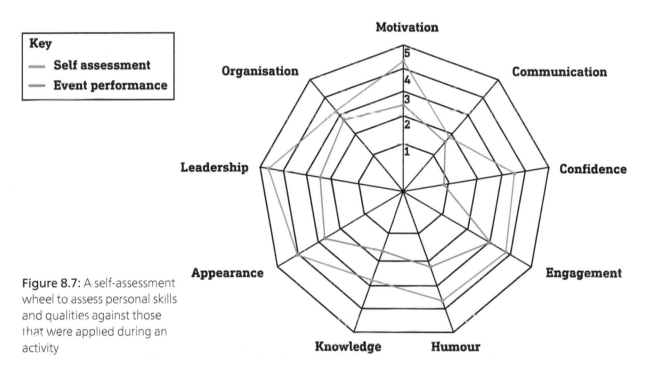

Figure 8.7: A self-assessment wheel to assess personal skills and qualities against those that were applied during an activity

B2 Skills needed to contribute to planning and delivering a sports event

Successful events are often the result of good organisation across a team. It is very rare that one person can be responsible for everything at an event.

Maintaining and evidencing the quality of individual contribution

The skills you develop from organising an event can be refined, allowing you to use them again in future events. Maintaining a record of evidence that logs the quality of individual contributions can be helpful for this future planning. Understanding your successes and establishing areas for improvement can help you develop and refine future exciting plans. It is best that all logs are in a written form (e.g. within a logbook – see Figure 8.7), and remember to keep this information safe as this recorded feedback might be useful for your next event.

EVENT LOGBOOK			
Event:		**Date:**	
		Duration:	
Venue:		**Age group of participants:**	
		Size of group:	

Staff responsibilities	
Staffing (separate sheet list names)	Equipment: ....<name(s)>..............
Event lead organise:........<name(s)>........	Refreshments: ....
Event planner:..	Health and safety (first aid / risk assessment): ....
Advertising:..	
Welcoming team:	Lost property area:.................................

Event aims & objectives:

Event components

Task (inc. time)	Component	Strengths	Weaknesses
Welcome / introduction	<Summary outline of content. Your plan will contain this section in greater detail>	<What went well?>	<What could be improved on?>
Warm up			
Main activity			
Cool down			
Close			

What were the strengths of the event?

1.

2.

3.

Future areas for development?

1.

2.

3.

Figure 8.8: Example of a logbook that may be used to record your progress, strengths and weaknesses

Being an active and positive member of the team

Teamwork is about working together. There are many elements that can contribute to the success of a team, however, good **COMMUNICATION** and **POSITIVE COOPERATION** between team members are essential. Positive contributions come from taking part, being proactive within the activities that are set, completing tasks to the standards and deadlines required and following instructions accurately. Becoming an active member of a group can help to encourage and motivate those around you, and leads to a positive working environment.

Demonstrating skills in teamwork, cooperation and leadership

Remember, though, teamwork is about working together. Having a group of individual positive and active people will not always make for a good team. If individuals are unwilling to work together then this will affect the overall team success. It is vital that everyone works together, as your team is only as good as its weakest member. If a member of your team fails to cooperate, or refuses to either lead or follow **LEADERSHIP**, then the team has the potential to break down. As an organiser of a team, it is important you inspire your team, so provide praise, identify areas of strength and weakness and use appropriate communication skills – all these will improve the team's outcomes.

Link it up

Communication skills and techniques are looked at in detail in Unit 3.

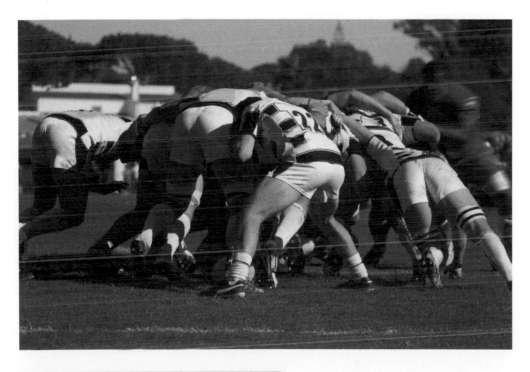

Working in a rugby scrum is a good sporting example of teamwork. All individuals work together to achieve group success.

Understanding the rules/guidelines

Game and activity **RULES AND GUIDELINES** are often developed to ensure that the activity is fair and provides structure. Their application can vary depending on the level of competition. National and international performances will often require strict adherence to rules, however, lower-level participation, such as a school sports day, would afford some flexibility in their application. For example, during a school basketball match, there may be greater flexibility on time allowance on different areas of the court. Game rules dictate that an attacking player should only be given three seconds within the attacking key, however, for young participants it is useful to provide greater flexibility to allow for much more game activity. A good understanding of the rules can allow you to provide the flexibility needed with the application of rules and enable the game to flow, reducing stoppages and creating greater enjoyment for all.

Agreeing, setting and following health and safety regulations

Remember also, as mentioned earlier in this unit, it is important to keep your participants safe. Safety should be a priority for all participants, and it is vital that you follow health and safety regulations regardless of how much flexibility you give in the rules. For example, if organising an athletic event, for activities such as throwing the discus, you should always ensure that spectators and waiting participants remain behind the cage. You should never hold a throwing event outside of the cage due to the safety risk to other non-throwing participants.

What if...?

You have been tasked by a sports event provider to create a new game that is exciting, interactive and inclusive. The game should be adaptable to support individual needs and promote fair play. It must be original and have a set number of rules and regulations that should be followed throughout.

1 Develop the game and include ten rules that must be followed by the participants. The following is the list of equipment that you can use. You do not need to use all the equipment, however, you are not allowed to use any more than that provided.

Your equipment is:

- 4 × gym mats
- 2 × crash mats
- 2 × tennis balls
- 4 × shuttlecocks
- 4 × large sponge balls
- 11 × cones
- 1 × whistle
- 2 × stopwatches

2 Once you have developed your game, play it with a small group to evaluate its success.

3 After you have finished playing the game, evaluate what went well and what areas for improvement you identified.

Contingency planning

As already mentioned, a contingency plan is a back-up plan that allows you to provide alternative or adapted activities, should you have difficulties beyond those originally planned. It is important you plan for the 'most likely' scenarios in order to respond or adapt during the event to overcome the barriers that may occur. Typical problems might include the following:

- *Weather conditions*: Some activities may require good weather, and on the day you might find it is too cold, too wet or too windy. Poor weather conditions can reduce your participants' enjoyment, or even make it unsafe, therefore having an alternative option, such as a sports hall, can help avoid this problem.
- *Equipment restrictions*: While you can prepare activity sessions to use specific equipment, there may be occasions when it is not available. This

may be because it is being used elsewhere, it has not been returned to its original place or there is insufficient equipment despite your original plan. To overcome this, you could develop alternative games/activities that use less equipment, or you could change group sizes or change part of the aims of a session.

- *Lost equipment or equipment broken during the activity*: It is not unusual for equipment to be lost or broken during an event. For example, a ball could be lost over protective netting or become flat. As for the considerations with the equipment restrictions, you should have alternative games, activities, group sizes and different aims that you can bring into action as an alternative.

- *Medical and first aid responses*: Not all events will run smoothly as accidents can happen. It is difficult to anticipate all possible problems, however, you need to take appropriate steps to avoid them as far as possible. You should be clear how you can respond to an incident, should it occur. A contingency plan can help you to prepare for how you will respond to an incident and what appropriate steps you will take to contain it. For example, if there is an accident (e.g. someone falls off a trampoline), how will you respond? What will you do with the other participants? How will you alert a first-aider or the emergency services? You should never leave these questions unanswered. Many accidents require a quick first aid response, and a lack of forward thinking could delay this. All medical and first aid facilities should be clearly displayed so that participants can locate where they are with ease. This can again reduce the response time to any incident or emergency. Remember, you should always ensure your participants feel and remain safe at all times.

Practise

1 Describe why is it important that first aid facilities are clearly located at an event.

2 Explain what is meant by the term 'contingency plan'.

3 Explain why health and safety is important when taking part in a sport and activity event.

4 Describe why a record of feedback can be helpful to plan future activity events.

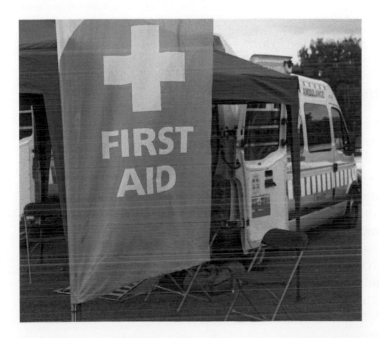

Clearly displayed first aid facilities are critical for the safe running of any event.

Skills and knowledge check

☐ What are the key components of teamwork?

☐ For a specified event, create a contingency plan.

☐ Explain how rules and regulations may vary for different activities.

☐ What are the most important health and safety regulations that should apply at all events?

☐ Why is it important to display first aid facilities at an event?

○ I can work as part of a team.

○ I can adapt existing plans and activities.

○ I can demonstrate leadership skills.

○ I can apply rules for fair play.

○ I can be proactive and enthusiastic at an event.

○ I can meet set deadlines.

If you have been unable to give positive responses to any of the questions or statements above, please go back and review the section.

C Evaluate your own contribution to an event and make recommendations for future improvement

The following section presents a range of methods for reviewing both your own performance and the success of your event.

C1 How to measure event success

Understanding the success of an event is very important as it can help you to reflect on recommendations for future improvement.

Using different methods to assess success

You can use different methods to assess the success of your event and how well you covered the planned components. These include asking questions such as:

- Did you meet your stated aims and objectives based on the planning you set out? For example, were all components in the plan completed successfully, including the physical activities and event preparation?
- Was your event completed safely? Were any incidents/accidents reported? If so, what were they (no matter how minor)? How do you think you could avoid them in the future? Reflect on how adequate your risk assessment was.

- Did the participants enjoy the event? Were there any complaints noted? If there were, do you understand the reasons why? Do you have any ideas for how these may be improved on? If positive comments were made, remember to record them for future use.

C2 Methods of reviewing own performance

You should keep any **FEEDBACK** you receive, both positive and negative, for future reference. Feedback is easier to recall when written down and kept safely, rather than relying on memory alone.

Feedback for review

In order to assess your own performance, you should take the opportunity to ask for and review feedback. Feedback can be valuable as it can help you assess what went well during the event, and what areas for improvement there are. It will enable you to reflect on how you could make changes in the future, should you need to, and set targets for your next session.

Link it up

Reviewing skills and methods for gaining feedback are also discussed in Unit 5.

Methods

Feedback can be gained from a range of sources, including the participants, the event supervisors and any spectators. It can also be gained through self-analysis. Two methods of self-analysis are SWOT analysis (see Figure 8.9) and a self-assessment wheel (see Figure 8.7 on page 249).

A **SWOT ANALYSIS** enables you to identify key areas of an event that went well, as well as areas that need improvement. It will also indicate how you can achieve the improvement, and what might create a barrier along the way. It is a useful method to assess not only your own performance, but also that of an event.

STRENGTHS	WEAKNESSES
What went well?	*What didn't go well?*
Where were the best contributions?	*What could be improved on?*
OPPORTUNITIES	**THREATS**
How can I / we make improvements?	*What could prevent me / us from making progress?*
What do I / we need to strengthen my / our weaknesses?	*What are the barriers ahead?*

Figure 8.9: A SWOT analysis can be used to identify personal and event successes or areas for improvement in the future

Link it up

You also look at SWOT analysis in detail in Unit 3.

The other methods you use for gathering feedback will vary and there is no one single method that is suitable for all occasions. Table 8.1 summarises some of the methods available to you and outlines their strengths and weaknesses:

Table 8.1: Feedback methods for assessing self and event strengths and weaknesses

Method	Format	Strengths/weaknesses
Questionnaires	Provide the participants with a question sheet that reflects on how they felt the event went. This can be handed out at the end of the event to gain their feedback on the success of your event, along with areas for improvement. See Figure 8.9.	**Strengths**: Can provide you with some summary feedback at the end of the event. You can provide a tick box format or have questions to be responded to. Participants can provide feedback on the questions you provide. Can be anonymous to gain valuable feedback. Easy to reflect on for future events as it is written down. **Weaknesses**: The feedback you gain is only as good as the questions. There should be an area for additional comments otherwise questions may be too restrictive. Not always ideal to complete at the end of an event due to time and participants wanting to leave.
Comment cards	Provide participants with a card on which they can make comments on what they enjoyed and what they found less exciting.	**Strengths**: Easy to manage the information as feedback can be brief and easy to gain at the end of an event. Feedback can be anonymous and placed within a comments box. Easy to reflect on for future events as it is written down. **Weaknesses**: Feedback can be limited depending on the participant, as some may write more than others. Not always ideal to complete at the end of an event due to time and participants wanting to leave.
Observation records	A supervisor observes an event and writes down feedback or records/photographs activities.	**Strengths**: Can be helpful to gain an independent review of the event. An observer can record information that you may miss in a self-analysis. Recorded footage and photographic evidence can be helpful to visualise strengths and areas for improvement. **Weaknesses**: Only as good as the observer. The success depends on the observer's experience as they may offer poor feedback. Participants can react differently if they feel like they are being observed.
Verbal feedback	Participants can give verbal feedback at the end of the event, commenting on the strengths and areas for improvement.	**Strengths**: Very easy to speak with the participants and gain views and opinions. You can react to their responses with further questions to gain additional feedback beyond that which you might gather from a paper questionnaire. **Weaknesses**: Participants may be intimidated by your questions and not want to upset you. One participant can dominate a conversation so not all have an equal say. Feedback is not written down therefore it can easily be forgotten.

Figure 8.10 shows an example of a feedback questionnaire that you could adapt for your own use.

POST-EVENT FEEDBACK FORM

Thank you for attending today's event, we hope you enjoyed it and will come again. We would like to gain your feedback about various aspects, as we aim to improve future experiences.

If you could take time to fill in this brief questionnaire it will be much appreciated. Many thanks.

Please rate your experience of the event below: (*tick*)

	Excellent	Good	Not bad	Could be better	Poor
How easy was your journey to the event?					
Did you feel welcome when you arrived?					
How comfortable did you feel throughout the event?					
How did you find the facilities for the event?					
How good were the refreshments?					
How enjoyable was the warm up and cool down?					
How organised did the activities feel?					
How would you rate your event leaders?					
Overall, how would you rate the event?					

	Definitely	Very likely	Maybe	Unlikely	Never
Overall, how likely are you to return for future events?					

Have you any comments that you would like to add? Was there anything we could improve upon?

Many thanks for attending today and we hope you enjoyed yourself. On behalf of the event organisers, we wish you a safe journey home.

Figure 8.10: An example of a basic post-event feedback questionnaire that may be used to assess an event's success

Practise

1 Create a questionnaire by constructing eight questions that may enable you to gain feedback on your event or performance.

2 Compare your questionnaire to that of a partner. What do you feel are the most appropriate and inappropriate questions within the two questionnaires?

3 Create a paired questionnaire that summarises both your questionnaires.

4 Present your findings to the group and discuss.

Strengths and areas for improvement

The main purpose of feedback is to try and identify both strengths and areas for improvement. You should consider asking for feedback in the following areas.

- *Planning*: Did your participants feel that the event was planned appropriately? Was there sufficient advertising, enough meet-and-greeters, equipment supervisors, adequate equipment availability, sufficient refreshments?
- *Content*: Did your participants feel that there was sufficient content within the event, or did they find it too limited? Were the participants easily bored or did the day/event sufficiently challenge their interests?
- *Organisation*: Did your participants feel that your event was prepared appropriately and that everything went smoothly? Did they feel that there were sufficient resources available, and were they where they should be at the right time, e.g. on a court or out ready for use? Were the facilities appropriate for all participants and the audience (e.g. parents)? Did the participants enjoy the games and activities? Did they feel that there was adequate communication between the event organisers and the participants, and if not, why not?
- *Attention to health and safety*: Did your participants feel safe throughout the event? Did they feel like the event environment was free from hazards and that appropriate steps had been taken to avoid harm to the participants?

C3 How to set targets for development

Gaining feedback on your event and performance will help you reflect on how successful your event was, and will enable you to set targets for future activities. Following a full review of your performance, you should consider how you can improve your event in the future. Consider the following.

- What went right?
- What went wrong?
- What could be improved upon?

A SWOT analysis is useful for setting targets in this way (as described above, Figure 8.9), as well as a post-event feedback form (also described above, Figure 8.10).

Your review can be used to reflect on not only your performance, but also the event itself. While you can use similar methods to achieve this, your understanding of the outcome should be different. The success of the event should be linked to the aims and objectives that you set at the beginning. This is one of the reasons why it is important to set out your aims and objectives clearly during the planning stage, as they then become your set success criteria. You should consider what you set out to achieve, and whether this was successful, by reflecting on the event feedback you have received from participants and other organisers.

As mentioned above, an assessment of individual performance can use tools such as a SWOT analysis or a self-assessment wheel. Questionnaires, comment cards, verbal feedback and logbook records can produce additional sources of reflective information. From these, you can identify areas of strength and areas for improvement for both future events and for individual performance.

SMARTER targets

To focus on areas of improvement, you can use **SMARTER TARGETS**. These aim to develop targets that are Specific, Measurable, Achievable, Realistic, Time-bound, Exciting and Recorded. Figure 8.11 shows one way of setting out your targets.

Link it up

To remind yourself of SMART targets, look back to Unit 5.

- *Specific*: This is where you focus on a specific element of the event. You should consider this carefully and not make it a general point. For example, naming a specific component of the main event, such as a skills development activity, provides you with something precise to develop for the future.
- *Measurable*: When you are developing an event you should ensure that any changes you implement can be measured. This could be assessed by reflecting on the outcome of any changes you implement. For example, if you change a development drill used within the event, think about whether it is successful. If it is not, could it be adapted for future performances? How can this success be measured? Will the participants be more able to perform the skill? How can this performance be measured?
- *Achievable*: Any target you set should always be achievable as there is little point in setting it otherwise. Do not set the bar too high. Unachievable targets will soon become meaningless, so it is important to ask yourself whether you can achieve your proposed development change at your next event. Is it suitable for the event and will the changes work?
- *Realistic*: Like achievable targets, any targets set should be realistic. There is little point setting a target that appears to be good for the future, but you have little chance of achieving it now. For example, if you are aiming to develop skills and activities by using a famous international performer to provide demonstrations, how realistic is this? While on paper it appears to be a fantastic idea, realistically not all events will be able to provide this. If on reflection your idea is unrealistic, think of an alternative.
- *Time-bound*: All targets should be time-bound, meaning that they should have a deadline within which they can be achieved. The time you set becomes the focal point as it creates a boundary for when you aim to achieve your goal. There is little point setting a target that has no end point. You should decide at the outset when your change can be realistically achieved.
- *Exciting*: When setting a new target, it is important to aim to make a positive change for the future. This means that it should enhance the event, making it more successful and exciting. Your participants are keen to enjoy your event, so any change should encourage this and be an improvement to its success.
- *Recorded*: When you have identified a specific target and reflected on how it can be measured, made achievable and realistic, along with making it time-bound and exciting, you should then write it down or record it for future reference. Once it is recorded you can always see the target you are working towards and review its progress in the future. Try to keep it somewhere safe and go back to it when setting any further targets.

Figure 8.11: Setting targets can be important for future improvements. Aim carefully to achieve success

Development plan

SMARTER targets are a valuable tool for reflecting on your own performance and reviewing previous activities and events. If carried out correctly, they can help you to prepare a new development plan for future events, and enable you to set improved aims, objectives and goals. For example, you might identify certain areas for improvement and begin to develop new ideas for achieving them in the future. To achieve this you will need to question whether the aims and objectives of your session are appropriate, and if not, why not? What could you change to develop this further and improve your next activity event?

What if...?

You have been asked to observe a sport and activity leader in order to assess their personal leadership skills. You are to assess their performance, using a post-event feedback form to gather the participants' views on the delivery provided.

1 Create an activity session for a leader to deliver to a small group of participants. This must be functional and last no more than 20 minutes.

2 Create a post-event feedback form for a group of participants to complete following the activity session.

3 The sport and activity leader should conduct the session, and participants should complete the feedback form immediately following the activities.

4 Using the feedback forms, describe the outcomes of the session based on the information collected.

5 Explain the strengths and weaknesses of the session and how any weaknesses could be overcome.

6 Analyse the feedback results and create SMARTER targets for the leader's future activity development.

Not all ideas need to originate from your own imagination or reflective thoughts. There are many other opportunities where you can gain additional skills from the sharing of good practice. When creating an event, coaching a session or leading a sports activity, you should always try to develop your ideas in order to make them more exciting for the future. Using the same activity session can leave both the participants and you bored over a period of time, so fresh ideas are always worthwhile. For example, when developing a warm up activity for a group of young children, consider how you could make it more exciting. For example, while using a jog followed by a range of STATIC STRETCHES may be suitable for some individuals, for young children this can become tedious and is not ideal. As an alternative you could play a game of 'tag' or 'stuck-in-the-mud'. These games can be good fun, create excitement while encouraging the participants to run and make frequent changes in direction in a confined space for the warm up.

Activities and opportunities

There are many training providers and courses that offer qualifications for future practice. For example, coaching qualifications are an ideal source of gaining inspiration. They can enable you to develop new skills and activities, and will provide you with a bank of fresh ideas for mini games and competitions. For qualification opportunities, check your national governing body as they will be able to provide you with the most up-to-date coaching and training certificates.

For additional self-development opportunities you can improve your event's activities by using online resources, workbooks and even through online training courses. Good activity downloads and details of self-development can be found online at the Sport England website (www.sportengland.org), and UK Coaching (www.ukcoaching.org). Developing your skills through opportunities such as these will continue to develop your confidence as a sport and activity leader.

Possible barriers to improvement

Leading events can be a process of trial and error, and it is these points that you need to develop for future reference. Possible barriers to improvement could result from a lack of resources or opportunities to practise, and might include:

- cost of qualifications
- lack of peer support for learning development
- lack of appropriate facilities
- inadequate access to resources
- lack of self-development
- lack of practical application opportunities
- lack of participant availability.

As you have learned on many occasions throughout this qualification, it is very important that as a sport and activity leader you promote inclusivity. Providing opportunities for all is your priority and you should always look for ways of overcoming difficulties and barriers to develop exciting activity-based events. You should always take steps to support future aspiring sport and activity leaders.

Skills and knowledge check

- ☐ Describe the importance of SMARTER targets.
- ☐ Explain the importance of health and safety within an event.
- ☐ Describe the strengths and weaknesses of different types of self-evaluation.
- ☐ Create appropriate questions that will help reflect on an activity session.
- ☐ Explain why is it important to develop your skills and qualifications for future events.

- ⚪ I can identify strengths and areas for improvement after an event.
- ⚪ I can ensure that health and safety rules and regulations are followed.
- ⚪ I can create an appropriate evaluation survey.
- ⚪ I can develop SMARTER targets following an event.
- ⚪ I can identify relevant training courses to develop my future skills.
- ⚪ I can create a questionnaire for an event review.

If you have been unable to give positive responses to any of the questions or statements above, please go back and review the section.

Ready for assessment (part 2)

You have been tasked to help prepare a charity five-a-side walking football tournament for a group of elderly and active retired participants.

You have been asked to prepare all the advertising, a risk assessment and an event plan for the day. You should include information on how to complete the warm up and cool down activities. There are mixed ages in the group and you must consider this carefully throughout your preparation.

There will be eight teams who all need to play each other in order to determine the tournament winner. You will need to provide a list of the team names to show the order of play throughout the tournament.

1 Complete a risk assessment of the area that you aim to use for your game.

2 Prepare an event plan including the introduction, warm up, main activity, cool down and close. The walking football team names will be determined by yourself, however, they should be presented ready to use in the most appropriate tournament format.

3 Develop a series of fun warm up and cool down activities. Remember that the participants are elderly and active retired, so you should consider this for any exercise. Make sure the activity is appropriate.

4 Prepare questionnaires to hand out to participants at the end of the event to review its success. Remember questions must be appropriate and aimed at getting feedback that will enable you to develop your strengths and areas for the future.

Good luck!

WORK FOCUS

HANDS ON

There are some important occupational skills and competencies that you will need to practise, which relate to this unit. Developing these and practising them could help you to gain employment as a sport and activity leader.

1 Work as part of a team.

- Select an example from an event where the importance of teamwork was key to its success. Provide four examples of how you could contribute to supporting teamwork at this event.

2 Show how you can motivate a group of participants at an event of your choice.

- Give four practical ideas for how you could do this.

3 Use appropriate verbal communication methods with children at an activity event.

- Give two practical ideas for how you could do this.

- Give two practical ideas for how these may be adapted for alternative specific populations, e.g. disability support needs, the active retired.

Ready for work?

Take this short quiz to find out whether you would be chosen for that dream job.

1 Motivating participants at an event is....
- [ ] A important but not essential
- [ ] B very important
- [ ] C something I should consider
- [ ] D something I have to do if I'm told.

2 Setting targets can....
- [ ] A help identify strengths only
- [ ] B help identify areas for improvement
- [ ] C be supportive though not essential
- [ ] D provide me with little information.

3 Self-assessment can help me....
- [ ] A provide evidence for planning future activities
- [ ] B identify individual attributes for appropriate roles at an event
- [ ] C identify team players
- [ ] D in no way at all help with my session.

4 Having aims and objectives can...
- [ ] A help me understand what I am doing
- [ ] B help me measure success
- [ ] C identify any facilities that are needed
- [ ] D develop SMARTER targets.

5 Creating an activity plan is...
- [ ] A unnecessary for communication
- [ ] B essential for communication
- [ ] C essential for parents
- [ ] D unnecessary for an emergency.

Your score:

If you scored mostly Ds, you may need to brush up on your interpersonal skills. If you scored mainly Bs then you are ready for employment; if you gained mainly As and Cs you should go back and read through the section again.

Answers to assessment practice questions

Shown below are some suggested answers to the questions in the assessment practice features in Units 1 and 2.

Unit 1

Assessment practice, page 7

Acceptable answers:

(1 mark for each correct answer, up to a maximum of 2 marks.)

- He might not believe he can take part because he doesn't have role models (1 mark).
- He might have an illness or injury (1 mark).

(Accept other appropriate answers.)

Assessment practice, page 11

Acceptable answers:

(1 mark for suggesting adaptations for each of the following for a selected sport or physical activity, up to a maximum of 4 marks.)

- activities (1)
- equipment (1)
- rules (1)
- playing area or environment (1)
- staffing numbers (1)
- participant numbers (1).

(1 mark for each advantage and disadvantage to the adaptations, up to a maximum of 4 marks.)

Advantages:
- Activities – playing small team games means that everyone is active at all times (1).
- Equipment – bigger or smaller equipment can be used to suit the individual (1).
- Rules – rules can be selected that are appropriate for the age and ability of the group (1).
- Playing area or environment – the area can be made smaller or larger or the location changed, e.g. inside or outside (1).
- Staffing numbers – more staff allow more one-to-one tuition and allow for those who need more help to receive it (1).
- Participant numbers – by allowing fewer people to participate, more attention can be given to those who need it (1).

Disadvantages:
- Activities – playing only one game may mean that some people do not know it and do not know the rules (1).
- Equipment – it is expensive to have lots of different sizes of equipment and difficult to store it all (1).
- Rules – for a diverse group it can be difficult to find rules that everyone knows and are not too simple or too difficult (1).
- Playing area or environment – it may not be possible to move the location of the activity if the centre is fully booked (1).
- Staffing numbers – staff may not be available to assist with the activity if they are working in other areas (1).
- Participant numbers – if there are fewer participants, less money is made from the activity session (1).

Assessment practice, page 15

1 Acceptable answers:

   (1 mark for identifying an appropriate aim.)

   - introduction to basic cricket skills (1)
   - introduction to fielding and batting skills (1).

   (Accept other appropriate answers.)

2 Acceptable answers:

   (1 mark for each piece of information, up to a maximum of 2 marks.)

   - the leader's name (1)
   - the emergency evacuation routes (1)
   - the timings of the session (1)
   - any specific information about the activity (1).

   (Accept other appropriate answers.)

3 Acceptable answers:
(1 mark for each correct description of part of a warm-up, up to a maximum of 2 marks.)

- pulse raiser, e.g. jogging or side stepping (1)
- movements that mirror the activity, e.g. batting, bowling, catching, throwing (1)
- stretches (1).

Assessment practice, page 20

Acceptable answer:
(1 mark for identifying participant type, 1 mark for describing how to use best practice in communication to meet their needs.)

When working with participants who are young children (1) a good way to communicate is to use a whistle to get their attention quickly and effectively (1).

(Accept other appropriate examples.)

Assessment practice, page 26

1 Acceptable answers:
(1 mark for each correct piece of legislation, up to a maximum of 2 marks.)

- Management of Health and Safety at Work Regulations 1999 (1)
- Health and Safety (First-Aid) Regulations 1981 (1)
- Control of Substances Hazardous to Health (COSHH) Regulations 2002 (1)
- Children Act 2004 (1).

2 Acceptable answer:
(1 mark for identifying a piece of legislation; 1 mark for describing a potential consequence.)

If an employer fails to comply with the Management of Health and Safety at Work Regulations (1) an employee could become seriously injured on a piece of equipment or in an activity area (1).

(Other correct examples are accepted.)

Assessment practice, page 35

1 Acceptable answers:

Severe injury or illness / Heart attack (1)

2 Acceptable answers:

Call 999 / Call an ambulance / Call for reception to call an ambulance (1)

3 Acceptable answer:
(1 mark for each correct response, up to a maximum of 3 marks.)

- Remove them from the area (1).
- Make sure they are with a member of staff (1).
- Reassure them that everyone is okay and the ill man is receiving medical assistance (1).

Unit 2

Assessment practice, page 48

1 Acceptable answers:
(1 mark for identifying an appropriate aim.)

- Basic volleyball skills (1)
- Introduction to volleyball skills (1)
- Volleyball skills (1)
- How to serve and volley (1).

2 Acceptable answers:
(1 mark for each role and responsibility, up to a maximum of 2 marks.)

- Selecting appropriate methods of communication (1) so that the group can understand what is being asked of them and clearly understand all rules and requirements of the session (1).
- Using appropriate behaviours (1) so that the group feel confident in the leader's ability and knowledge (1).
- Personal qualities (1) using humour, empathy or gestures to make the group feel at ease (1).
- Leadership styles (1) this will change depending on the needs of the group, e.g. command style/authoritarian or more relaxed/laissez faire (1).

3 Acceptable answers:
(1 mark for identifying how to make the session accessible; 1 mark for describing how this can be done, up to a maximum of 2 marks.)

- How the activity will be organised (1) – adults will be in one large group to learn skills and split into smaller groups for practices (1).
- Realistic consideration of cost (1) – no new equipment would be needed and one member of staff is sufficient to run the activity (1).
- Logistics (1) – the sports leader is free before this activity and can make sure the equipment is set up and can meet the participants as they arrive for the activity (1).
- Technical competence of the leader and participants (1) – the leader will need to know the rules and regulations of the sport and have experience in delivering volleyball skills (1).

4 Acceptable answers:
(1 mark for identifying each piece of legislation, up to a maximum of 2 marks.)

- Management of Health and Safety at Work Regulations 1999 (1)
- Health and Safety (First-Aid) Regulations 1981 (1)
- Control of Substances Hazardous to Health (COSHH) Regulations 2002 (1).

Assessment practice, page 57

1 Acceptable answers:
(1 mark for each environmental consideration, up to a maximum of 3 marks.)

- the sports facility itself (1)
- the indoor sports hall (1)
- the changing rooms (1)
- the toilets (1).

2 Acceptable answers:
(1 mark for identifying a social consideration; 1 mark for describing how it can be included in planning, up to a maximum of 2 marks.)

- opinions (1)
- thoughts (1)
- beliefs (1)
- concerns (1)
- prejudice (1)
- stereotypes (1).
- Social considerations need to be planned for so that the adults do not experience barriers to participation, e.g. comparing themselves unfavourably to others (1)
- The session needs to make the adults feel comfortable with their own ability/confident/happy (1).

Assessment practice, page 60

1 Acceptable answers:
(1 mark for each barrier, up to a maximum of 2 marks.)

- social (1)
- economic (1)
- access to provision (1)
- historical (1)
- educational (1)
- fashion/trend (1)
- ability level (1)
- cultural background (1)
- role of the media (1).

2 Acceptable answers:
(1 mark for an appropriate activity.)

Free sessions/cheap sessions for £1 – of indoor football/badminton/basketball/mixed sports sessions/trampolining/baseball (1)

(Accept other appropriate responses.)

3 Acceptable answer:
(1 mark for explaining how the activity meets the need; 1 mark for explaining how it reduces a factor affecting their participation.)

Free indoor football can help to reduce the economic barrier because the activity can be accessed by all teenagers (1). Because there is no fee for the activity the teenagers do not need to worry if they can afford to attend (1).

(Accept other appropriate responses. Learners' responses must link to their suggested activity in Question 2.)

Assessment practice, page 62

1 Acceptable answers:
   (1 mark for each barrier, up to a maximum of 2 marks.)

   - social (1)
   - economic (1)
   - access to provision (1)
   - ability level (1)
   - cultural background (1).

2 Acceptable answers:
   (1 mark for each method, up to a maximum of 2 marks.)

   - social – group activities (1)
   - economic – low price (1)
   - access to provision – the organisation and its facilities need to be easily accessed (1)
   - ability level – by aiming the activity at all ability levels (1)
   - cultural background – the session will be advertised in a place where people from many different groups will see it, e.g. a community centre/a school (1).

3 Acceptable answers:
   (1 mark for each justification of how the methods overcome the barriers, up to a maximum of 2 marks.)

   - Social – group activities allow participants to meet new people and make friends (1).
   - Economic – low price activities allow everyone to be able to attend sessions (1).

   (Accept other appropriate responses.)

Assessment practice, page 67

1 Acceptable answers:
   (1 mark for each key skill, up to a maximum of 2 marks. 1 mark for each additional key skill, up to a maximum of 2 marks.)

   Key skills:

   - communication (1)
   - organised (1)
   - approachable and personable (1)
   - being authoritative (1)
   - motivating others (1)
   - demonstrating (1)
   - problem-solving (1)
   - being knowledgeable (1)
   - understanding (1)
   - having confidence (1).

   Additional key skills:

   - understands activity structuring (1)
   - uses target setting (1)
   - can use appropriate language (1)
   - collects effective feedback (1)
   - carries out evaluations (1).

2 Acceptable answers:
   (1 mark for identifying adaptations to each key skill identified in Question 1, up to a maximum of 2 marks.)

   - Communication can be adapted by using more gestures/less formal or more formal language/ verbal and non-verbal cues, depending on the group (1).
   - Direction and control can be changed from being more authoritative with the teenagers than with the adults (1).

   (Accept appropriate responses for the any of the key skills.)

Glossary of key terms

ABUSE: an action by another person that causes significant harm

ACCESSIBLE TO ALL: making it possible for everyone to access both the facility and the activity

ACTION PLANNING: helps to focus ideas and gives detailed steps of how to achieve specific goals

ACTIVE LISTENING: where the listener concentrates on what is being said and responds to the speaker to show they understand

ACTIVITY DAYS: are usually one-off events targeted at a specific age, gender or ability

ACTIVITY ENVIRONMENT: the location where an activity takes place

ACTIVITY-LIMITING HEALTH CONDITIONS OR PHYSICAL LIMITATIONS: anything that prevents an individual from performing everyday activities

AIM: the main goal you want your participants to achieve by the end of the session

AMATEUR SPORTS COACH: someone who offers coaching services on a voluntary basis

AMPUTEES: people with partial or total absence of limb or limbs from the body

APPROPRIATENESS OF ACTIVITY: must meet the participants' needs, wants and abilities

AUTOCRATIC: this type of leader tells the players what they want them to do. They make all the decisions and have complete control

BAME: black, Asian and minority ethnic

BARRIERS TO PARTICIPATION: these are particular needs preventing people from participating regularly in sport and physical activities

BEST PRACTICE: the standard and most effective way to carry out a task or how to follow instructions

BME: black and minority ethnic

BODY IMAGE: how you perceive your body – either positive or negative, consciously and subconsciously

CHILD PROTECTION POLICIES: legal obligations outlined in the Children Act 2004. They must be followed in order to protect the safety and welfare of participants under the age of 18

CLASSES: timetabled activities, which happen at the same time every day or every week

CODE OF CONDUCT: a set of rules that dictate how people should behave in certain situations

COLLABORATION: the action of two or more people working together to achieve something

COMMUNICATION: the exchange of information using verbal or non-verbal methods

COMPETITION FORMATS: competitions may take the form of round-robin or knockout tournaments (among others) and allow participants to compete against each other

COMPLEX EQUIPMENT: may consist of many components and be heavy or unwieldy

COMPLEX SKILLS: skills that require coordinated movements needing control and concentration

COMPONENT: an individual part of a session: usually warm up, main content and skill development, cool down and plenary

CONDITIONED GAME: a game where the rules are changed to work on a particular skill

CONTENT OF THE ACTIVITY: how the activity will be organised

CONTINGENCY PLAN: a back-up plan that allows you to provide alternative or adapted activities, should you have difficulties beyond those originally planned

CONTRAINDICATION: a reason or factor that prevents someone from participating in exercise or certain activities

COOPERATIVE GAMES: games for working as part of team, developing communication skills and working towards group achievement

CORE RESPONSIBILITIES: ensuring you follow appropriate professional conduct, maintaining event health and safety and providing inclusivity and equality

DECISION MAKING: when a problem occurs during an activity, it is up to the leader to find, and choose, a solution to solve it

DEMOCRATIC: this type of leader involves players in all decisions. Everyone is given the opportunity to share their opinion

DEMONSTRATION: show a participant what you would like them to do and how

DISABILITY SPORT: any activity played by individuals with any partial or total mental or physical impairment which makes it difficult or impossible to perform daily life activities

DISCLOSURE AND BARRING SERVICE (DBS): helps employers make safer recruitment decisions and prevents unsuitable people from working with vulnerable groups, including children

DIVERSE GROUP OF PARTICIPANTS: groups can be defined by specific characteristics they share which might be physical, social, psychological, health-related, skill-related or developmental

DIVERSE NEEDS: include different needs between groups, the factors that influence them, the aims of activities and expected outcomes related to these needs

DRILLS: where participants repeat an exercise or set of exercises

DROP-IN SESSION: give participants an opportunity to try a sport or physical activity and to come at a time which suits them

DUTY OF CARE: a legal responsibility to safeguard people who are in their care or taking part in their activities

EMPATHY: the ability to share and understand someone's feelings

EMPLOYER: a person or business that pays a salary or wage to an individual in exchange for them completing a job or a task

ENDORPHINS: hormones that reduce feelings of pain and trigger positive feelings in your body

ENERGY: the capacity to be physically or mentally active

ENTHUSIASM: having strong excitement or interest about something you enjoy

EQUALITY: treating all participants as equal

EQUALITY AND DIVERSITY ISSUES: aim to eliminate discrimination, harassment and victimisation, and to advance equality of opportunity and foster good relations between different parts of the community

ETHNICITY: state of belonging to a social group that shares a common and distinctive culture, religion or language

EXPECTED OUTCOMES: the effect you expect to see from an instruction or event. For example, when teaching someone to kick a football, the expected outcome is that they will be able to move the ball along the ground with their foot

EXTRINSIC MOTIVATION: having the desire to succeed due to the reward it may bring, such as money or trophies

FACILITY: the place where the session takes place

FEEDBACK: when information about someone's performance of a task is used as a basis for improvement

FIRST AID RESOURCE: a basic first aid kit or a dedicated facility and staff

FORMATIVE FEEDBACK: ongoing feedback from an instructor, highlighting strengths and areas for improvement

HAZARD: something that is identified as having the potential to cause harm

HEALTH AND SAFETY HAZARDS: hazards or threats caused by objects, facilities or people which will or might cause an accident or incident that is harmful to people's safety

HEALTH AND SAFETY ISSUES: concerns about hazards and potential hazards relating to maintaining health and safety

HEALTH AND SAFETY LEGISLATION: provides specific rules that need to be followed to ensure the health and safety of all

HEALTH AND SAFETY OBLIGATIONS: ensure that all the participants who take part in the coaching activity do so in a safe and suitable environment

HEALTH AND SAFETY POLICY: a set of rules and instructions that cover all processes and procedures relating to health and safety within an organisation

HEARING IMPAIRED: has a partial or total loss of hearing

IMPACT AND COMBAT SPORTS: sports/activities where there is a significant forceful contact with the body

INCLUSIVITY: not excluding anyone based on race, gender, disability, culture, sexual orientation or any other factor

INITIATIVES: ideas which have been made into a programme, event or scheme, which help to promote something and raise awareness of it

INTRINSIC MOTIVATION: having the desire to succeed purely for sheer enjoyment and the satisfaction of achievement

LAISSEZ-FAIRE: this type of leader steps back and lets the group make decisions for themselves. The group has a lot of freedom

LEADER: someone who provides direction, instruction and guidance to a group

LEADERSHIP: defined as guiding a group of people or an organisation

LEARNED BEHAVIOURS: the reactions people apply to specific situations that they repeat each time they encounter that situation

LEGAL OBLIGATION: a requirement by law

LIABILITY WAIVER: a legal document that acknowledges that the participant is aware of the risks involved in any activities they undertake

MEDICAL CONDITION: a disease or disorder of the body

MENTALLY REHEARSE: run through a plan in your head before the session so you understand what you will be doing at each point

MOTIVATION: the drive within you to achieve your goals

MUSCULAR ENDURANCE: the ability for one muscle or a group of muscles to keep working for a long period of time without getting tired

NATIONAL GOVERNING BODIES (NGBS): organisations that govern and regulate a sport or activity

NEGLECT: failing to meet a child's basic needs

NON-VERBAL COMMUNICATION: expressing yourself without words, using body language, facial expressions and gestures

OBJECTIVE: how you are going to achieve your aim

OUTDOOR ACTIVITIES: leisure pursuits completed outdoors, often in a natural environment or at a purpose-built facility

PART INSTRUCTION: the process of taking a skill or activity and breaking it down into smaller individual components

PARTICIPANT NEEDS: must be identified and understood to engage and motivate them

PARTICIPANTS: the people who are taking part in the activity

PATIENCE: the ability to accept delays or problems without becoming annoyed

PERCEPTION: the way you think about or understand something

PERFORMANCE PROFILING: a tool that helps you to identify your strengths and weaknesses by analysing your current performance

PERSEVERANCE: continually determined to do something, despite it being challenging or difficult to achieve

PHYSICAL ACTIVITY READINESS QUESTIONNAIRE (PAR-Q): a form that assesses an individual's medical history and needs to see if they are ready to take part in physical activity or exercise

PHYSICAL INJURIES: some are minor, such as a sprained ankle or a pulled muscle. Others can be more severe, such as a broken limb or a joint injury

PLANNING TEMPLATES: provide prompts as to what you need to consider and include in a session

POTENTIAL CONSEQUENCES: possible outcomes of an instruction or event; for example, a potential consequence of leading a football session outside is that it might rain

POSITIVE COOPERATION: comes from taking part, being proactive within the activities that are set, completing tasks to the standards and deadlines required and following instructions accurately

POSITIVITY: showing a positive attitude

PRIVATE SECTOR: provides sport and activity services that are owned by an individual or a group

PROFESSIONAL CONDUCT: standards and behaviours you must follow in the workplace

PROFESSIONAL SPORTS COACH: paid to coach full-time

PROFESSIONALISM: demonstrating the skills and behaviour expected of a person who is trained to do a particular job

PROBLEM-SOLVING: finding a solution to an issue

PUBLIC SECTOR: funded and paid for by the local government out of taxes and sometimes National Lottery money

RACISM: the unequal treatment of an individual based on their race or ethnic group

RAPPORT: good rapport is a positive working relationship between the leader and the group

REFEREE: a person who can provide information (hopefully positive) to a potential employer about your skills, attitudes and personality

REFERRAL PROCEDURES: when to refer, how to refer and the role of the designated safeguarding officer

RELAY: a race between two or more teams where team members take turns to race

RESPONSIBILITY: having a duty or control to deal with someone or something

RISK: the likelihood of someone being harmed by a hazard

RISK ASSESSMENTS: reviews of health and safety which look at the participants and their environment ahead of the planned activity

ROLE MODEL: an individual whose behaviour, attitude, actions and success are emulated by others

ROLES AND RESPONSIBILITIES: the leader needs to select appropriate methods of communication, behaviours, personal qualities and leadership styles. The participants must also display appropriate behaviours, personal qualities and methods of communication

RULES AND GUIDELINES: developed to ensure that the activity is fair and provides structure

SAFEGUARDING: protecting people's health and well-being and allowing them to live free from harm, abuse and neglect

SAFEGUARDING LEGISLATION: these are legal obligations outlined in the Children Act 2004, and must be followed in order to protect the safety and welfare of participants under the age of 18

SAFEGUARDING PROCEDURES: steps you must follow to safeguard yourself and others as well as understanding what to do if you suspect a safeguarding issue

SAFE WORKING ENVIRONMENT: employers have to make the place of work safe and must minimise or remove all risks and hazards where people work

SEDENTARY LIFESTYLE: one with limited or no physical activity

SELF-CONFIDENCE: having the confidence and trust in your own abilities and judgements

SELF-ESTEEM: how you feel about yourself as an individual – positive self-esteem means you feel good about yourself and gives you that 'go get' attitude

SELF-EVALUATION: where you review your own progress and development by highlighting your strengths and areas for improvement

SELF-SUFFICIENCY: being able to rely on yourself without the need of external assistance

SEND: Special Educational Needs and Disability

SENSITIVITY: being able to consider and respond to another's feelings

SESSION PLENARY: takes place at the end of the session and is where a coach will recap what was learnt in the session

SIMPLE EQUIPMENT: easily moved and set up

SIMPLE SKILLS: consist of basic movements and require little concentration, such as catching a ball, a vertical jump or a short football pass

SMALL-SIDED GAMES: fun games that have fewer participants in a smaller area

SMARTER TARGETS: targets that are Specific, Measurable, Achievable, Realistic, Time-bound, Exciting and Recorded

SOCIALISATION: the activity of mixing socially with others

SPECIFIC OR ADAPTED FACILITIES: are designed primarily for a target population, such as the disabled

SPONSORED CHARITY EVENTS: these are non-competitive events, including walks, bike rides and fun runs. Participants can have fun and raise money for charities

SPORT AND ACTIVITY LEADER: the person responsible for leading the participants in the activity

STATIC STRETCHING: stretching muscles when the body is at rest

SUBSIDISED ACTIVITIES: reduced prices for those on low income or income support

SUMMATIVE FEEDBACK: a formal assessment at the end of a unit

SUMMER CAMPS AND HOLIDAY ACTIVITIES: are usually aimed at children and take place during school holidays

SWOT ANALYSIS: a common way of assessing performance in four areas – strengths, weaknesses, opportunities, threats

TARGET SETTING: a process of gathering and analysing information that can then be used to set challenges for improvement to be made

TASTER SESSIONS: might be added to a timetable to introduce groups of new participants to a sport or physical activity, or they might be offered to existing participants to try a sport or physical activity they haven't done before

TEAMWORK: where a group works together cooperatively to achieve a shared goal

TOURNAMENTS AND COMPETITIONS: are run by centres, gyms and sport and physical activity clubs to allow participants or groups to compete

VERBAL COMMUNICATION: expressing yourself through language and sound

VISUALLY IMPAIRED: has a partial or total loss of sight

VOLUNTARY SECTOR: a not-for-profit sector, which is neither private nor public

VOLUNTEER: someone who gives up their time for no financial gain to complete a job or a task

WHEELCHAIR SPORT: any sport where a participant is in a wheelchair that can be adapted to suit the requirements of the sport, e.g. long-distance performance, impact performance, increased manoeuvrability

WHOLE PRACTICE: a method in which you try to practise the exercise activity as one

WHOLE-PART-WHOLE INSTRUCTION: practising a skill as one, then breaking it into its smaller components to practice each individually, and finally put the components back together as one complete performance

Index

W